Theories of Human Development
Part II

Professor Malcolm W. Watson

THE TEACHING COMPANY ®

PUBLISHED BY:

THE TEACHING COMPANY
4151 Lafayette Center Drive, Suite 100
Chantilly, Virginia 20151-1232
1-800-TEACH-12
Fax—703-378-3819
www.teach12.com

Copyright © The Teaching Company Limited Partnership, 2002

Printed in the United States of America

This book is in copyright. All rights reserved.

Without limiting the rights under copyright reserved above,
no part of this publication may be reproduced, stored in
or introduced into a retrieval system, or transmitted,
in any form, or by any means
(electronic, mechanical, photocopying, recording, or otherwise),
without the prior written permission of
The Teaching Company.

ISBN 1-56585-822-0

Malcolm W. Watson, Ph.D.

Professor of Psychology, Brandeis University

Malcolm W. Watson received his B.A. in Psychology from the University of Utah in 1967. After living in Berlin, Germany, then serving in the Medical Service Corps of the Army in Vietnam, he pursued his graduate education in Developmental Psychology at the University of Denver. He received his Ph.D. in 1977.

Dr. Watson has been on the faculty at Brandeis University in Waltham, Massachusetts, since receiving his Ph.D. He has been Chair of the Psychology Department and is currently a Professor of Psychology and Chair of the Social Science School Council at Brandeis. He has also taught at Boston College and been a member of the John D. and Catherine T. MacArthur Foundation Network for the study of transitions in early child development.

Dr. Watson received the first Michael Laban Walzer Award for Excellence in Teaching at Brandeis. He has taught courses on research methods, developmental psychology, theories of development, and the development of play, art, and creativity. His research has been in four areas: the development of symbolic play in children, the development of drawing and art in children, children's understanding of family roles and conflicts, and the causes of aggression and violence in children and adolescents. He has published numerous articles in journals and books and has edited several books. The National Institute of Mental Health and the National Institute of Child Health and Human Development have funded Dr. Watson's research.

Table of Contents

Theories of Human Development
Part II

©2002 The Teaching Company Limited Partnership

Theories of Human Development

Scope:

This 24-lecture course provides an introduction to six highly influential theories of human development and the theorists who developed each theory. It is difficult to comprehend human nature without understanding our origins and the processes that guide our development from conception to maturity. Thus, the study of human development is a valuable tool, not only for understanding children and helping them to develop optimally but also for understanding ourselves as adults. The key to gaining insights into the phenomena of human development is to organize facts and data into coherent, scientific theories. Without such theories, scientists, including developmental psychologists and other students of human development, would make little progress in devising meaningful studies that further our understanding or in applying what we know in a way to benefit others. These lectures compare the historical and philosophical backgrounds from which each theorist emerged and the domains of development that each theory can explain. By examining the important points of each of the theories, the lectures help the student to compare them and see how they differ, where they converge, and how they complement one another to explain universal patterns of human development, individual differences, and abnormal development. Real-life examples and findings of major scientific studies are used to clarify the main points of the theories. In the end, the student will be prepared to judge which theories are valid and how each theory is valuable in giving us understanding of children and developmental processes.

The first lecture provides an introductory background for the study of the six theories and discusses the value of scientific theories generally. Lecture Two begins a discussion of the history that set the stage for the systematic study of child development. It covers the early history of conceptions of children before any scientific study of them existed. Lecture Three compares two major worldviews of human nature and development, as seen in the thinking of two influential philosophers, Locke and Rousseau. Lecture Four concludes the history of child study and the ways in which the major theories emerged.

The subsequent lectures discuss each of the six theories in turn. Lectures Five through Seven discuss Freud's psychodynamic theory as it applies to child development, particularly to personality development. These lectures provide insight into the roles of the unconscious, competing drives, and the ways in which a person develops the ability to adapt to various demands from within and from the environment. Lectures Eight through Eleven discuss Erikson's Psycho-social theory and how it developed from Freud's influence to become the first theory to describe development across the entire life span. Lectures Twelve through Fifteen discuss the theory of infant attachment, as developed jointly by Bowlby and Ainsworth, and how this theory explains both early attachments and the development of close relationships throughout the life span. Lectures Sixteen and Seventeen discuss Bandura's social learning theory and his related self-efficacy theory and provide examples of how his theory explains the crucial role of imitation in our learning and socialization. Lectures Eighteen through Twenty-One describe the most influential theory of development that has yet emerged, Piaget's cognitive-developmental theory. The universal processes of development and the stages that Piaget theorized are explained. Lectures Twenty-Two and Twenty-Three describe the last major theory, Vygotsky's cognitive-mediation theory. Vygotsky's theory has emerged as a prominent one today, especially in influencing educational practices. The integrated cognitive and social focus of the theory is described. Lecture Twenty-Four provides a conclusion to the course by discussing how the various theories may be compared and integrated.

    ©2002 The Teaching Company Limited Partnership

Lecture Thirteen
How Nature Ensures That Attachment Will Occur

Scope:

This lecture describes how the ethologists influenced Bowlby. Ethology theory contributed the concept of innate releasing mechanisms, which are a central part of attachment theory in explaining how parents and infants become attached to each other. The lecture then discusses the allure of babyish features and their role in attachment and concludes with a description of the development of attachment in the first year of life.

Outline

I. When John Bowlby rejected Freudian psychodynamic theory as inadequate to explain how attachment develops, he turned instead to *ethology theory.*

   A. Ethology theory first emerged in the mid-20th century from the work of three European naturalists: Karl von Frisch, Nikko Tinbergen, and Konrad Lorenz.

      1. Ethology theory is a general approach to studying animal behavior and development in which the focus is on how behaviors that have adaptive importance and evolutionary significance have evolved in a given species.

      2. The ethologists carried out detailed, systematic observations of different species to describe how certain complex behaviors worked to bring about this adaptation, and they tried to explain why certain behaviors would have evolutionary significance.

      3. Certain complex action patterns or instincts would accomplish this adaptation at certain critical periods in an individual's life. A *critical period* is defined as a time in the course of development for a given species when the individual is particularly sensitive to certain environmental cues and primed to respond to them. Outside this critical period, an individual may not respond the same way. Thus, certain skills or reorganizations of the neural system are likely to occur during critical periods.

B. A prime example of a complex action pattern and a critical period can be seen in the construct of *imprinting*, which was first explained by Lorenz.

1. In imprinting, a newborn animal responds to the movements of another object in proximity to it and forms neurological connections or patterns that then keep the newborn wanting proximity to the object. The individual will follow and seek the proximity of that object. If too much time passes, the critical period passes, and the imprinting will no longer occur to a moving object.

2. Imprinting in birds occurs when a bird, such as a duck, hatches and imprints on the first moving object of a certain size. This is usually the bird's mother. In ducks, the ducklings are now permanently bonded to the mother and follow her around.

3. Imprinting was thought to occur in any species where the need for parenting was great, such as in birds and mammals. This system had evolved to ensure that the parent-child relationship would emerge and continue.

C. Ethologists believed there were cues of color, patterns, or actions that were built into the species that signaled to others in the species to respond in a certain way. These signaling patterns were called *innate releasing mechanisms.*

1. One example would be the movement of the mother duck as a releasing mechanism for the ducklings to follow the mother. Another example would be the red spot on the beak of a seagull as a releasing mechanism for the baby gull to peck at the parent's beak, which in turn, was a releasing mechanism for the parent gull to open her beak and let the baby gull eat the food she had collected.

2. In primates, there are several signaling or releasing mechanisms in one member of a species that elicit specific responses from another of the species.

II. As Bowlby theorized, there are also innate releasing mechanisms in humans that elicit attachment patterns quite similar to the imprinting of some lower species.

  ©2002 The Teaching Company Limited Partnership

A. What are some of the primary releasing mechanisms in an adult—the mother—that elicit proximity seeking and attachment formation in babies?

1. Babies respond to the soft, warm feel of skin and cloth. They cling and grasp automatically when they come in contact with hair, skin, or soft cloth, and they are comforted by this physical contact.
2. Babies respond to faces, especially to eyes, and like looking at them. Particularly after about eight weeks after birth, babies like making eye contact.
3. Babies respond to smiling, which after about eight weeks after birth elicits an automatic smile from the baby.
4. Babies respond to and prefer the sound range of the human voice, particularly female voices, and seem to be calmed by voices.

B. Reciprocally, what are some of the primary releasing mechanisms in a baby that elicit proximity seeking and attachment formation in adults, e.g., the mother. Some of the same releasing mechanisms work both ways.

1. Adults respond to the soft feel of babies. In particular, adults like the feel of a baby who clings and grasps them.
2. Adults like looking at the eyes of another person and particularly like making eye contact with a baby.
3. Just as babies do, adults automatically respond with a smile when someone smiles at them, particularly a baby. They find watching a baby smile or laugh to be extremely pleasurable and rewarding. Smiling in humans seems to convey a universal message regardless of culture. The message is: I like what is happening; keep it up.
4. Although adults like the sound of a baby, they find a baby's cry extremely distressing. It is a negative releasing mechanism that is nearly impossible to ignore. Like smiling, crying in humans seems to convey a universal message regardless of culture. The message is: I don't like what is happening; change things.

III. Lorenz argued that one particular set of innate releasing mechanisms elicits nurturing behavior in fellow members of a species. He called these releasing mechanisms features of *babyishness.*

    A. What are these babyish features in humans?

        1. Babies typically have extra large heads in proportion to the total body size and extra large eyes in proportion to the head.

        2. Babies have a large forehead in proportion to the head.

        3. Babies have soft, fatty, rounded, and non-angular features. For example, they have a rounded chin; a small, rounded nose; large, puffy cheeks with no visible cheekbones; and soft, dimpled hands, fingers, and limb joints.

    B. Similar babyish features are also found in several other species, such as rounded, non-angular muzzles and faces; large eyes; and fat, round bodies in puppies. However, these common babyish features appear only in species that have a period of immaturity and complex parenting behaviors. For example, lizards, which have no parenting period, are born looking like miniature adults with no babyish features.

    C. Whenever one human perceives babyish features in another, that person automatically feels a release of feelings of nurturance toward the babyish individual.

        1. According to an ethological approach, in response to releasing mechanisms that signal that someone is immature and unable to take care of himself, we have evolved this nurturing reaction. This adaptive response ensures that nurturance and protection will occur.

        2. We can't help ourselves; we want to cuddle and nurture and protect the person with the babyish features. This occurs in children responding to a baby, in adolescents, in childless adults, and in parents.

        3. This automatic response even occurs across species. We respond with nurturance and attraction to puppies, kittens, baby gorillas, and ducklings. There is some evidence that individuals in other species reciprocally respond with nurturance to the babyish features in human babies and children.

©2002 The Teaching Company Limited Partnership

D. The result of this reciprocal eliciting system is so strong that adults even respond with nurturance and protection to other adults with babyish features.

1. Leslie Zebrowitz has carried out many studies to show that we see adults with baby faces as being more immature, kind, innocent, and in need of help but less competent and responsible for their actions than mature-faced individuals.

2. These perceptions and biases that we have are independent of attractiveness in others, and they influence who we choose for certain positions and responsibilities, how we choose jurors, how we decide guilt or innocence in court cases, and how we choose partners for various activities.

IV. What is the normal course of development of these early attachments?

A. Some significant changes in the first few months seem to coincide with the onset of the signaling behaviors called releasing mechanisms that we discussed above. These changes show the reciprocal nature of the attachment process. The parent is becoming attached to the baby at the same time that the baby is becoming attached to the parent.

1. In the first three weeks after a full-term birth, the baby emits some releasing behaviors, such as grasping, clinging, cuddling, and crying; nevertheless, mothers usually report feeling exhausted and frustrated with their parenting.

2. From about four to six weeks after birth, the baby's routine stabilizes, and the confidence of the mother increases.

3. At about seven to eight weeks, major portions of the baby's cortex are first able to fire—that is, to function—and with these brain changes come behavioral changes that affect the attachment process. This period is often called the *seven-week shift.*

4. The baby now begins visually to track a person's face and make clear eye contact. In addition, the baby begins to smile in response to what another person does. Not surprisingly, at this time, the mother often says, "My

baby is now a real person," "My baby knows me," or "He is now a lot of fun."

5. At about three to four months, turn-taking in talking and listening and in playing simple games, such as peekaboo, emerges. At this time, the mother often reports that she needs the baby and cannot live without him.

6. By about five to six months, it is clear that the baby has specific preferences to only a few other people and shows signs of specific attachments.

7. Between seven and 12 months, two significant behaviors appear in the baby. First, most babies begin to show *separation fear*. When the person to whom the baby is attached is not present, the baby shows distress, often crying or cowering and looking for the attached person.

8. Second, most babies also show *stranger fear*. When a stranger comes near the baby, the baby freezes, watches the stranger carefully, clings to the parent or hides behind the parent, and often cries.

9. These two behaviors demonstrate extreme discrimination and preferences for a specific attached person.

10. Mothers will often admit that they secretly like this behavior in their children because it demonstrates that the children prefer her to anyone else.

B. As children develop secure attachments, they acquire the sense of a secure base, which we discussed last lecture, and they are able to explore their environments and make contact with other people. Thus, securely attached children gradually branch out to form additional relationships and to become attached to other people, as well.

Supplementary Reading:

Bowlby, *Attachment and Loss*, Vol. I: *Attachment*, Parts 3 and 4.

————, *Attachment and Loss*, Vol. II: *Separation, Anxiety and Anger*, Parts 1 and 2.

Questions to Consider:

1. Why do you think it is important for the survival and adaptation of our species to have not only infants who are predisposed to becoming attached to their parents but also parents who are predisposed to becoming attached to their infants? What are

some of the factors that may disrupt this normal system from occurring?

2. Do you think there is anything biological or "built in" to make the mother a more likely attachment figure for the baby than the father or some other person who is close to the baby?

Lecture Thirteen
How Nature Ensures That Attachment Will Occur

In our last lecture we introduced attachment theory; and as I mentioned, we're going to talk about attachment theory in the next few lectures. Today I'd like to talk about how nature works to ensure that attachments develop and also introduce the Theory of Ethology, what that theory is all about, and explain how ethology theory was used to explain this theory of attachment. But I'd like to particularly focus on the idea of innate releasing mechanisms, and I'll explain what those are. Then, we'll conclude with a romp through the course of development of the onset of attachment to show how these attachments get started from birth and in the first few years.

As I mentioned, John Bowlby and Mary Ainsworth were the two people who jointly formulated attachment theory. We're mainly going to talk about John Bowlby's work today. When John Bowlby rejected the Freudian psychodynamic theory as an inadequate way to explain how attachment develops, he turned instead to ethology theory. Now ethology theory first emerged in the mid-20th century and it emerged from the work from mainly three European naturalists, Karl von Frisch, Nikko Tinbergen, and Konrad Lorenz. Later on, they actually won a Nobel Prize for their work. Ethology theory is really a general approach to studying animal behavior. These folks were biologist naturalists, but they studied behavior in animals and development of behaviors in animals that focused on the adaptive importance of particular behavior patterns. They were interested in the evolutionary significance of certain behaviors and how these behaviors then had evolved in a particular species. They carried out a lot of detailed systematic observations of different species, and they described how certain complex behaviors worked to bring this adaptation about. They tried to explain why certain behaviors would have evolutionary significance.

Certain complex action patterns, often called instincts, seem to accomplish this adaptation, and these instincts would kick in at critical periods in an individual's life. These are the ideas that came out of this ethology theory. A critical period is defined as a time in an individual's life, in any given species, in the course of its development when that animal is particularly sensitive to certain environmental cues, and primed to respond to these environmental cues. If the individual's in that critical period and something happens

 ©2002 The Teaching Company Limited Partnership

in the environment, some signal is given, the individual will respond, and will thus maybe develop a certain pattern and have a normal development. Outside of this critical period, either before it or after it, the individual may not respond the same way. So, certain skills or reorganizations of the neural system are likely to occur during critical periods. The critical period primes that individual to develop or to have a neurological change.

There's a prime example of this action pattern in a critical period that's seen in the idea of imprinting. Konrad Lorenz first explained imprinting; he gave it the name. In imprinting, a newborn animal responds to the movements of another object or the features of another object in close proximity to that animal and forms, obviously it has to form some kind of neurological connections or patterns of firing that now make the other object a preference and will keep the animal trying to seek the proximity of that other object or thing. If that sounds sort of vague, let me give you some specific examples in just a minute. Let me mention though, it happens in a critical period. If time passes and the critical period is gone, imprinting won't occur. In imprinting, the connections have to be made during this period when it seems like through genetics this animal is predisposed to respond. Imprinting mainly took place in birds, although it could occur in other animals as well.

When Lorenz studied it, he looked at ducks, geese, and animals like that. When a duck hatches, it will imprint on the first moving object of a certain size—usually about the size of the duck's mother, but any size from a loaf of bread up to the size of a small person—and what happens is that when the duck hatches at that point there's a critical period in the duckling's life and the first moving object is what the duckling responds to, and then will follow and seek the proximity of that object. Now normally, the first object would be the duck's mother. The egg hatches, there's the mom, she walks around and the duck starts to follow her—or the goslings do this with a goose mother. But the neat thing was that you could do this kind of experiment to show that it worked with other objects beside the mother. This was a way, by the way, that made sure that the child or the young stuck with the mother, this imprinting was a way to make sure they were bonded, and this attachment emerged and then continued. Let me give you an example of the kind of study that Lorenz did.

He took the eggs and had them hatch without the mother being present. And, you could put something else there, you could have an artificially animated breadbox walking around and the ducklings or the goslings would follow the breadbox. The famous study that he did was he took the eggs, put them by themselves, when they hatched he crouched down and walked around and the goslings followed him around. There are some famous pictures—you may have seen one—of Konrad Lorenz walking around the yard doing his chores with this whole string of goslings following him around. He became their mother, permanently bonded for the rest of their youth. In their childhood, if you will, he was their mother.

Now, ethologists believe there are certain cues in a particular individual or object that then end up releasing these signals so that a person will then respond and imprint to this person. The cues may be colors, or patterns, or certain actions; and whenever you see these signaling patterns, another individual will respond in a certain way. He called these *innate releasing mechanisms*, these cues or patterns. So, movement in a mother duck is an innate releasing mechanism for the ducklings to follow the mother. Some of you may have seen on seagulls, different kinds of gulls, a red spot on the beak of the adult gulls. That red spot is an innate releasing mechanism, a signal to babies to peck at it. That part's built in—in some way they've developed, and they can't help themselves—when they see that red spot, they want to peck at it, and that pecking at it is then an innate releasing mechanism that signals the adult to then open its beak. And so, the mom or dad will open its beak, typically they've gone and picked up a lot of food for the young. When the young sees the beak she pecks at it, when she pecks at it the mother or father opens the beak and the baby eats. So here's another form of an innate releasing mechanism. And there are several innate releasing mechanisms in primates as well, that seem to elicit specific responses.

So Bowlby theorized that there would also be innate releasing mechanisms in humans that would elicit attachment patterns quite similar to the pattern of a lower species. In humans, we don't have imprinting and we don't have critical periods that are so absolutely set—the way you find them in birds, for example—but he argued that we do have something like imprinting that works in a similar way and we do have something like critical periods, and most people agree. It's a little hazier for humans; we're not locked into instincts, but there's something there.

 ©2002 The Teaching Company Limited Partnership

So there would be some kind of mechanism that would elicit proximity seeking and then attachment formation in babies. They would respond to something the mother was doing, or some way, the way she looked. Now—by the way, I've mentioned this before, but when I use the word mother, I mean a parent or another caretaker, whoever is playing that parenting and mothering role—babies respond to soft, warm things like skin and cloth. If you ask what are the innate releasing mechanisms in a mother or the parent that would elicit these kinds of behaviors from the babies—softness, warmness, cloth; they cling and they grasp automatically. I don't think they can help themselves. This is not a learned behavior; they come into the world doing this, and everything they do tends to indicate that they like this, that they prefer it, this kind of physical contact. In fact, there's a lot of other work with some kinds of primates, with some kinds of monkeys and primates, who do the same thing. They tend to have a strong preference for what's called *contact comfort*, comfort and softness and being able to cling to it.

Babies also respond to faces. So faces are innate releasing mechanisms, signals that the baby likes these faces, they like to look at these faces. They particularly like eyes; and studies show that if you put different stimuli up to a baby to look at, babies will prefer a face to other kinds of stimuli. If you put a face up, they tend to look at the eyes more than anything else once they've developed at a certain level of the visual system that they can control their looking—which is at about seven to eight weeks after birth. They like to make eye contact or, from the baby's standpoint, they like looking at faces and they do make eye contact. What else do they respond to? Smiling. So smiling in the mother or in adults is an innate releasing mechanism to the baby. So, after about seven to eight weeks of development after birth, if you smile at the baby, it elicits an automatic smile back from the baby, and babies tend to like that and will look for smiling, and they quickly learn to try to elicit smiling. Babies also respond to the sound range of the human voice. If you give them music—they may like music they may like other things—but what they particularly like is sound in the range that the human voice is in, particularly female voices. Female voices tend to calm them; and some people have argued they've been conditioned to this in utero. Maybe, maybe not; but they come into the world liking this level of sound.

©2002 The Teaching Company Limited Partnership

Let me give you a demonstration, or at least talk you through a demonstration. If you want to impress people with how good you are with babies—they have to be about seven to eight weeks of age, but sometime in there you get a three-month baby—if you get down close to the baby's face and you bob up and down and move your face and open your eyes really wide and your mouth very wide and exhale delightedly, babies will smile and everyone will tell you that you really have a good way with babies. But, in fact, you are giving innate releasing mechanisms or signals that the baby can't help himself, he smiles because he sees the big face and the big mouth moving, he sees the big eyes, and he sees some of that movement. That's what he likes.

Now reciprocally, there ought to be some releasing mechanisms in babies that would then turn on mothers and fathers, because the attachment system is reciprocal. You remember last time we said that if you want the baby to be attached to the mother, you want the mother to be attached to the baby. You want them both to stick together; and so, we're all in the same species, you might expect that these releasing mechanisms are really going to be similar, parallel releasing mechanisms, and they are. So what do we adults like in babies? Well, adults respond to the soft feel in babies. In particular, adults like it when a baby clings and grasps them. So, no matter how hard and tough you think you are, most of us have this good feeling when a baby sort of molds herself to you and clings and sort of cuddles. That feels good to people.

Adults also like looking at the eyes of another person, particularly babies, but all of us like eyes, and we like to make eye contact with babies; it turns us on. Just as babies do, adults automatically respond to smiles. When somebody smiles at you, you usually smile back and you really can't help yourself. In babies, we love it when they smile and we love it when they laugh. We find that rewarding. I say that "we" do; this is not something that only people learn like mothers, but children respond that way, teenagers respond that way, males respond that way, females respond that way, whether you're a parent or not. Maybe not everyone in the world responds that way, but that's the tendency. Smiling seems to be a universal message, regardless of culture. It doesn't matter where you come from; when somebody smiles at you, the message is, "I like what's happening, keep it up," and we find that smile rewarding.

 ©2002 The Teaching Company Limited Partnership

Adults maybe like some sounds from babies, but they have one particular sound that they respond to, and it's a distressing, aversive sound. When babies cry, that's an innate releasing mechanism to adults. It's highly aversive and it's distressing. It's meant to be. It's almost impossible to ignore. We can cry, but it's difficult. It's meant to be aversive, it's an innate releasing mechanism to get us to respond to the baby because, like smiling, crying in babies conveys a universal message regardless of culture, and that message is when somebody cries, the message is, "I don't like what's happening, change things." When we hear that in a baby, we have a tendency to want to respond.

There's one set of innate releasing mechanisms that Konrad Lorenz argued elicit, in particular, nurturing behaviors in fellow members of particular species, and he called these releasing mechanisms, these features, set of features, babyishness. All animals that have an extended period of immaturity and parenting, tend to have young offspring who don't look like the adults of the species, but have certain features that we'll say, are babyish features; and, of course, we have these babyish features in humans as well.

So what are they? These features of babyishness—which remember are innate releasing mechanisms to bring people closer together—I have to say; I don't know where they started. The baby's features are probably just some mechanical result of the way we develop physically; but the argument is the way we've evolved, that when we see these features, we're drawn to them. We're attracted to them and they release a certain kind of behavior pattern in us. So, babies typically have very large heads in proportion to their total body size. A large head relative to the whole body is a baby's feature. They also have extra large eyes in proportion to their head. But before I sound like we're getting into the Little Red Riding Hood story, they don't have extra large teeth, for example, or extra large ears. They have large heads, large eyes. They also have a very large forehead in proportion to the whole head. If you look at a baby, the eyes, the features of the face are relatively low with a big head, a big forehead; but they tend to have soft, fatty, rounded and not angular features. So, for example, they have a rounded chin. They have a small and rounded nose. They have large puffy cheeks with no visible cheekbones. They have soft, dimpled hands. They have joints with dimples and roundness. All of these things are baby's features in humans.

You can find some of these same babyish features in other species. So, in a lot of species you can find rounded, non-angular muzzles, for example, on a cat or a dog. You can find large eyes, fat round bodies—if you think of a little puppy with a fat, round tummy and non-angular sort of short noses—some of the same features. But remember, they only appear in the species that have complex parenting behaviors. I keep going back to lizards as my extreme example. Lizards, when they're born, don't have baby features. They're small, but they look the same as adults. They're miniature adults. They have no baby features, because they have no parenting; and there are other species like that.

So, whenever one perceives babyish features in another person, this person feels this release of feelings of nurturing towards this other person. So the innate releasing mechanism is a set of features, and what it releases, the behavior it releases, is this feeling of wanting to protect, nurture and take care of the other person. We can't help ourselves. We want to take care of people. We want to nurture people. We want to protect people who have babyish features, namely babies. We can't help it. In fact, it works across species at times. So you have humans who see a little puppy or kitten, and what do they do? They say, "Oh, she's so cute." They want to pet it and cuddle it and take care of it. The same with a cat, the same with a gorilla baby, we usually don't hold them, but we see that and we have that same kind of reaction, we want to protect that person.

Of course, it happens with human babies too. You see a baby, and if the baby has a lot of these babyish features you go, "Ooooh!" is your response. This happens again in adolescence, in childless couples, in males and females, as well as parents. So Bowlby argued it's an automatic response; we can't help ourselves. There's even some anecdotal evidence that it happens the opposite way across species; for example, dogs will sometimes be more tolerant of babies than they are of adult humans. You'll sometimes hear stories of dogs protecting babies or young children. There's the recent case of a little girl who fell in the gorilla area of the zoo and the gorilla mother went over and protected her. It even works, and we actually used it this way, in dolls. If you think of how dolls work for little girls—really for all of us—dolls are made with baby features, extremely large heads relative to the volume of the doll. They have extremely large eyes, rounded features, the kind of things that will elicit nurturance and this reaction, even from kids.

It works with makeup. So for women, very often what they're doing when wearing makeup is emphasizing the babyish features of their face. You maybe didn't realize you were doing this. You put makeup on your eyes to make the eyes look bigger and stand out relative to the size of your face. You put lipstick on in a way to make your eyes look rounder and puffier. I don't think all makeup makes women look like babies, and maybe not all of it is intended to, but there's a lot of makeup that makes women look more babyish, whether they realize it or not. Why would that be? Well some people have argued that it's stressing innocence, a need to be protected, and a need for nurturance. In fact, in women, if you think about it, in some ways they have on average more babyish features than men, in the sense that they have less angular and more rounded features. That's maybe one reason they get treated the way they do, in some small part.

There's a social psychologist, Leslie Zebrowitz, who has even shown that these babyish features continue in our species. Maybe they're meant to have this response of mother to child, but we respond that way even adult to adult. So, there have been many studies that Leslie Zebrowitz carried out to show that we respond to people who have baby faces, or immature faces as adults, in a different way than we respond to people who have mature faces. At least, there's that tendency. We see people who have baby faces as being more innocent, kinder, and more honest, those are good features. But we also see them as being less confident, less responsible than mature-faced individuals; and these perceptions and biases are independent of the attractiveness of others. You can have two people that you rate on attractiveness or sex appeal, and they can be equal; but you see these differences if one is more baby-faced than another. In fact, the research has shown that it influences flatly, how we choose people for different positions of responsibility, how we choose jurors, how we decide guilt or innocence in court cases, how we choose partners for various activities.

For example, in court cases, in criminal cases, if someone is a defendant and has a baby-face, that person is more likely to be found guilty of crimes of negligence, when they didn't do what they were supposed to do, but less likely to be found guilty of crimes that were pre-meditated, of careful planning. It doesn't mean that this is the only thing that controls our behavior; it's just one slight tendency or push in that direction.

So you can see that baby-facedness seems to be a strong way that we respond to others. This is across cultures, by the way, with people doing studies in another culture or another ethnic group. It seems to be there early on in babies, and it seems to last throughout life. Bowlby argued this is one of the main features, which we use to bring babies together, to bring mothers and babies together so they want to be together, they have this closeness.

Let me now shift for a minute and tell you about the normal course of development of these early attachments. I've given you this sort of background process that happens. There are some significant changes in the first few months, and they coincide with the onset of certain signaling behaviors and these releasing mechanisms that we've discussed, and they also show the reciprocal nature of attachment, that it's happening for both the parent and the child. The parent's becomes attached to the baby, at the same time the baby's becoming attached to the parent.

In the first three weeks after birth, after a full-term birth, the baby emits some of these releasing methods or behaviors. They grasp, they cling, they cuddle, they cry. They have some of the babyish features. Nevertheless, moms and parents usually report feeling exhausted and frustrated with their parenting; and the one thing that seems to be missing in these first few weeks is the babies aren't smiling, they're not making eye contact, and they don't have the full-blown babyish features, the real pudginess and fatness about them. In about four to six weeks though after birth, the baby's routine stabilizes. They're more predictable in what they're going to do, and the confidence in the mother increases when you talk to mothers and they talk about what's happening in their parenting behaviors.

At about seven to eight weeks, there's a major shift in that a lot of the cortex now kicks in, it's a mylanization of neurons that now, a lot of the cortex can now fire that was not possible before about seven weeks. They call it the seven-week shift. It seems to be a maturational process. It doesn't have much to do with the way a baby's treated or brought up. When this cortex kicks in, there are association areas that then allow voluntary kinds of behaviors, and after about seven weeks, babies change. They start sleeping for longer periods of time. But the important change is, for our discussion today, is they start making clear eye contact. They'll track the eyes of the mom or somebody else, and they start smiling. So, you smile at the baby now, and the baby looks at you and smiles back. Surprise, surprise! In seven to eight weeks, mothers report, "This baby is a real person! I love this baby." So, at the time that this happens for the baby, the mothers now get excited and life becomes better. They say, "My baby's a real person; my baby knows me. He's a lot of fun."

At about three to four months, turn-taking starts kicking in. It's a gradual process; that is, babies start listening, and they play simple games like peekaboo. At this time, the mother starts reporting, "I need this baby. I can't live without this baby." You could say that she's primed by culture to think that way, but now they report it; it's a gut feeling. At about five to six months it's clear that babies have specific preferences for only one or a very few individuals. You could say that they really have attached; they prefer one person and they don't prefer another. At five to six months you see that; and, of course, the mother's like that too. They've already said, "I can't live without this baby."

Starting at about seven months, and between seven and 12 months, two really significant behaviors appear in babies. First, most babies begin to show *separation fear*. That is, when the person that they are attached to leaves and is not present, they show extreme distress. They cry, they cower and they look for the attached person. They don't like it when the person is separated. The second thing they do is they show *stranger fear*. So when a stranger comes into the room or comes near the baby, the baby freezes, watches the stranger very carefully, often hides behind the mother, and sometimes cries. These two behaviors demonstrate an extreme discrimination and preference for a specific, attached person; and mothers, even though they'll tell you, "Oh, I don't know why he's acting like that; I'm sorry," privately admit they love it because it says, "My baby likes me more than he likes you," and that turns them on.

We're now going to finish this discussion; but next time, we will continue with a discussion of the development of attachments, how insecure and secure attachments develop, and what they mean.

Thank you.

Lecture Fourteen
Development of Secure and Insecure Attachments

Scope:

This lecture describes the normal development of a secure attachment and Ainsworth's *strange situation task*, which has become the most popular assessment for secure attachment. It then discusses insecure attachments and how they predict several psychopathological problems in development. The lecture also looks at two major causes of insecure attachments, bad parenting and the child's innate temperament, and concludes with a way these two causes may be complementary.

Outline

I. As we discussed in the last lecture, humans are predisposed to form strong parent-infant attachments. According to Mary Ainsworth, secure attachments versus insecure attachments are made when parents are consistent in their interactions with their children.

    A. Schaffer and Emerson, for example, showed that babies develop strong attachments with the people in their lives who are the most emotionally and socially interactive with them.

        1. A child forms a strong attachment to a person who talks to her, hugs her, plays with her, and laughs with her.

        2. The person who meets the child's basic needs by feeding her and changing her is not necessarily the person to whom the child becomes attached.

    B. Several researchers, including Condon and Sander, Stern, and Kaye, showed that, almost at birth, infants begin coordinating their movement to the sounds and sights associated with humans, and quickly learn to take turns with their parents.

        1. The infant moves, then pauses and waits for the parent to respond. After the parent responds, she pauses and waits for the infant to respond again.

        2. This turn-taking develops into consistent parent-child interactions.

        3. This type of give-and-take interaction seems to be a part of the development of secure attachments.

II. To assess the type of attachment that had formed between a parent and child, Ainsworth developed a technique she called the *strange situation task.*

A. This task consists of a series of events for the infant and parent, usually the mother.

   1. The infant is first placed in a room with the mother alone. In one phase, the mother leaves the infant alone. In another phase, the mother returns. In another, a stranger enters. In another, the mother and stranger are both present with the infant.

   2. The task presents several chances to observe the baby's reactions to separation from the mother, to a stranger, and to reunions with the mother.

   3. Certain patterns of distress shown by infants on separation from their mothers and on encountering strangers were observed. Most important, certain patterns of reactions of the infant to reunion with the mother were also observed.

B. Based on extensive research, Ainsworth classified the patterns found during the strange situation task into three main types of infant attachment.

   1. Type A is called *avoidant attachment.* In effect, the baby seems to ignore the mother, to show minimal distress when she leaves, and avoid her upon reunion. The baby seems to be detached from the mother.

   2. Type B is called *secure attachment.* The baby shows distress when the mother leaves and seeks her proximity, affection, and contact when she returns. The baby shares feelings easily and is easily comforted by the mother. Most children show this type.

   3. Type C is called *anxious-ambivalent attachment* or *resistant attachment.* Babies seem to be ambivalent and inconsistent in their distress and reunion responses. Upon reunion with the mother, the baby often moves toward the mother, then away from her; the baby sometimes acts as if he or she is attempting to punish the mother.

C. Ainsworth, and many other researchers including Main, Vandell, and Easterbrooks, have found that the classifications on this strange situation task do indeed predict the types of attachment that a child develops and subsequent outcomes from these attachments.

1. Children with secure attachments form more secure and normal peer friendships during the preschool years.
2. Children who show the insecure types of attachment are more likely to have behavior problems as children and in school. This is especially true of those who have a resistant or ambivalent attachment type.
3. Children with an avoidant attachment type are more likely to show problems with depression and mood disorders.

III. Ainsworth stressed that almost all children form some type of attachment as infants. The problems come when they form insecure attachments rather than secure attachments; insecure attachments are primarily the result of inconsistent parent-child interactions.

A. Some researchers, such as Brazelton and Tronick, have shown how mothers who don't respond to their infants— "stone-faced" mothers—create infants who attempt to avoid the mothers.

B. Pre-term infants are more at risk for developing insecure attachment styles and having parents who abuse them.

1. Because these pre-term infants are delayed in development, they often do not show some of the releasing mechanisms, such as smiling and making eye contact, until later ages. They also are less predictable and stable in their responses and routines.
2. As a result of early hospitalization of these infants, parents are sometimes separated from them for longer periods of time.
3. Therefore, parents have a more difficult time forming normal attachments to pre-term infants, and insecure attachments can ensue.
4. Because of the research done in this area, hospitals and pediatric care specialists are now able to help parents of pre-term infants adjust to these differences.

 ©2002 The Teaching Company Limited Partnership

5. For example, Tiffany Field showed that extra handling of pre-term infants increased the speed with which they caught up in body weight and in neurological development.

IV. Others have questioned whether the quality and consistency of parenting is the main cause of the development of insecure attachments, as Ainsworth argued. Might not the problem be caused by some characteristics of the child? One cannot blame the problems entirely on the parent.

   A. The infant's innate temperament may have a lot to do with the type of attachment that is formed.

      1. Jerome Kagan has found that some babies are born with an extremely inhibited temperamental style of dealing with the world.

      2. These inhibited infants are extra sensitive to stimulation, especially new aspects of their environment.

      3. They respond with wariness, caution, and an inhibition of behavior, which shows up in their emotions and physiology, as well.

      4. Hill Goldsmith and others found that highly inhibited children are more likely to develop type C attachments—anxious-ambivalent or resistant—which would go right along with their temperaments. For example, these children show more separation distress and stranger fear than most other children. They have a difficult time with changes in their environments.

      5. Children who are extremely uninhibited—at the other extreme in terms of temperamental style—are more likely to develop a type A attachment, one of being avoidant.

      6. Nevertheless, temperamental style alone does not predict problem behaviors the way attachment style does.

   B. Most researchers agree that the development of secure or insecure attachment styles is important for healthy development. Most of them also believe that the development of a particular attachment style depends on a combination of factors from the child's temperament and the way the parents respond to the child.

Supplementary Reading:

Ainsworth, Blehar, Waters, and Wall, *Patterns of Attachment.*

Bowlby, *Attachment and Loss*, Vol. III: *Loss.*

Questions to Consider:

1. In your experience with children, both your own and others, how do you think their individual attributes and temperamental styles interact with the ways their parents treat them to determine the characteristics and styles they develop? How does their nature and predisposition affect the way people treat them and vice versa?

2. What do you see as the major problems that may occur in a child's life if she has not formed an early secure attachment with a parent or parent substitute? Do you see examples of problems occurring when secure attachments are not in place?

©2002 The Teaching Company Limited Partnership

Lecture Fourteen
Development of Secure and Insecure Attachments

Hello. In our last lecture we talked about the early development of attachment and some of the processes that lead to attachment. We particularly talked about the work and theorizing of John Bowlby. In this lecture, I want to discuss the development of secure and insecure attachments and talk about attachments when they do not work in an optimal fashion; and I'd like to talk about Ainsworth's classification of types of attachments, and I'll also discuss the results that occur when children have insecure attachments.

Now, as we discussed in the last lecture, humans are predisposed to form strong infant-parent attachments. According to Mary Ainsworth, secure attachments can also become insecure or, that is, some attachments may not work properly. Mary Ainsworth thought that the primary reason for insecure attachments developing was because of the inconsistent care and interactions that parents showed to their children. John Bowlby was the one who introduced ethology theory, and had a view of attachments forming in sort of a lockstep, automatic way. Ainsworth had more of a view of the strong influence of individual differences from parents—and we're going to talk about that today.

Let me begin by talking about some research that leads up this view of positive and negative kinds of attachments forming. There was some early work by two researchers, Schaffer and Emerson, in which they simply did observations of attachments forming. They went into homes and observed kids interacting with their parents. They looked at what happened when you had stranger fear, when strangers entered. They looked at what happened during separation, when the mother or father would leave. And, they wanted to find out how these attachments would occur, more about this kind of process. What they discovered was first, although a lot of kids develop one single strong attachment to one person, usually the mother, very often kids develop multiple attachments, even from the beginning. So, very often it's the case that a child forms a strong attachment to both the mother and the father at the same time, or often to the mother and an older sibling, or maybe to the mother and an uncle. So different attachments can form early on.

The aspects that seem to really determine which individuals became the attached figures for the babies were the aspects of how these people treated the babies; and what they found in their research was it wasn't dependent so much on *which* people did the caretaking for the kids—that is, who fed the baby, who washed the baby, who put the baby to bed—what was really important were the interactions of who talked to the baby, who hugged the baby, who played with the little child, who laughed with the little child. Very often, it's one and the same person who does this; but, for example, in one family, if the mother does all the caretaking; washes, feeds, cleans, takes care of all the basic needs, spends more time with the baby—90 percent of the time the baby might become attached to the dad or someone else in the family if that's the person showing more of the emotional, social interaction. So that aspect is very important.

There are other researchers that also looked at the early relations between a parent and child and the interactions between them, and the interactions would seem to have to do with the way the attachments would form. Condon and Sander were two researchers that filmed babies right at birth, and what they found was that, even at birth, babies begin coordinating what they do to sounds and eventually to the sights and actions of other people. So, for example, if they played music for a newborn baby, the baby might listen, but the baby wouldn't coordinate his or her actions to the music. If they played human speech, human sounds for that baby, the baby would coordinate the movements, the turning, and the actions in coordination with this human speech. In fact, even if you had nonsense—if you took human speech and parceled it up into making nonsense words or sentences—the baby would still respond. The baby would respond regardless of the language. You could take an American baby and play Chinese speech and the baby would still respond. It was the human speech, that level, that tone, that the baby coordinated to and this was at birth—for all intents and purposes, at birth.

Dan Stern was another researcher who looked into the early interactions of babies to their parents or to other people, and he found that very early on, there was a turn-taking that started to develop, so that babies and moms start to take turns. Moms seem to do this automatically, they don't necessarily think about it, and the babies learn it pretty quickly. The mother will talk to the baby. The baby pauses and looks. Then the mother will stop and pause, and the baby will do something. The mother will do some action; the baby will watch. Then the mother pauses and the baby will do something. So for example you say, "Hi, are we having a good day today?" The baby is watching very carefully, and then the mom stops and looks at the baby and the baby says, "Aaaaaaaaaah!" and flails about; it's turn-taking. Then the mothers start playing games with babies, and the early turn-taking type of games are peekaboo, pattycake. In things like peekaboo you ask, "Where's the baby?" and you put some type of cloth up over the baby's head. The baby pauses—if you watch babies play this game they're still, maybe there's some heavy breathing because they're emotional—you say, "Where's the baby?" and then you stop and the baby rips off the cloth and maybe makes sounds and flails about—the baby's turn.

So right away, Dan Stern and other researchers are showing that we start turn-taking, and turn-taking is learned extremely early. It's very handy in all social interactions that require turn-taking, and particularly in language communication; but it seems to be part of this early attachment process as well.

Ken Kaye did a wonderful experiment, I think, and I remember seeing the videotape showing this experiment. He set up the situation where he wanted mothers to teach their baby to do something, at least that's what he told them. In fact, hardly any mother could teach their babies to do this; the babies were only a few months old. But, he really wanted to watch the way they interacted, the way they went about it. And what he did was he had the mother have the baby sit on her lap in front of a barrier; it was actually a transparent, Plexiglas barrier. He would have the mother get the baby interested in something like a set of keys and jiggle them around, and then put the keys behind the barrier where the baby could still see the keys. The mother's job was to try to get the baby to learn to reach around the barrier to get the keys, to have to not go directly through it, but how you could reach around to get it. So, mothers were really motivated to show how smart their babies were and tried to get them to do this. Remember, almost no mothers got their baby at this really young age to do this. What he was really interested in was the process, what they would do.

What he found again and again was that mothers would give the keys to the baby; the baby would play with them, mouth them, suck them, do these things, and then, after a while they would stop. As soon as the baby stopped, the mother would then take the key and shake them and do things like that, and then the baby would take over again. Eventually, the mother would take the keys and put them behind the barrier and the baby would get excited and bang on the barrier and try to get them, and couldn't get them, of course. Then the mother would pause and do nothing while the baby was responding. When the baby stopped—and very often when they stopped, they would look back over at the mom; it's almost as if they were saying, "I don't know what to do now mom. It's your turn." Then the mom would reach around and shake the keys and the baby would go at it again. Or, maybe the mom would pull him back and try to show the baby that they went around the barrier, pull him a little closer, and then the baby would take a chance.

The point is that it was constant turn-taking. Mom would wait while the baby practiced. Then the baby would pause and wait for the mom to do something. This seemed to be the interaction that was occurring. This give and take interaction then, seems to be part of this process of learning to be attached, of becoming attached. In order to assess the types of attachment that formed though, Mary Ainsworth developed a technique that she called the *strange situation task*. The strange situation—sounds like a science fiction movie—if you recall, I mentioned that first she did a lot of her work in Uganda, and then in Baltimore. This is some of the research that she did, particularly in Baltimore.

This was actually an experimental condition or task that was set up to elicit the kind of attachment, the style or type of attachment that babies would have. It consisted of a series of events for the infant and the parent, usually the mother. I can't keep track of the exact order, but essentially what it was, is the infant is first placed in a room with the mother and the two of them are there alone. They sort of get used to the room, a few toys, and the things to do there. Then at one point, the mother gets up and leaves. Now the mother's directed what to do, and all of this time they're videotaping or observing what the infant does. In another phase the mother returns. In another phase a stranger enters. In another phase the mother and the stranger are both present. In another phase the mother leaves, then the stranger leaves. In effect, it's a series of events that they then observe the baby's reactions to separation from the mother, reactions to a stranger, and reactions to a reunion with the mother;

and they looked at certain patterns of distress that the infants would show upon separation from the mother and on encountering a stranger. But most importantly they looked at the patterns or the reactions of the infant upon reunion to the mother. The reunions were as important, if not more so, than what the babies did when moms left or when strangers entered.

They did extensive research with many, many families; and from this, Ainsworth classified the various patterns that she found in the strange situation task, and she came up with three main types of infant attachment. Now, as a caveat, it isn't the case that kids fall in only one type and they lockstep in that type forever and ever. They're not that separate; it's a gradual blending if you will. Sometimes they might do a little bit of this type, sometimes a little of that type. But, they were able to classify kids as to their predominant or dominant type of attachment. She had Type A, Type B and Type C. Type A she called *avoidant attachment*—and by the way, these same labels are used today and in hundreds of studies these labels for these types of tasks have been used.

The Type A, or avoidant attachment is, in effect, a case where the baby seems to ignore the mother, or pretty much so. It shows minimal distress when she leaves, and upon reunion, when she returns, avoids her. The baby does not seem to be too emotional, does not seem to care when she leaves or when she comes back. There isn't too much response. In fact, almost stays away and sometimes won't make eye contact. This is an insecure attachment type, according to Ainsworth.

The Type B attachment she called *secure attachment*, and babies in this case showed a lot of distress when the mom left. They tried to seek her proximity and affection and her contact when she returned. They would rush to her. They shared their feelings easily, whether they were negative and they were upset, or whether they were positive and they were happy; and they were easily comforted by the mother upon her return. So, even if they were distressed, the mother returned, all was right with the world. The mother comforted them and then they were fine. And most children show this type. So, if you look at any thousands of families, most kids are going to fall in this middle range.

Type C you could argue is maybe at the other end; and Type C she called *anxious-ambivalent attachment* or *resistant attachment.* It goes by two names: Anxious-ambivalent—my favorite—or resistant attachment. Babies in this case, in the ambivalent case, seem to be ambivalent, seem to be inconsistent in the distress they show, when they're separated and in the reunion responses. So, in reunion with the mother, they would often rush towards her and then back away; and they sometimes act like they're trying to punish the mother. They make approaches, they touch her, they get a hug and then maybe they'll even hit her or look away or push off and try to get away. Some people will even point out, sometimes when they've left a baby and the baby's upset, and they come in, they think—"Oh, my baby's trying to punish me because he's so upset that I left." If this is the predominant form, if this is what happens most of the time, they call it the anxious-ambivalent form; and it was also an insecure attachment type.

You see, for Ainsworth, except in rare cases, she didn't believe that there were cases where a kid was not attached—of course there are, a child is left alone to fend for herself with no adults—but in most cases, she said that we're all attached. We can't help ourselves, that's the way we've become as a species; we're all attached. But some attachments are strong and secure, and some attachments are insecure. It's just different kinds of attachments. So, Ainsworth was followed by many researchers, some of them her students, who used this classification system and the strange situation task to indeed show that they [these attachments] exist, not just in her studies, but also time and time again. Actually, these types of attachments will predict different aspects of how the child develops, subsequent outcomes that occur because of these attachments. Mary Main, Deborah Vandell and Ann Easterbrooks are three researchers who come to mind who have done a lot of work on the effects of insecure and secure attachments.

Here's just a sampling of the findings. Children who show very secure attachments to their parents as babies are much more likely to show secure attachments to friends during the school years and to have normal peer relationships or peer friendships. So, kids who have early relationships that are in the secure pattern now form friendships pretty easily. Those who are in one of the two insecure patterns are more likely to have problems with peer relationships and friendships. So, already we see a strong and important result at these

 ©2002 The Teaching Company Limited Partnership

kinds of attachment patterns. Children who show the insecure type of attachments also have more behavior problems when they enter school; they have more problems with teachers, in getting along, and following the rules. This is especially true with the resistant or the anxious-ambivalent type. These kinds of kids seem to be having problems, and they argued that it's at least predicted by attachment type. It's not the full cause, but at least it's predictive.

Children in the avoidant attachment type are more likely to show problems with depression, and mood disorders. So, if you're an avoidant attachment type as a baby, you're more likely to have mood disorders later on as you go through school and become an adolescent. You could ask what are the reasons for forming secure or insecure attachments, and Ainsworth again argued that the main reason is insecure parent-child interactions. In fact, this puts the blame mainly on parents or mothers, so this is a controversial point. But in her research and experience, this is what she argued happened.

Let me now give you some research that was done to show how this inconsistent pattern—the processes that could occur—how this might lead to insecure attachments, and then we'll talk about the idea of whether this is the cause or not. I'm going to talk about some research that was done by T. Barry Brazelton, a pediatrician, and Ed Tronick, a developmental psychology researcher, who did research on what I'll call the "stone-faced mothers," for lack of a better title, for these kinds of studies. The argument here was that mothers didn't respond to their babies. We talk about how they have to because of these built-in releasing mechanisms, but not all people have the same level of these mechanisms. What if a mother or father doesn't respond? The babies make responses, but all the time *they* don't, or are really inconsistent in showing this response to babies. What would happen?

Well, at first Ed Tronick set up a study to try to demonstrate this. Again, I've seen the videotapes of this, and they're quite compelling when you actually see it demonstrated. What he did was he had some mothers come in with their babies, with their little infants a few months old—six to seven months, and he sat the baby in an infant seat in a situation to look at the mom. The mom would stand in front of the baby and he would tell them to not act in your normal way, "I want you to show no emotions or no response to this baby. In other words, I want you to have a stone face. Whatever that baby of yours does, you stand there. Don't smile, don't laugh, and don't frown, no expression—stone face." Then he videotaped the baby to see what the baby's response would be at the same time he videotaped the moms to see what they were doing at this time.

What he found was this sequence of events for the babies. The babies would first look at the mother who came in and stood there, and look very excited. These were babies that were attached to their mothers. These were normal babies, by the way, who were securely attached, and they would flail about and smile and make excited noises, happy to see their moms, and the moms would do nothing. The baby would pause—the turn-taking I told you about. It was sort of a turn-taking but the mother didn't respond; it was her turn but she did nothing. The babies would look at her. So they'd try harder. They'd try more exaggerated movements and more excited noises. They'd smile and they'd do everything and they'd pause—it's mom's turn—and the mother would do nothing. They would try harder again to get her to respond; and then, after a while, they would try tricks that we'll call flirting—which I have a tendency to think that even babies have and maybe we don't have to learn them; they're just part of our nature. They would turn away and look back, sort of coyly, and smile at the mother. The mothers wouldn't respond. It always worked in the past, and now it wasn't working!

They would try everything; and after a while—a few minutes of this—the babies would turn away and not look at the mother. They wouldn't make eye contact with her. Once in a while they'd look back and even smile, and if she hadn't changed, they'd look away. By the end of this study, they were looking away and were slumped down in their seats. They would just sort of melt and slump into the infant seat. It got so bad they had to stop the study because the mothers couldn't take it anymore, it got to the point of seeming to be abusive to their children, it made them so sad. It looked like the babies were depressed, like something was wrong with them, and it happened within a matter of minutes. So his argument was, what if this happens over and over again, if this was the way the parents respond or very often respond?

Let's say the mother is depressed or has some kind of disorder, something's happening. By the way—remember it's reciprocal—moms had a hard time doing this study. Not only would they get upset at their babies looking like this, but when the babies would coyly look at them and smile and try to get them to smile, you'd see mothers who could hardly stand to keep the stone face. They started to grin and they had a hard time following the directions.

Barry Brazelton did a similar study, but this time in nature. He did a case study of a mother who was blind who had a sighted child and seemed to be pretty well attached. The father could see and the baby seemed to be very well attached. But he filmed in detail the sequences that they would go through, and what he found in the filming was that the baby had learned to not make eye contact or facial contact with the mother. So the baby would not look at the mother's face and would look away, and yet they had a strong attachment because the mother compensated; she did a lot of rubbing and hugging and talking and the baby was attached to her. And the baby would make normal eye contact with the father, but not the mother. In this case it was a normal attachment, but some other things compensated it. OK. This is a case then that maybe shows the processes that one might go through in developing insecure attachments.

There's another case where you could talk about it as a natural example for insecure attachment. In pre-term infants, babies are often born without the releasing mechanisms that we talked about. The full baby's features might be a little bit more skinny or shriveled up. They don't have quite the babyish features. They don't respond. Because they're delayed in development, they don't show eye contact, the smiling we talked about until a later age; and they're also less predictable, they're less stable as pre-term infants, their routines don't get stabilized as soon. In fact, there is more of a problem of attachments forming in pre-term infants, of stable secure attachments. There's more likely to be insecure attachments. This is particularly true if you had an infant that had health problems that had to be hospitalized for some time after birth.

In fact, they found that the visiting patterns of parents predicted whether secure attachments would form or problems would form. Parents who visited daily, who spent a lot of time with their infants in the pre-term nursery, tended to do better; parents who stayed away, often because it was so upsetting and they didn't know how to respond, and they cared deeply but they didn't visit and they didn't make this contact, often had more problems with insecure attachments later on. So, what they found was that the babies who showed these problems, and the parents who understood what was going on with pre-term problems and could adjust or compensate for what was happening to them, would do OK. In fact, now when you have pre-term infants, hospitals will encourage parents to take part in the care. So, for example, Tiffany Field has found that if babies that are pre-term are rubbed and rolled around, these little fragile-looking babies, in fact, will increase significantly in body weight and in neurological development at a faster speed than those babies who don't have this kind of rubbing and treatment. It's changed the way we look at treatment of pre-term infants.

Others have questioned whether the quality and the consistency of parenting is a main cause of insecure attachments. So, even though Ainsworth said it had to do with inconsistent parenting, might there be some other reason for this as well? Do we have to blame the parents entirely? Well, the main other reason that's given is an infant's innate temperament. It may have a lot to do with just the innate style of the infant on whether secure or insecure attachments form. Jerome Kagan is one such researcher who found that babies are born with different styles of temperaments, even at birth. Some kids have this extremely inhibited style. They're extra sensitive to stimulation from outside; but being extra sensitive, they tend to freeze up and be wary and cautious, especially to new aspects of their environment. Something happens, something comes into their view, they freeze, they look around, and they can't function. Other infants are born with an extremely uninhibited or outgoing type of temperament. Nothing fazes them; they're not as sensitive to change. And most people are somewhere in between. In fact, what Kagan found was this inhibited temperament has a stable, lasting influence. Over time, these inhibited kids are more likely to become shy kids as preschoolers, and as school age kids. They're more likely to be kids who have more problems with change and newness, novelty in their environments.

Hill Goldsmith and others have taken this information and looked at attachment styles, and they have found that highly inhibited children are more likely to have the Type C attachment style, of being anxious-ambivalent or resistant. For example, these children show more separation distress, stronger stranger fears than most other children. They have more difficult times with changes in the environment. Children who are extremely uninhibited, at the other extreme, are more likely to develop the Type A attachment style,

 ©2002 The Teaching Company Limited Partnership

being avoidant, and of not caring. So, temperament from the child may determine the way they develop attachment, not so much the way that the parents treat the child. Kids are just born this way and it's the luck of the draw, so to speak. And, surprise, surprise, most kids are in between.

Most researchers would agree now that it can't be one or the other. It's probably a combination of temperament and also the way they're treated, because one thing that temperament style does not do, it doesn't predict the problems that develop from these insecure attachments that you get just from insecure attachments. So it's probably some combinations, which is probably the best way we should look at it at this time.

Next time we're going to talk about a further consequence of attachment style, and that is the relation of attachments to further relationships in adulthood.

Thank you.

Lecture Fifteen
Early Attachments and Adult Relationships

Scope:

This lecture concludes the discussion of attachment theory by discussing the long-term relations between early attachment and later relationships. The lecture first describes Bowlby's concept of an *internal working model* of the child's attachment and its functions in providing constant security. The internal working model also influences all subsequent attachments. The lecture describes an example of this relation found in Everett Waters's study of the continuity between infant attachments and adult attachments. The lecture concludes with a discussion of how early attachments also influence adult romantic relationships and styles, as shown in studies by Shaver and Hazan.

Outline

I. In the last lecture, we discussed the influence of secure and insecure attachments on a child's development. Parent-infant attachments influence subsequent peer relationships, but they also have an influence on relationships in adulthood. Recall that one of the major functions of early attachments is thought to be its influence on the formation of future relationships. In other words, a healthy parent-infant attachment may make subsequent healthy relationships possible.

II. As part of Bowlby's theory of attachment formation, he proposed that during the first two years of life, children develop an *internal working model* of each of their primary attachment relationships.

  A. Why is this construct called an internal working model?

  1. It is *internal* because it is a mental representation of the person to whom the child is attached, including his or her behaviors and the actions and emotions involved in the relationship between the attachment figure and the child himself.

  2. It is a *model* in that it is a prototype or copy of the person and relationship to which the child can refer or think about.

  3. It is considered a *working* model for two reasons: It is

 ©2002 The Teaching Company Limited Partnership

constantly changing or under revision, as in "a work in progress," and it is constantly being used to recall and think about the attached person. The person works with his model.

B. Internal working models are thought to develop when the child is separated from the attached person.

1. When the attached person is not present, the child's secure base is also unavailable; therefore, the child feels insecure.

2. It helps to have some reminder of the attached person available to function much like a security blanket. We all find it comforting at times to carry an object related to our attached person or a picture of the person, perhaps even a "piece" of the person, such as a lock of hair or piece of clothing.

3. As children develop the ability to use symbols and represent absent objects, they become more adept at creating their own internal "security blankets," so to speak. They develop a model or representation of the person to carry around with them at all times and use when the person is absent to provide the secure base. They do not need an external object.

C. This internal working model provides more than a secure base, however. It is also a model for subsequent relationships.

1. When a child encounters a new person and begins to form a relationship with that person, she needs something to guide her as to how she should respond and interact.

2. By turning to her internal working model, she already has the model she needs.

3. The working model is dynamic and changeable. The experiences of subsequent relationships can modify the representation one carries around of the attachment relationship.

D. Freud proposed that *transference* occurs when a person transfers representations and emotions related to one person, such as one's mother or father, onto a new person, such as one's therapist or spouse.

    1. Freud's concept of transference is related to Bowlby's internal working model.

    2. In a sense, the child transfers her experiences with the original attachment figure to the new person simply to figure out how to deal with the new relationship.

    3. Thus, it is not surprising that experiences we have had in previous relationships guide how we respond in new relationships.

    4. The important point made here from attachment theory is that our earliest close relationships start off the transference process and provide the foundation for our internal models.

E. The influence of the internal working model extends beyond childhood. Adults also use their representations of their parent-child relationships as models to guide the ways in which they interact with their own children when they become parents. Thus, they repeat some of the same patterns of parenting that they experienced as children.

F. People may also use their representations of their parents' relationship to each other as the model to guide the ways in which they will now interact with their own spouses or intimate partners. Thus, they repeat some of the same patterns of interacting in intimate relationships that they witnessed in their parents' interactions with each other.

III. Recent research provides evidence for the relation of the earliest attachments to subsequent attachments.

A. Everett Waters, who was a student of Ainsworth, and others were able to re-interview people in their 20s who had been tested in Ainsworth's strange situation task when they were babies to determine the stability of their attachment styles.

    1. From infancy to young adulthood, 72 percent of the people continued to have the same secure or insecure attachment styles with their own children and spouses that they had shown in their attachments to their parents as babies; 64 percent stayed in the same exact category of attachment style with their own children and partners that they had had with their parents.

2. However, early attachment style does not automatically control what one will experience for the rest of one's life. In the study, stressful life events often changed one's attachment style.

3. If a person had an insecure attachment style with his own parents, he was more likely to show more jealousy and controlling behaviors toward his spouse.

4. If a person showed derogation and anger toward his parents, he was more likely to show this same behavior toward his spouse.

5. If a person perceived his parents as being care-giving and care-seeking toward each other, he was more likely to be more loving and show less jealousy and aggression toward his spouse.

B. In other research, Phillip Shaver and Cindy Hazan used Ainsworth's three attachment classifications to explain interaction styles found in romantic relationships.

1. The *secure* style involves a balance of a preference for closeness and a need for autonomy. In some ways, it is reminiscent of Erikson's accomplishment of both a secure identity and a sense of intimacy. These people share feelings easily, have little fear of abandonment, find relationships easy, and tend to prefer sexual relations as part of their commitment to another person.

2. The *anxious-ambivalent* style involves inconsistency in feelings for another. These people are often overly invested in a relationship and, thus, exhibit a lot of jealousy and striving for control and fear of autonomy. They tend to have lower self-esteem when it comes to the romantic relationship, and they like physical contact but often have problems with actual sexual behavior. Often, they drive their partners away by smothering and inconsistent behavior.

3. The *avoidant* style involves a focus on autonomy to the exclusion of closeness. These people don't share feelings easily and experience repeated break-ups and failed relationships. They experience less grief with a break-up, yet they are lonelier. They tend to have more promiscuous sexual relationships, in other words, sex without a commitment to a relationship. In some ways, this style is reminiscent of Erikson's failed intimacy stage in which a person experiences isolation.
4. In their research, Shaver and Hazan found that young adults who rated the style of their current romantic relationship as being predominantly secure also reported having secure attachment styles with their own parents. They remembered their parents as warm and affectionate, and their current parenting to their own children tended to be sensitive and non-compulsive.
5. Adults who rated the style of their current romantic relationship as being predominantly anxious-ambivalent reported having anxious-ambivalent attachments with their own parents. They remembered their fathers as being unfair, and their current parenting to their own children tended to be compulsive.
6. Adults who rated their current style as being predominantly avoidant reported having avoidant attachments with their own parents. They remembered their mothers as being cold and rejecting, and their current parenting also tended to be rejecting.

IV. In conclusion, what seems to be the current status of attachment theory?

A. Most developmentalists today accept that the attachment system develops and functions essentially as Bowlby and Ainsworth described it.

1. Currently, there is much research that is based on attachment theory or has been influenced by it, and there is strong empirical evidence for the processes occurring in humans as Bowlby and Ainsworth theorized.

©2002 The Teaching Company Limited Partnership

2. The processes laid out by the theory are more precise in explaining the development of relationships than are the more general descriptions found in Freud and Erikson's theories.

3. There seems to be increasing evidence for the long-term positive and negative influences, respectively, of secure and insecure first attachments.

4. Attachment processes are now used to explain many related behaviors, including homesickness, the process of infatuation, and the shifts in relationships over time when a marriage or intimate relationship fails.

5. Attachment theory has been highly influential in changing policies of allowing parents to stay with their children in hospitals, of placing newborns with their mothers right after birth, of the way we handle pre-term infants and the way we handle separations of children from their parents, and in other important parent-child practices.

B. However, the theory does have some shortcomings and points of contention.

1. It is still unclear what the causes of insecure attachments are and how much influence comes from the parents' behaviors toward their children.

2. Many see the theory of an internal working model having a strong control of future relationships as metaphorical at best and, indeed, misleading at worst.

3. A more parsimonious view would be that we encode or represent observations and habits from all our experiences, then use what we have learned in future encounters and relationships, but that we do not need some magical construct of an internal working model to explain this process of learning. In fact, the earliest relationships may have only limited influence on future relationships. More likely, all experiences influence subsequent experiences.

C. Attachment theory does organize and simplify the account of a real relationship process that occurs in humans and allows us to understand it, whether accurately or not.

Supplementary Reading:

Waters, Vaughn, Posada, and Kondo-Ikemura, eds. "Caregiving, Cultural, and Cognitive Perspectives on Secure-Base Behavior and Working Models: New Growing Points of Attachment Theory and Research."

Hazan and Shaver, "Romantic Love Conceptualized as an Attachment Process." (Article in the *Journal of Personality and Social Psychology*.)

Shaver and Hazan, "Adult Romantic Attachment: Theory and Evidence." (Article in the book *Advances in Personal Relationships*.)

Questions to Consider:

1. Does it seem to you that in your life and the lives of those you know best, people usually repeat the same patterns from one relationship to another? For example, do people tend to marry spouses similar to their own parents, or do they get involved in romantic relationships that repeat the same patterns with similar partners to those found in earlier relationships?

2. Does it seem to you that attachment theory is a valid explanation for real-life development, that it is not just a fictional story? Why or why not?

©2002 The Teaching Company Limited Partnership

Lecture Fifteen
Early Attachments and Adult Relationships

Hello. In our last lecture, we discussed the influence of secure and insecure development on a child's attachment. Parent-infant attachments influence subsequent peer relations, but they also have an influence on relationships in adulthood. You may recall that back a few lectures ago we talked about the various functions of this reciprocal attachment system, and one of the major functions is thought to be the influence on later or future relationships, on earlier relationships. In other words, healthy parent-infant attachment may make healthy subsequent relationships possible. So today we're going to discuss how these relations between early and later attachments come about, and what the nuances of these attachments are. We'll conclude today with an evaluation of attachment theory. Last week we talked about some work mainly instilled by Ainsworth's theory and her research. Today, we'll switch back more to Bowlby's theory and what he gave us.

Bowlby proposed that during the first two years of life, children develop an *internal working model* of each of their primary attachment relationships, and he called it an *internal working model.* What does this construct mean? Why would he give it this title? Let me break this down. It's *internal* because it's a mental representation. It's a mental representation that the child makes of the person to whom the child is attached, and also the behaviors and the actions and motions that are involved in this relationship between this person that's the attachment figure, and the child himself. It's a *model* because it's a prototype and a copy of the person and the relationship. It's a model or this copy to which the child can refer to and think about. And, it's considered a *working* model, the key word *working* here for two reasons. First, it's constantly changing; it's under revision. Think of it as a work in progress. And second, it's constantly being used. It's used by the child who forms this model to refer to; so think of it as a person working with this model.

Therefore, internal working models are what children develop and are thought to develop when children are separated from the attachment person. If we were never separated from the people we were attached to, we would probably never have to develop working models. If all of our needs were met instantaneously, we would never have to worry about it. But of course, that's never going to happen.

When a child's secure base is not available, the child's going to feel insecure, and so it helps to have some kind of reminder of that attached person. That reminder, being around to work sort of like a security blanket works for children. Now if we think about this on the adult level, it will make sense of what children are going through too.

When we leave someone that we're very close to—we go away on a trip for example—when we're going for some period of time and we're attached to these people and we know we're going to miss them, very often we take something with us to remind us of this person. We carry around a picture of the person. We even take a piece of the person. I think more in old days you would take a lock of hair or a piece of clothing, a woman's handkerchief. We also take things that might be valuable and remind us of this person or belong to them. These are like our security blankets, for one thing they do for us is to remind us of this person—having him or her there, with us. Children do this same thing, but children develop the ability to use symbols and represent absent objects—somewhere in the second year of life they get pretty good at this—and when they have this ability, they get pretty adept at creating some internal security blanket, so to speak, rather than carrying around some external piece of the person or having the person there. They can carry around the person inside.

When they develop this model or representation of the person, they can have the person with them at all times. They don't need an external object. So, the idea of an internal working model, even though it's a fancy term, is simply that the person has a working representation of the attached figure and all that goes with that relationship, and can carry this around with them, and therefore always has a secure base. So now, when the child is not with the mother, the child is away at daycare, the child still has a secure base. And that's the purpose, according to Bowlby, of the development of this internal working model that you think of as just this representation. That's what you have throughout life. We can, throughout our life, carry around representations or models of other people.

But, there's a very important by-product of this development of working models, and that is that the model is around now to also become a model for subsequent relationships. So now, when a child encounters a new person—the child's off at daycare now and encounters a new peer, a new person—what's the child do? How does the child know how to behave? If the child likes the person and wants to form a relationship, what can she do? She needs something to guide her. She needs to know how to respond and interact with another person; and by turning to her internal working model, she already has a model of what to do. This is the idea that Bowlby tried to present. This working model is dynamic and changeable. It isn't always static. So, it started with a model from the earliest attachment relationships, but subsequent relationships can modify it. So, a representation that you first had, and developed as a baby with your parents, you now can carry around. But as you make new friends—peer relationships—that's going to modify your model, as you've gained more experience. And you'll have other models, maybe several different kinds of models that you can combine and put together and use to give you information about how to interact with others.

I want to switch to another interesting point. Freud proposed a concept called *transference*, and transference occurs in Freudian terms when a person transfers representations and emotions related to one person onto a new person. So emotions from a relationship that one had with one's mother or father is now placed on a new person, such as one's spouse or the therapist. And for Freud, transference was extremely important as part of his therapy, in using this in therapy. But the point of transference that I want to focus on is how this concept may be related to Bowlby's internal working model, because, in sense, the child transfers in an internal working model the experiences from the original attachment figure to the new person. He's simply trying to figure out how to deal with this new relationship. It's not surprising then that experiences we've had in previous relationships now guide us in responding in new relationships.

When Freud explained transference, it sounded sort of magical; but there's really not much magical about it. It's simply a common occurrence in which we use what we've learned before in experiences, in new situations and new relationships. In Freudian terms, the action of transference can happen in many situations. It can happen as you form new friendships, as you form new intimate relationships. It can happen in different kinds of relationships. You can transfer the parent-child relationship to a teacher-student relationship. You can transfer the parent-child relationship to a therapist-patient or client relationship. You can do many things. You can transfer your intimate spousal relationship to some other kind of relationship. Sometimes it gets you in trouble, because they're not the same kinds of relationships. Other times it's a pretty good way for how to respond in new situations.

The influence of an internal working model then, just like transference in Freudian terms, extends beyond childhood. You see, adults use these representations, the parent-child relationship, as a model to guide how they react later on with their own children. This was the point of Bowlby's working model, as well. When you become a parent, it's the first time. Now, you may have taken a parenting class, but for those of us who have taken a parenting class and then become parents for the first time, you realize it doesn't quite cut it when you get to the real situation. What do you do? How do you behave? And the argument is that you have this internal working model, and you start doing things as your parents related to you. Thus—surprise, surprise—you start repeating some of the same patterns that apparently you experienced when you were a child; and you can repeat the positive very good things, and you can also repeat the negative, maladaptive ways of being a parent, depending on what you experienced.

I have a very good friend who's a teacher, a schoolteacher, who was one day on the playground, and kids were driving him crazy that day. And he started to yell at someone to get them to behave and he said, "As I was yelling at them, I heard my mother calling out to these kids. I looked around to see where she was and I realized it was coming out of me!" So we do repeat the things that we've learned. People also use the representations of their parents in forming relationships with other people, not just parent to child, but in friendships or intimate relationships. So now you're in intimate relationships. How do you behave? What do you do?

The argument goes that you can go back to your parent-child relationship, but now you've incorporated as part of this model the way your parents responded to each other. You look at how they responded as spouses, mom and dad, and use that from your model to learn or to gain experiences on how you would respond to somebody. So in this case, a man now might start responding to his

   ©2002 The Teaching Company Limited Partnership

wife or his partner the way his dad responded to his mother—and the same thing goes the opposite way for a woman. There's a lot of recent research that provides evidence that there's a relation before the earliest attachments and subsequent attachments. This is the crux of this. If this is a good theory, if this really explains things, then it really should be these early relationships relating and influencing later relationships.

So let me tell you about one set of stories to begin with. Everett Waters and several other colleagues did this. Everett Waters was a student of Mary Ainsworth. He did something that we've been waiting for, for some time—this is a fairly recent study. People had not done longitudinal studies, they speculated about this and even asked people how things were when they were children with their own parents. But think about it, none of us can really remember what it was like when we were babies with our parents. So, if you ask somebody and say, "What was your relationship like with your parents," most of the time adults are talking about what it was like when they were teenagers, maybe a little earlier. But you don't get a whole picture. When you do a retrospective study like that, you have some problems. We needed a longitudinal study; but this was a fairly recent concept and people had yet to have done it. Everett Waters and his colleagues have now done this.

What they did was they went back to the people who as babies were interviewed using Ainsworth's strange situation tasks; and they looked at these same people who were now in their mid-20s approximately, and found enough of them, a whole slew of them, that they could actually accept their attachment styles now and what's going on in their life, and they have the actual data and the attachment types and patterns that they showed when they were babies. What they found was, from infancy to young adulthood, people in their 20s, there was a fairly stable style of attachment. 72 percent of all of these people that they tested and interviewed continued to have the same either secure or insecure attachment styles, in general. If you had a secure attachment style when you were a baby, you were more likely to have a secure attachment style now. And they had the same style with their own children, the way they responded to their own children and also the way they responded to their own spouses. Sixty-four percent of them stayed in the exact category. If they were anxious-ambivalent when they were babies, they had an attachment style with their kids that showed an anxious-ambivalent style with their own kids. If they were avoidant as babies, they had an attachment style that they were avoidant with their own kids.

However, 72 percent, 64 percent—that isn't the entire sample. There are a lot of people who did not stay in the same attachment style, they switched; and so they wanted to try to understand which people switched. What they found was that the majority of people that switched from one attachment style as a baby to another attachment style as an adult, had major stressful life events that would seem to be antecedents of these shifts. So for these people, there was a death of an attached figure when they were children, there was a major illness in their life, or in the lives of those important to them or their family, there was a divorce of their parents, there was severe child abuse. Something was going on; it wasn't a routine life, if you will. Some major stressful life events had occurred, and this was the case for most people that switched styles. So, in fact, what they concluded was you stay in the same style unless something comes along in your life that pushes you out of it and you switch. That seems a little bit general, but that's the best way of explaining it right now.

If you look spousal relationships, not just parental relationships, a person who had an insecure attachment style with his own parents was much more likely to show jealousy and controlling behaviors with his or her spouse. If you were insecure as a baby, you were more likely to show high jealousy and more likely to be a control freak in your spousal relationship now. If, as a child, you showed a lot of derogation and anger towards your parents, you were more likely to show this same kind of anger and derogation towards your spouse. If you saw your parents as being very helpful and care giving and care seeking towards each other, saw their relationship of how they were to each other, you were more likely to be loving and show less jealousy and aggression towards your spouse in the current time. You can also see some of these same parenting styles with their kids. I've already mentioned this, but if you had an avoidance style with your parents, you were more likely to be avoidant with your kids, or they were more likely to have an avoidance style to you as the parent, and so on.

There are actually several places in the Bible, the Old Testament, that give quotes like this—I found this in Exodus 24:7, in the last part of that verse there's an injunction of the consequences that happen from certain kinds of bad behavior and it says:

> Visiting the iniquity of the fathers upon the children, and upon the children's children unto the third and to the fourth generation.

Now, it occurs to me that this statement may actually be a statement that reflects the natural order of things, that a natural consequence of whatever happens early on is passed on from generation to generation. It's not automatic, it doesn't mean that we're locked into this forever; but it means certain problems that you had as a child, you're more likely to pass on. Good things are also passed on, and it may go from generation to generation.

Let me now tell you about some other research that was done on early relationships to later relationships, and this is on the topic of influences on romantic relationships. This research was started and done by Phillip Shaver and Cindy Hazan. They used Ainsworth's classification of three attachment types once again, as a model to try to explain interaction styles that we find in romantic relationships in young adults. Their argument is that it would work for adults at any age; but remember they went back to all the literature on attachment to form this basis. Now, the way they assess what your intimate or romantic relationship style is now is to ask a lot of questions that a person will then fill out. These questions deal with different styles. In the long run, what you end up getting from this person is strengths and weaknesses, which questions he would agree with and where he fall on these questions. What you can do then is give someone a rating or a score on each different attachment style. What they're looking for is not absolutely one kind of style in a person, but the predominant style—even though we vary in relationships, the predominant style that we show. Let me read you some statements. This comes from Shaver and Hazan:

> I'm going to read you this statement. You think to yourself and answer honestly. Do you agree with this statement, does it apply to you specifically? Does this explain the way you are, or does it in fact not fit in at all? Here's the first one:
>
> I am somewhat uncomfortable being close to others. I find it difficult to trust them completely, difficult to allow myself to depend on them. I am nervous whenever anyone gets too

close. And often, love partners want me to be more intimate than I am comfortable being.

Do you agree with that for you? Does that fit you or not? Here's another one:

I find that others are reluctant to get as close as I would like. I often worry that my partner doesn't really love me, or won't want to stay with me. I want to get very close to my partner and this sometimes scares people away.

Is that you? Here's a third one:

I find it relatively easy to get close to others and I'm comfortable depending on them. I don't often worry about being abandoned or about someone getting too close to me.

Does this apply to you?

Well, the first case really was based on an avoidant attachment style. The second case was based on an anxious-ambivalent attachment style. The third case was based on a secure attachment style. So the way they translated these attachment types or styles from adult romantic relationships was a secure style. It shows really a balance or need for closeness and a need for autonomy. In some ways it's reminiscent of Erikson's accomplishment of both a secure identity and a sense of intimacy. These people share feelings easily. They have little fear of abandonment; they find relationships easily. They tend to prefer—this is what Shaver and Hazan found in interviewing people—people who say they agree with these statements tend to prefer sexual relations as part of their commitment to another person. They like sex, but they like it in committed relationships.

The anxious-ambivalent style involves sort of an inconsistency in feelings towards another person. People are often overly invested in the relationship and thus they exhibit a lot of jealousy and a striving for control. They often fear autonomy and they're fearful that the person will leave. They tend to have lower self-esteem when it comes to romantic relationships. They like physical contact, they report, but often have problems with actual sexual behavior. They often drive their partner away by smothering the partner or their inconsistency in behavior.

And the avoidance style involves a focus on autonomy to the exclusion of closeness, if we're talking about both the

 ©2002 The Teaching Company Limited Partnership

connectedness, the independence that we had discussed earlier. These people don't share feelings easily. They had faced repeated breakups of relationships. They experience less grief when they break up, yet they also report being lonelier. They tend to have more promiscuous sexual relationships; in other words, they have sex without commitment to a relationship. And in some ways, this style is reminiscent of Erikson's failed intimacy stage in which a person experiences isolation even though they have social relationships. Now I realize this is sort of setting it as absolute. Like I said, people sometimes waver; they tend to be in between. But Shaver and Hazan found that a lot of people have a predominant style, a more modal style that they go to. They found that young adults that rated their style of their current romantic relationships as being predominantly secure, also from the assessments they gave reported all evidence that they had secure attachment styles with all parents. They remembered their parents as being warm and affectionate, and the current parenting to their own children, if they'd been married and had children, also tended to be sensitive and non-compulsive.

Adults who rated their styles in their current romantic relationships as being predominantly anxious-ambivalent reported having anxious-ambivalent attachments to their own parents and they remembered in particular their fathers being unfair. When they had children currently, their parenting styles with their own children was somewhat compulsive. And adults who rated their current styles as being predominantly avoidant, reported again having avoidant attachments to their own parents, and they remembered their mothers as being cold and rejecting quite often, and when they were parents they tended to be more rejecting in the relationships.

Now I have one caveat for these studies. It seems from several different pieces of research that this way of classifying a romantic style seems to hold up. But as of this time, we really haven't done longitudinal studies where we've taken people that we know exactly what went on in their childhood and now related it to their romantic styles in adulthood. These have only been retrospective studies, so we have to be very cautious about any causal effect about what happened earlier and its later relationships.

Let me now conclude by giving you a short critique of this theory of attachment, what are the good points as I see them. Well, most developmentalists today accept the attachment system, how it develops, how it functions. They have essentially accepted it as its been described by Bowlby and Ainsworth. Currently, there is a lot of research that's based on attachment theory, or has been influenced by it; and there's strong empirical evidence for this process occurring in humans as Bowlby and Ainsworth theorized. It seems to be the modal way that we form relationships early on, and it seems to happen automatically. The mechanisms laid out by this theory are certainly more precise in explaining the development of these relationships than the more general descriptions that Freud and Erikson gave us. And, there seems to be increasing evidence for long-term positive and negative influences from secure and insecure first attachments.

These attachment processes explain a lot of related behaviors, like homesickness, like how we stay attached to people even after we split up relationships. So very often, as Robert Wise pointed out, even if a marriage fails, we still are strongly attached to this person. We don't think we love the person anymore, we may be angry toward the person, but we can still have a strong attachment staying over for some time. Attachments end very slowly when we're strongly attached to a person. So there's a lot of research and ideas on how these relationships are related to attachment. Attachment theory has also been highly influential in changing policies. I've mentioned some of this as we went along. Things aren't the same now. Parents stay with their children in hospitals. In newborn nurseries, mothers get to see their children, have them right after birth. This wasn't the case or the way it was years ago. In pre-term nurseries and for pre-term infants, we changed the way we handle them and the amount of interaction that parents have with their children, so there are many different parent-child practices that have been influenced by this theory.

But there are also some shortcomings to the theory. One of the main ones is that it's still very much unclear what causes insecure attachments. If you recall, Ainsworth tended to blame the inconsistency of parenting behaviors, but it's probably some very complex mix of that and the attributes of the child. Many see the aspect, the construct of an internal working model as a strong control of future relationships, as being metaphorical at best, and in some ways misleading. A more parsimonious view that many people would take: Is it simple? Why bring in an internal working model construct to explain it? Simply put, we gain experiences in

 ©2002 The Teaching Company Limited Partnership

everything we do in life, and when we have experiences or things we've learned in one situation, we apply them to future situations.

So our first relationships were with our parents or our first attachment figures, and of course, that gives us experience and representations, it's true, that we then use in subsequent relationships. But think of it as a chaining effect, our subsequent relationships are now changed and developed; and these, along with the first ones, influence the next set of relationships. All along the way, any relationship will give you experience or representations that you can use in subsequent relationships. Therefore, the first attachment relationships are important because they started things off, but they don't control everything. All relationships along the way are important. I think this is the main way to look at attachment theory and it's value today. It seems to simplify an account of this process. It seems to help us to look for the mechanisms behind the process, and it seems to help us to predict future relationships, though I think it is far from over. If you want to talk about a working model, this is a working theory that probably will be changed by the current research that's being done.

In our next lecture we're going to shift to our fourth major theory, Bandura's Theory of Social Learning, and we'll start that next time.

Thank you.

Lecture Sixteen
Bandura's Social Learning Theory

Scope:

This lecture introduces the fourth major theory: Albert Bandura's social learning theory. It begins with an introduction to some basic principles of learning theory, which include the relation between stimulus input and response output and the influence of reinforcements in changing behavior. The lecture then shows how Bandura added a cognitive focus to learning theory by showing how the influence of what one expects to happen is more important than what actually happens. This focus led to the concept of *vicarious reinforcement*. The lecture then discusses the primary role of observational learning and imitation in human development. The lecture concludes with some basic principles of how imitation functions.

Outline

I. Albert Bandura's *social learning theory* was a modification of traditional learning theory, and traditional learning theory grew out of the behaviorist approach of John Watson and others, including B.F. Skinner. Before discussing Bandura's theory, we must discuss some basic premises of traditional learning theory.

   A. The basic model of a behaviorist and learning tradition is what is often called *S-R associations.* The *S* and *R* refer to *stimulus* and *response*.

   1. All that an individual can do and all that it learns is dependent on stimulus input to the organism. A stimulus—the *S*—is picked up by the senses; for example, we see an object, such as a donut, in our visual field. The stimulus excites afferent, i.e., incoming, neural pathways that then connect to the brain and cause associative firing of neural connections in the brain. From there, a signal is sent out efferent, i.e., outgoing, neural pathways that have only two types of connections in the organism. Neurons connect to either a muscle, causing the muscle to contract, or a gland, causing it to release a hormone. We then respond—the *R*—by the combination of muscle contractions and hormone

 ©2002 The Teaching Company Limited Partnership

releases; for example, we salivate on seeing the donut, reach for it, and eat it.

2. *Reinforcement* is simply a term for a positive or rewarding effect caused by our responses that increases the likelihood that the organism will respond the same way the next time the stimulus excites the neural system. Likewise, *punishment* refers to negative or aversive effects caused by particular responses.

3. For example, feeling full and gaining sensory pleasure are reinforcements for the behavioral response of eating a donut, while feeling nauseous and vomiting would be a punishment for eating a donut.

4. When an association is made between the stimulus and the response and this association has rewarding results, the pathway becomes stronger and the likelihood of the response occurring in the future is increased. Thus, the stimulus-response connection will be repeated and can become habitual. Learning can be defined as this change in response rate.

5. Most of learning theory and the research that it elicited has concerned itself with explaining the conditions and patterns that would come with this basic model of S-R and how reinforcers create the learned habits or pathways.

6. This approach has developed some highly effective behavior modification techniques to change the behaviors of others or even to apply to oneself.

B. If one considers the basic mechanistic approach that we discussed earlier in the lectures, one can see that learning theory developed from a mechanistic worldview.

1. The organism waits to respond to stimuli from outside.

2. Learning is explained by basic laws of association, but the workings of the association areas of the brain are not considered to any great degree because the approach focuses on what comes from outside in, not inside out.

3. Learning theory was opposed to Freud's psychodynamic theory, with its putative internal motivations, conflicts, and mechanisms.

4. Thus, learning theory is a theory of behavior, not a theory of motivations or cognition.

5. Learning theory does not consider the laws of learning to be any different for infants, children, adults, or indeed, other animals. The same principles are seen to apply to all organisms, and no stages of development are theorized.

II. Bandura was trained in this learning theory tradition.

A. He was born in 1925 in Canada and received his Ph.D. in 1952, from the University of Iowa. At that time, Iowa was a primary center of research in psychology in the learning tradition. Bandura then became a professor at Stanford University, where he still is today.

B. Expanding on the work of others—for example, Miller and Dollard had coined the term s*ocial learning* in 1941— Bandura added two crucial changes to traditional learning theory.

1. He explained the mechanism of reinforcement in terms of *expectancies*, which added a cognitive focus.

2. He described the primacy in humans, as opposed to lower animals, of the process of *observational learning* through *imitation* of others.

3. This focus on our learning from others made this type of learning social.

III. First, we will discuss Bandura's view of expectancies.

A. Unlike most learning theorists, Bandura discussed the processes that occurred in the brain that change behavior. This new emphasis on internal processes added a cognitive focus to behaviorism, a focus that extreme behaviorists rejected.

B. When a rewarding outcome occurs after one emits a behavior, it cannot have any effect on the behavior that was just emitted. The only effect can be on future behaviors.

1. Thus, it is one's expectation of reward in the future, not past behaviors per se, that actually changes, that is, reinforces response rate in the future.

2. To have an expectancy of some outcome, one must believe that there is a *means-end contingency*, that when some response occurs to some stimulus condition, and then a particular effect is also likely to occur.

 ©2002 The Teaching Company Limited Partnership

3. The expected contingencies, and under what conditions they can be expected, are what are learned. One need never really be reinforced; one only has to believe in the expected contingencies between response and reinforcement to act on them.
4. Learning causal relations in this manner is not a mindless, reflexive association but a cognitive process.
5. For example, if you believe, based on past experiences, that when you say "please" while asking for something, another person is more likely to give you what you want, then you will say "please" more often. In some cases, you may believe there is a contingency where none exists, but you will, nevertheless, act according to what you believe or expect to happen.

C. The focus on contingency expectations determining what outcomes act as reinforcers for behavior led Bandura to discover an important process—*vicarious reinforcement.*
   1. Even if a person were never reinforced for emitting a particular response or performing a particular behavior, that person might increase the rate of responding in a particular way simply because she had seen others being reinforced for responding in that way.
   2. Indeed, one need never be reinforced to experience the effects of reinforcement because one might come to expect a contingency between a response and the outcome. This learned contingency is socially learned from observing others and is called *vicarious reinforcement* because it only happens to the person vicariously, not directly.
   3. For example, a child, Suzie, might see another child, Sammy, hit a playmate and take away the playmate's toy. Suzie might then see Sammy playing with the new toy with no ill effects and no intervention from adults. From this observation of others, Suzie may process a putative contingency between hitting and taking away toys and getting new toys to play with as one's reward. Suzie might now be more likely to also hit and take away toys. Of course, one can also develop expectations of negative outcomes and punishments.

4. Vicarious reinforcement explains many conditions in which humans learn new behaviors or change the response rates for old behaviors even though they are never directly rewarded or punished for these behaviors.

5. Vicarious reinforcement also assumes some complex cognitive processing. For example, one must see a similarity of oneself to the other person and believe that the contingency that occurs for another person will be valid for oneself as well.

IV. Bandura's other major contribution was the astute observation that much of what we learn, even as young children, comes not in situations in which we are reinforced or punished for responding in a particular way or in conditions in which we learn by repeated trial and error, but in cases in which we simply observe others behaving, then imitate, or copy, the behaviors we have seen modeled or performed by others.

A. The strength of observational learning is that a person can learn a new behavior with no previous trials. Thus, observational learning is efficient and powerful and increases the rate and complexity of learning in humans far beyond the levels of lower animals.

B. Learning by observation without trial and error, depends on cognitive processing; Bandura described a two-phase process to such learning—*acquisition* and *performance*.

1. During the acquisition phase, a child needs to attend to the model and use some mechanism to encode the observed actions into his memory storage.

2. Bandura believed that a person uses two main symbol systems to encode the observed information: either by imaging—creating mental pictures of what one had observed—or by verbally encoding—translating the observed action into a linguistic narrative. Others believe that these two symbolic processes do not adequately explain the complex ways that humans represent and encode their experiences in memory.

3. In one experiment, Bandura randomly assigned his child subjects to one of three groups, one that verbally narrated what they saw a model do, a second that counted out loud to interfere with symbolic encoding,

 ©2002 The Teaching Company Limited Partnership

and a control group that did nothing. He found that the verbal narration group showed the most imitation of the model; the control group, the next most imitation; and the interference group, the least.

4. Bandura argued that this experiment showed that cognitive encoding during the acquisition process was important to learn a behavior through observation.

C. According to Bandura, after acquisition of an observed behavior has occurred, there is often a performance phase.

1. One may have encoded and, thus, learned a behavior, and may have encoded an expectation of contingencies for what will happen when one performs the behavior. However, performance of the behavior will only occur when one believes the appropriate contingencies are in place.

2. A person may have learned a behavior by observing others but carry it around inside his mind for a long time before ever actually imitating the behavior. The behavior will, nevertheless, be available if the person decides to use it.

3. For example, a child may observe his mother and father yelling and swearing at each other, encode the behaviors, and develop some beliefs as to what will happen if one performs these behaviors—acquisition phase. Then, several days later, he may yell and swear at his brother in the same way when he wants to control his brother and his parents are not around to punish him— performance phase.

4. In one simple but cleverly elegant experiment, Bandura randomly assigned child subjects to one of three conditions. In one condition, the children saw a model being rewarded for acting very aggressively. In a second condition, the children saw the model being punished for acting aggressively, and in a third condition, the control, the children saw no reward or punishment being given to the model for acting aggressively. Afterward, the children who saw the model being rewarded showed the most imitation of aggression; the children from the control condition showed the next most imitation of aggression; and the children who saw the model being

punished showed the least imitation. These results were expected because of vicarious reinforcement.

5. However, the next part of the experiment was the most important. All the children were then asked to show the experimenter what the model had done. When requested, all the children imitated all the aggressive behaviors they had observed. There were no differences between the groups. In other words, the expectations, through vicarious reinforcement, affected performance of imitation, but acquisition of the behaviors was already in place for all children.

6. These principles of observational learning are profoundly important when we consider the effects of media violence on children or the idea that children observe others and learn from them all kinds of behaviors, both good and bad.

Supplementary Reading:

Miller, *Theories of Developmental Psychology*, chapter 3.

Bandura, *Social Learning Theory*.

Questions to Consider:

1. Some people argue that learning theory in general, including Bandura's Social Learning Theory, is mechanistic in its underlying assumptions. In particular, it treats humans as functioning like machines and as only reacting to the environment, rather than acting on it. Do you see this underlying focus in Bandura's theory? Is this approach necessarily invalid? Perhaps this view of humans does represent their real nature.

2. What do you see as examples of the benefits to human development, which ensue because we have a predisposition to learn through observation? What do you see as examples of how we can quickly acquire dangerous and negative behaviors, as well?

 ©2002 The Teaching Company Limited Partnership

Lecture Sixteen
Bandura's Social Learning Theory

Hello. In this lecture and the next lecture, we're going to discuss the fourth theory in our sequence of theories of human development, and this is Albert Bandura's Theory of Social Learning. But before we talk about his theory, first I believe we need to discuss some traditional principles of learning theory. And after that, I'd like to give you a little bit of a background about Bandura and his history, and then we'll discuss his main theoretical concepts and some of his research.

Albert Bandura's *social learning theory* was a modification of traditional learning theory, and traditional learning theory grew out of a behaviorist approach that, as you'll remember, was really started by John Watson and then was passed on to others. B.F. Skinner was one of the important and main people in learning theory; another was Clark Hull, who influenced Bandura. So, I'd like to give you some basic premises of this traditional learning theory, because these are the aspects, the principles that then influenced Bandura.

The basic model of a behaviorist or a learning tradition is what is often called an *S-R association*. The S refers to *stimulus*, and the R refers to *response*. It's called an S-R Stimulus Response Theory because in this theory, the stimuli from the world, and the responses or behavior that the person emitted, are what is important; and the internal aspects, what happens in the brain is really not covered. The mind is really not looked at. The basic argument is, if A, the things from the world, leads to B, what happens in the brain, and B leads to C, the responses, the behaviors, then A leads to C, and we don't have to worry exactly about the internal processes. You can't see them anyway; you'll get it wrong. All that an individual can do, all that it learns is dependent on stimulus input in this model, the input coming in through the senses to the organism. A stimulus—this is the S, you remember—is picked up by these senses.

For example, we see an object such as a donut in our field of vision. The stimulus then excites afferent neural pathways, that is incoming neural pathways, that then take this incoming information to the central nervous system in the brain and it then causes associative firing and neural connections in the brain. From there, a signal is sent out on efferent or outgoing neural pathways that are connected to only two types of places in the organism. First, a connection can be made to a muscle, causing the muscle to contract. Second, an efferent connection can be made to a gland, causing the gland to release hormones. And so, the R, the response, everything we do is simply a combination of muscle contractions and hormone releases. So, for example, we see the donut, and now, because of hormonal releases, we might get excited, we also salivate because of hormonal releases, and because of muscle contractions, we reach for the donut and we eat it.

Reinforcement—this is a big idea in learning theory—can be learned simply as a positive or rewarding effect that is caused by the responses we emit. This positive effect then increases the likelihood that an organism will respond in the same way the next time that a stimulus excites the neural system. Likewise, *punishment* just refers to a negative or aversive effect that's caused to certain responses; it follows that same pathway. For example, we've eaten our donut and now if we feel full, and we've gained a lot of sensory pleasure that acts as reinforcement for the behavioral response we went through eating the donut. We're more likely to eat another donut the next time we see one, when it presents itself. But, if we feel nauseous and vomit after eating the donut, it's going to be a punishment, and the next time we see a donut, we'll be less likely to eat one.

When the association is made between a stimulus and a response, this association then, if it has rewarding results, causes the pathway to become stronger, and it's more likely that this response will occur in the future, and the stimulus response connection will be repeated and will become habitual. Learning can be defined as a change in this response rate. You see, in learning theory they were trying to reduce things and trying to explain them in some basic way. Most of learning theory and the research, the numerous studies that were elicited from learning theory, concerned themselves with explaining the conditions and the patterns that would come with the basic model of S to R, and how reinforcement creates these learned habits or pathways, and the details of how reinforcement works and under what conditions.

Now this approach had developed some highly effective behavior modification techniques. Some techniques to help change behaviors in others and also that we can even apply to ourselves that really work. If one considers this learning approach, and also considers the

©2002 The Teaching Company Limited Partnership

basic mechanistic worldview approach that we talked about earlier in these lectures, you should be able to see that learning theory really developed from this mechanistic theory of the world, the organism waits to respond to stimuli from the outside. The basic laws of association explain learning; but interestingly, the workings of the association areas of the brain or the mind are not considered to any great degree, because the approach focuses on what comes in from the outside—outside in, not inside out. That's a basic mechanistic approach.

Learning theory was also opposed to Freud's psychodynamic theory, because in Freud's theory there was so much punitive internal motivation and internal conflicts and mechanisms that learning theory couldn't get at. They wanted to stay with what was really observable. Learning theory thus became a theory of behavior, not a theory of cognition or intrinsic motivation. Also, learning theory does not consider the laws of learning to be any different for infants, or children or adults—or indeed, for other animals. So, the same principles seem to apply to all organisms, even across species. There are no stages of development that are theorized. This is not a stage theory.

Now with that background, I want to mention that Bandura was trained in this learning theory tradition. This was how he started. He was born in 1925, in Canada. He received his Ph.D. degree in 1952, from the University of Iowa, and at that time, the University of Iowa was a hotbed of research and theorizing, and important work being done in the learning tradition. He then became a professor at Stanford University, and he's still there today. Now, he expanded on the work of others; in particular, two people named Miller and Dollard who did some work in the early '40s, and in 1941, coined the term *social learning theory*. Bandura worked with what they had already offered; but he added two crucial changes to this traditional learning theory, even to the social aspects of it.

He explained that the mechanism of reinforcement could really be understood in terms of the expectancies that we processed. At the time—I don't know if he would have defined it this way—but he added a cognitive focus. He came along with a precursor to what would later be the cognitive revolution, the way we look at development and all of psychology. He also described this primacy in humans—as opposed to lower animals—as an *observational learning process*, that we learn through observing others and *imitating* them, and this is different for humans than for other animals. He separated them.

So, first let's turn to Bandura's view of *expectancies*, this first part that he added. Unlike most learning theorists, he discussed this process that occurred within the brain to change behavior. The new emphasis for him was on internal processes. So, again he added this cognitive focus to behaviorism. In fact, at the time that he came up with his social learning theory—and for some time afterwards—the extreme behaviorists rejected this theory and did not like it because of where he was going with it. He said that when a rewarding outcome occurs, this outcome becomes reinforcement, if you will; and since it occurs after we have already emitted a response, a behavior, it can't possibly have an effect on the behavior that was just emitted. That's in the past. The only possible effect it can have is on the future.

So, you can't argue about reinforcements changing past behaviors; it's one expectation of reward in the future, not past behavior per se, that actually changes or reinforces the response rate in the future. It's not the reinforcement you got. If you really want to be technical, it's what you believe, what you expect; and in order to have an expectancy of some outcome, you have to believe that there's some *means-end contingency*, that when some response occurs to some particular condition or stimulus condition, there's also a particular effect that's going to occur. You have to see that as causal and related in some way; and these expected contingencies and under what conditions that you expect them, these are the things that are learned. Does that seem different to you from what learning theory posits? Well, it's a subtle, but I think an important change. One need never be really reinforced, you see. One has only to believe that there's an expected contingency between a response and a reinforcement to act.

You can be right or wrong. You really don't have to have all of this experience, this condition. Learning causal relationships is also an important cognitive process. It isn't a mindless reflex if you look at Bandura's approach. For example, you may believe from past observations and experience—things that you've seen—that if you say, "please" while you're asking someone to give you something, you're more likely to have the person give you what you want. You

 ©2002 The Teaching Company Limited Partnership

may have never done it before—in fact, it may not work—but you believe it does and so you're more likely to say please when the situation arises and you want something, because you're going to act according to what you believe. Now my guess is that if you say please, you are likely to get a better response and more likely to get something you want. But you can believe something that actually may not be true, but it's what you believe that counts. So the focus is on the contingencies, the expectations that determine the outcomes.

Along with this, this belief in expectations and contingencies, Bandura discovered a very important process he called *vicarious reinforcement*. You see, even if a person were never, ever reinforced for emitting a particular response or performing a particular behavior, that person might increase the rate of responding in a particular way simply because she's seen others reinforced by responding in that way. So, we don't ever have to be reinforced to experience the effects of reinforcement. That's the change that he made. We might expect a contingency, but we don't have to experience it firsthand. This is a learned contingency by observing others; therefore it's social. You can see why it's social learning. It's called vicarious reinforcement because it only happens to a person vicariously, not directly. We're reinforced by it vicariously, but not in real life.

Let me give you a real live case. This happened just recently on my son's playground. There were some problems with bullies and some of the older kids were really picking on some younger kids. Now they had been taught in this school to go contact an adult and the adult would take care of things. They had a "zero tolerance" view of aggression. But they had a playground monitor, one adult, who did not really follow that approach. She was from the old school, and that approach was, "boys will be boys" and you have to learn to work out your own problems. So, when some little kids went to her to complain about the bullying they'd received, and the other kids were there, the kids that had been picking on them and the other kids were also hanging out, the teacher said, "Come on you kids. You have to work it out for yourself." Guess what happened? Bullying increased significantly because the kids observed the adult interacting with these other kids. They learned the expected contingencies, and now kids who had not been bullies previously, started picking on other kids, and the bullies started doing even more of it. The contingencies were learned.

Vicarious reinforcement explains many conditions in which humans learn new behaviors or change the response rates for old behaviors, even though they're never directly rewarded or punished for these behaviors. And, vicarious reinforcement also assumes some complex cognitive processing. For example, you have to see a similarity of yourself to the example, the other person; to believe that the contingency occurs not only for that person but it's also valid for yourself. So you could argue that this is a precursor to seeing that children need to develop some level of perspective-taking to see the cognitive connections between how they do things and the viewpoint of how others do things. This came along before Piaget's theory influenced others in this country, but perspective-taking would be arguably necessary to be able to see these kinds of contingencies and to use them effectively.

Now Bandura's other major contribution, besides this other idea of expectancy that led to vicarious reinforcement, was the observation that much of what we learn, even as young children, comes not in situations in which we're rewarded or reinforced or punished— responding in a particular way—but under conditions in which we observe others. It's certainly related, we don't learn just from repeated trial and error, but in cases where we simply observe others behaving and then we imitate or copy the behaviors that we've seen modeled or performed by another person. So in this case, the child is the imitator, and the person she observes is the model, and the strength of observational learning for humans, which you don't see in lower animals, is that a person comes to learn a new behavior with no previous trials.

Learning theory focused on conditioning: how over a period of time you'd experience these reinforcements, and over a period of time you could set up these conditions and get someone to change their behavior. Bandura came along and said that people walking around see all kinds of things. They learn just like that. If you have to, you try it. You learn all kinds of things that you never have done just by observing them. So, observational learning is efficient, it's powerful. It increases the rate and complexity of learning in humans far beyond levels of lower animals. For example, if you ever tried to teach a kid to tie his shoe, it's very difficult to teach a kid to tie his shoe with giving him rewards or shaping him to just the right moves. It's very difficult to teach a kid to tie his shoe by explaining 'first you take this side and loop it over here, put it around here, flip it around here…' Try to explain yourself the process of tying your shoe. But all you have to do is show him fairly slowly a few times, and kids will get it. In relatively few times, they'll get it. You don't even have to reinforce them so long as they have some kind of intrinsic motivation to learn it. All they have to do is observe it.

Complex behaviors can be learned through observation and imitation that would take us a hell of a long time to condition, through just using reinforcement. This depends on cognitive processing. In cognitive processing and learning through observation, Bandura described a two-phase process for such learning; and the two phases he called *acquisition* and *performance*. Acquisition was really the learning phase, and he separated it from performance, which was what learning theorists had always talked about. So let me go back through these two processes.

During the acquisition phase, a child needs to attend to a model. The child not only needs to attend to a model to watch what's happening, the child needs some mechanism to encode the observed actions, to put the actions in his memory storage. Bandura is getting more and more cognitive, talking about the internal processes. Bandura believed there are two main symbol systems that a person uses to encode the observed information. The first is imaging; we'll call it imaging. It's creating mental pictures of what one had observed. And the second is verbal encoding, or translating an observed action into some kind of linguistic narrative. Now, in today's work and research on cognitive processing, I think people would think this is very simplistic to just talk about verbal encoding or pictorial imaging. Cognition and the way we encode things is probably a very complicated mixture. It involves other kinds of propositions and other kinds of symbol systems.

But let's go with what Bandura had at the time; and before I go with it, let's be clear. When we have imaging, we do use that from time to time. It may not be the only form we use, but we do it. Right now I want you to picture the door to your house or your apartment. Now go to the doorknob. Can you see the doorknob? Go to the right of the doorknob. Can you see what's there? You can do it, probably most of you can. If I say, "Picture a dog. Now picture that dog being a

German Shepard. What do the ears look like on that dog?" Can you do it? This is imaging and we encode a lot of stuff this way. But we also use linguistic or verbal encoding to a large extent. So, as I'm driving someplace, very often I'm giving myself directions. I'm saying, "Go four lights. Now here's the first, here's the second. Now turn left and stay in the left-hand lane." Have you ever given yourself directions like that? All kinds of things—you give yourself directions, and very often you can encode yourself and often think of what you're doing by verbal encoding. So, we do use both these forms.

Let me tell you about a very simple experiment that Bandura did to illustrate this kind of acquisition and encoding phase of learning in the sense of imitating or observing others. He randomly assigned a bunch of kids to one of three groups. By random assignment, it means that there is no systematic bias. For all intents and purposes, in each group the kids were equally smart, equally motivated and equally functional because, if you have a big group of kids, you get the same mixture in each group. In this random assignment to these three groups he had one group observe a model do something, and while they observed, he asked them to, out loud, verbally narrate what was happening. So, they might say, "Now the model takes the block and sets it over here. Now the model does this," and they were supposed to talk out about what was happening and narrate it. In the second group, he had the model count by twos or some kind of counting task that he wanted to be interference. So part of their brain, if you will, has to focus on the task of counting and part of it was observing the model, see what the model is doing.

Now in the first task, he wanted facilitation. He wanted to increase the encoding, if you will. In the second task he wanted to interfere with it; and in the third task, he wanted a control condition. They just observed and did nothing. Then later on, he told all of these kids very simply to, "Do everything that the model did and I'll give you a reward. You get these toys over here; you get these candies for how well you do." This is the way you motivate kids to do it. It's a no-brainer. The kids are going to do some kind of task that they found the model doing. It wasn't completely simple; it was a sequence of things. And guess what he found. Think about it; it's easy. In the group that had been facilitated, that verbally narrated what had happened, in that group they showed the most imitation, in fact, maximum imitation. They did everything that they observed the model do, for all intents and purposes. In the group that was the control condition, that observed and did nothing, they showed the next most imitation of the model; and in the group that had counted and had interference; they showed the least amount of imitation. That's a pretty simple experiment. But the argument he made was that the acquisition phase, the ability to encode this information and learn it, depends on our symbolic processing. You can either facilitate it or interfere, but this makes a difference.

According to Bandura, after you've had an acquisition phase and you've observed a behavior, then you have a performance phase. This is what all the behaviorists have been talking about. So you've encoded something, but you only will perform it if you've also encoded the expectation of contingencies for what you'll get for doing it and if you see a situation as being appropriate that these contingencies are in effect, then now's a good time to do it. So he argued that a person might have learned a behavior, but carries it around inside one's mind having encoded it, and carry it around for a very long time. We have a lot of deferred imitation. We can carry it around for hours or days or years, and we'll never actually act on it, we'll never actually perform it, yet it's learned. It's available if we need it. So you or a child may have learned his mom and dad yelling or swearing at each other in a fight and he'll encode those behaviors, he'll pay attention and develop some belief about what would happen if he does those things. This was a way that mom and dad solved their problems. Several days later, he's in an argument with his brother, and he starts yelling at him and swearing at him in the same ways he saw his parents do it, and he does this much later.

Let me tell you about another experiment that Bandura did to compare the acquisition and the performance phase. I think this is a very simple but clever and elegant experiment. Bandura then randomly assigned child subjects to one of these three conditions. In the first condition, the child saw a model rewarded, being given a reward and praised by others for acting very aggressively. So this would be vicarious reinforcement, if you will. In the second condition, the child saw the model being punished for acting very aggressively. So somebody came in and yelled at the person and took something away. In the third condition—it was a controlled condition—the person acted really aggressively, but there was no reward, no punishment. Then afterward, the child was put into a room with the same materials, a BoBo doll, some stuff to be aggressive with, and just left there. He said, "Do what you want. Play." And, surprise, surprise, in the condition in which the kids had seen the model being rewarded, they showed a high level of aggression, in fact, maximum imitation of the aggression of the model. In the control condition, they showed a moderate level of aggression; and should this surprise you? And, in the punishment condition, they showed very little aggression, almost none. So, in fact, there was vicarious reinforcement. They had learned the contingencies and were following these, and what was appropriate.

Now the next part of the experiment was really the most interesting and the most important. After all this was done, and you found these levels depending on the vicarious reinforcement, then Bandura went back and he asked all the children—he didn't reward them—he just said, "We're trying to see if you really remember what the model did. Can you show me exactly what the model did?" He said this to all of the kids and guess what—there were no differences. All the kids now imitated everything the model did at the highest level, regardless of the reinforcement condition they had seen.

So the reinforcement was a contingency that they had encoded about what would happen to them if they did it; but they had acquired the behavior in all conditions. They had encoded the behavior, along with the reinforcement contingency. It was there and they could do it. You see that difference?

Now, why is that important? Because these principles of observational learning are then profoundly important when we look at certain behaviors that kids may pick up. One of the main areas that Bandura looked at was aggression, and how aggression develops in kids. He was one of the first people to really do a lot of strong studies on aggression. He was one of the first to do work on the effects of the media on violence on children, on the effects of TV on children. In the early 60s, he started doing some of this work, and this has been subsequently followed with work on both the positive aspects that children can gain and learn from observing TV and models on TV, as well as the negative aspects. But he found early on, through this approach that we'll talk about, that children, when they observe aggression in others, could sometimes simply learn new behaviors, behaviors that they never had before. They get new ideas, and we see this sometimes nowadays in school shooters. Sometimes

 ©2002 The Teaching Company Limited Partnership

they can learn, have a facilitation of behaviors they already know, but make it easy because they see contingencies on maybe when they'll get reinforced. Sometimes it will disinhibit them from performing something; and sometimes they simply become desensitized. They see something enough times that they no longer have an emotional reaction to it, like seeing violence and goriness, and they're no longer inhibited from doing it because it doesn't bother them the same way. Observing media violence then has all of these effects, and this research has shown that.

In our next lecture, we're going to continue with Bandura's theory. We're going to add a new twist that Bandura talked about, a twist to understanding intrinsic motivation, and that is the importance of the sense of self-efficacy.

Thank you.

Lecture Seventeen
Bandura's Self-Efficacy Theory

Scope:

This lecture discusses a further cognitive focus in Bandura's theory in which he argued that a person's development of a sense of self-efficacy or belief that one can have an effect on some aspect of one's environment guides what tasks or challenges one will attempt and how one will develop further skills. The lecture gives examples of the development of self-efficacy. It concludes with a discussion of how Bandura's theory is not tied to specific ages or stages of development and what implications this has for understanding human nature.

Outline

I. In the 1980s, Albert Bandura presented a second theory called *Self-Efficacy Theory*, which is connected and complementary to his social learning theory. This theory has had a substantial influence, not only on researchers in child development, but also on researchers of adult development and aging.

A. In this theory, Bandura became even more focused on internal cognitive processes in explaining learning and development and, thus, further distanced himself from the classic learning theorists.

B. *Self-efficacy* can be defined as the belief that one can cause some effect on one's environment.
    1. A person's self-efficacy is, in effect, the way a person perceives his own abilities and competence in dealing with a problem or challenge. A person can perceive his abilities in a particular domain to be high or low.
    2. How a person sees his abilities will determine to which source he attributes successes and failures—either to himself and his ability or lack thereof or to the situation or others. These attributions of success and failure and beliefs about one's level of efficacy in being able to accomplish something will then determine what kinds of tasks a person will try, what challenges he will take on, and what he will shy away from.
    3. For example, I may believe that I have a high level of social skill and am extremely appealing to women. In

©2002 The Teaching Company Limited Partnership

this case, I am likely to approach women socially and with confidence and be rather assertive and outgoing in my initial social interactions with them. On the other hand, if I believe that my level of social skill and appeal with the opposite sex are rather low, I am likely to be reluctant to approach women socially and will be rather shy and non-assertive in my interactions with them.

4. We likely have different levels of self-efficacy for different skill domains such as for skiing, social interactions, math, and music. However, overall, we may develop a general level or sense of self-efficacy based on our various experiences.

C. Bandura discussed an important concept that is intimately related to self-efficacy, the concept of *reciprocal determinism.*

1. The idea of reciprocal determinism is that a person's skills and developmental level are not only determined by the environment and others in the environment; the person also creates or determines her own environment by making modifications in it.

2. If a person believes that she will fail in certain tasks and in certain social situations, she is likely to avoid those tasks and situations. If she thinks she will be successful in other tasks and other social situations, she is likely to seek out those situations.

3. As a person selects specific environments, the tasks in turn influence what the person will learn and develop. The person will then be even more likely to pick the environments in which she feels competent and comfortable.

4. This process of reciprocal determinism is greatly influenced by our sense of self-efficacy, and our sense of self-efficacy will increase or decrease in particular areas because of the ongoing process of reciprocal determinism. This chaining of events creates what are called *self-fulfilling prophesies.* Whatever we believed will happen is validated because we have brought these beliefs and predictions to fulfillment.

5. In the example above of the person who had a high sense of self-efficacy in his social skills and appeal to the

opposite sex, he will place himself in situations in which he gains a lot of practice at these skills and acts as though these attributes are already present. It is highly likely that he will become the kind of person he already believed he was.

D. How does this sense of self-efficacy develop? Bandura believed there were four primary sources of information or input that act to increase or decrease our sense of self-efficacy.

    1. First and perhaps most important, our own personal successes and failures change our self-efficacy through reciprocal determinism. In a sense, "nothing succeeds like success." For example, if we constantly get high grades on math exams, we will come to believe that we have high math skills and can take exams with confidence.

    2. Second, through observational learning, as discussed in the last lecture, we gain vicarious reinforcement. We see the successes and failures of those whom we perceive are similar to us, and we think these attributes must apply to ourselves as well. For example, if we see a person we identify with being successful at public speaking, we may think we are like him in that way and have the same ability. We are likely to imitate him.

    3. Third, what others say about us influences how we think about ourselves. In addition, we will be influenced by what others say to persuade us of our ability level. For example, if a child's teachers and peers constantly tell him he is stupid at math or persuade him to work harder because he is failing, he will likely change his sense of self-efficacy in math skills to match what he has heard.

    4. Fourth, the emotional state and the physiological pain and pleasure we feel internally in the context of performing a task will influence the sense of self-efficacy we develop. For example, if while giving a public talk, a person has sweaty palms and a racing heart and feels lightheaded and nauseous, the person is likely to develop a lower sense of self-efficacy about his public speaking ability.

II. Several other researchers have developed theories of motivation similar to Bandura's self-efficacy theory. This convergence of theorizing and empirical evidence tends to strengthen the validity of this conceptualization.

A. In 1959, Robert White wrote a highly influential paper in which he argued that when humans have met their basic needs, such as for food, water, and rest, they don't simply shut down like machines or like many lower-level animals. Instead, at those times, they are most intrinsically motivated to act on their world.

1. These times are frequent in our lives.

2. At times like these, we seek out challenging tasks, we want stimulation and excitement, and we want to avoid boredom.

3. When we seek challenges that push us to our limit and are successful at a task, we feel a strong sense of efficacy, of having affected our environment and accomplished something.

4. This sense of efficacy feels good and motivates us to seek it often. In the process, we are more likely to develop mastery and competence in our lives.

5. White argued that this *mastery*, or *competence motivation*, was highly adaptive. Because of it, humans remain flexible and ever learning.

6. Susan Harter added to this theory by giving examples of how one's history of successes and failures over time actually change one's level of motivation to seek challenges or avoid them.

B. Martin Seligman developed a highly influential theory of *learned helplessness*. A person often learns to be helpless because of continuous experiences with failing at a task or not having the ability to effect a change in her environment. In a sense, a person tends to give up if she thinks she is helpless to have any control.

C. Based on Seligman's work, Carol Dweck then developed a theory about how we come to believe what our basic skills and abilities are, to what sources we attribute our abilities. She focused mainly on people's conceptions of their intelligence.

1. Dweck showed that when a person primarily has experiences in which she has been made to believe that she can change an attribute or ability by her own efforts, she will come to believe that the ability is not a fixed amount or level, that effort determines the skill level she can develop. In this case, a person will be more likely to try harder after failures and accept challenges that give her a chance to develop her skills.

2. On the other hand, Dweck showed that when a person primarily has experiences in which she has been made to believe that an attribute or ability is some fixed entity or amount within her, that she was born with it, so to speak, she comes to believe that she cannot change her skill level. In this case, a person will be more likely to avoid challenging tasks that might show her to be incompetent and to give up in the face of challenges.

III. In conclusion, what can we say about the value of Bandura's combined social learning theory and self-efficacy theory?

A. Before Bandura, learning theory did not take account of cognitive processes, nor did it account for the great importance of observational learning. Bandura's theory is still mechanistic and grounded in the behaviorist traditions of learning theory, but he added a cognitive focus and a focus on beliefs, attributions, and expectancies.

B. Bandura's theory has had a great impact on research on the development of aggression, the development of phobias, the lack of motivation to attempt tasks in older adults, and successful ways of dealing with and treating various problem behaviors and disorders. In an applied sense, his theory has been highly successful.

C. Because Bandura was grounded in the processes of learning, he tended to equate development with learning. In his theory, it seems that all of development is simply what we have learned. Others would argue that he has failed to explain major reorganizations in the structure of thinking and skills.

D. In terms of child development, Bandura's theory focuses on processes, rather than structural or stage-like changes.

 ©2002 The Teaching Company Limited Partnership

1. The processes he discussed—vicarious reinforcement, observational learning, reciprocal determinism—function independently of the age of the person.
2. This approach has a tendency to treat children as miniature adults, less experienced and skilled, it is true, but functioning with the same nature and internal processes that can be found in adults.
3. Because of this lack of focus on the unique features of childhood and the way they change from birth to maturity, many believe social learning theory misses important aspects of development and, indeed, of human nature and falsely attributes some adult-like abilities to children that they don't possess at young ages.

Supplementary Reading:

Bandura, *Social Foundations of Thought and Action.*

———, *Self-Efficacy: The Exercise of Control.*

Questions to Consider:

1. Bandura's concepts of reciprocal determinism and self-efficacy are revolutionary in one sense. They shift the focus of learning from the view of the environment controlling the child's development to the view of the child in large part controlling his own development. Do you see the constant reciprocal effect of the environment on the child and the child on the environment as being a valid explanation of what happens for most of us?
2. What do you think the relation is between one's sense of self-efficacy and one's self-esteem? Do you think they are the same thing? If not, how do they differ?

Lecture Seventeen
Bandura's Self-Efficacy Theory

Hello. In the last lecture we discussed Albert Bandura's social theory and his conceptual contributions of expectancies and vicarious reinforcement and how they drove learning, and also the research he did regarding observational learning. In this lecture we're going to continue to discuss Bandura's work. We're going to discuss a related theory, self-efficacy theory, which takes the cognitive process of one's expectations and beliefs even one step further. We'll also discuss other related theories of self-efficacy to gain a fuller view of how this important concept fits into human nature; and then we're going to conclude with an evaluation of Bandura's theory.

In the 1980s, Albert Bandura presented his second theory, called *Self-Efficacy Theory*. It's connected, and I think complementary, to his social learning theory. This theory had a substantial influence, not only on researchers in child development, but particularly on researchers of adult development and aging, as well. It's valuable across all ages; it's not tied to any particular age. In this theory, Bandura became even more focused on internal, cognitive processes in explaining learning and development; and by doing it he further distanced himself from the classic learning theorists. Bandura is still a learning theorist, but he doesn't fit that classic mode.

Now, what is self-efficacy? *Self-efficacy* can be defined as the belief that one has that one can cause an effect on one's environment, the belief or the extent that a person believes that she or he is effective, has an influence. That's why it's called efficacy; a person's self-efficacy, in effect, is the way that a person perceives his own abilities and confidence in dealing with various problems and challenges. A person can perceive his abilities in a particular domain to be very high; and in another domain, can be very low—I can know that I am really good at skiing, and really lousy at tennis—and so, how a person sees his abilities will determine to which source he attributes success and failures. If he sees abilities, or his successes, as coming from his own abilities, and if he sees his failures coming from his own abilities, he may see himself as not being very good. If he sees them [his failures] as coming from some other situation, and it's not really his fault, maybe then he still will have a high self-efficacy. So these attributions of success and failure, and the beliefs that we have about our level of efficacy and how we can accomplish things, will

 ©2002 The Teaching Company Limited Partnership

determine what types of tasks we will try, and what challenges we'll take on, and what kinds of tasks or challenges we'll shy away from.

Let me give you an example. If you're a man, and you happen to believe that you have a high level of social skill and you're extremely appealing to women and you have a social skill in getting along with women, you might be more likely to approach women socially and with confidence and be rather assertive and outgoing in your initial social interactions with them. On the other hand, if you believe that your level of social skill and your appeal to the opposite sex is really quite low, then you're likely to be reluctant in approaching women socially, and you'll be sort of shy and non-assertive in your interactions with them.

Now we're likely, as I mentioned, to have different levels of self-efficacy for different skill domains. I mentioned skiing and tennis. We could talk about emotional interactions as an area of skill. We could talk about mathematics and music, and so on. However, over all, we might develop a general level or sense of high self-efficacy based on the various experiences we've had, or we may over all develop some kind of low level of self-efficacy, or something in between. So Bandura discussed an important concept to try to explain this level of self-efficacy and how it influences development and our learning. And, he explained another concept that's intimately related to self-efficacy. This is the concept that he called *reciprocal determinism*. The idea of reciprocal determinism is that a person's skills and developmental level are not only determined by the environment and by others in the environment, but also that a person creates or determines her own environment by making modifications to it. So, it's reciprocal, and it's determined reciprocally; because not only does the environment influence you in how you develop and the skills that develop; but in turn, you select the environment that you place yourself in. You change your environment, in effect. You only allow certain areas or certain things in the environment to affect you, and not other things. This is important because it gets away from that purely reactive-passive view of humans, that the environment is out there doing things to you and molding you. You see, it goes both ways; it's an interaction.

Whenever we think of the environment having an influence on us as learning theory did, you can also think—yes, but we change our environment. We create our environment and allow it to have this influence on this. If you believe that you're going to fail at a certain task or at a certain social situation, what are you going to do? You're likely going to avoid that task and that social situation. If you think you're going to be successful at a particular task, you're likely to seek out that task and that social situation. This isn't always true, but I've generally observed that people really like what they're good at and they keep doing the things they're good at. They don't tend to like what they're bad at and they tend to avoid doing those types of tasks and being in those kinds of situations.

So, as you select a particular type of environment, then the tasks in turn will have an influence in helping you to learn development. You gain more experience in some areas than in other areas. You're likely to pick the environment where you feel somewhat comfortable and competent in. Some people have a word for this; they call it niche picking. Isn't that clever! OK, niche picking is you pick your niche, the one you're comfortable in. So whenever you say, it's not my fault, I was forced into these situations in my environment; my friends did this to me—remember, in this kind of reciprocal determinism, we also pick the environment and the niches.

Now, this process of reciprocal determinism is greatly influenced by our sense of self-efficacy, will increase or decrease in particular areas depending on the influences we have and the experiences we have from reciprocal determinism. But, our sense of self-efficacy will determine what we pick. So this chaining of events creates what we call a *self-fulfilling prophecy*. You may have heard that term before. The idea is whatever we believe will happen, is then validated subsequently because we brought about the situation that bring these beliefs and predictions into fulfillment. For example, if that person I told you about has this high sense of self-efficacy about his social skills and his appeal to the opposite sex, he'll place himself in situations where he gains a lot of practice in these skills and he'll act as though these attributes are already present. It's highly likely he'll become the kind of person he already believes he was; and, of course, this can work for people having negative self-efficacies in believing they're not good at something.

Let me tell you about a piece of research that just recently came out that's quite interesting. This was based on a view that women in general—we realize there are many exceptions—women in general do worse than men on math tests. And the research showed that

   ©2002 The Teaching Company Limited Partnership

women do worse than men on math tests, but only when they're first told that the test assesses gender differences in math abilities. If you don't tell the people taking the test that this is what it's all about, they don't differ from men in how well they do on the test. But if you tell them what it's about, that we're going to look for gender differences in their math abilities, I believe that their beliefs about their self-efficacy caused this self-fulfilling prophecy. They lose their confidence; they think they're going to do worse—Voila, they do worse.

Now how does this sense of self-efficacy develop? Bandura believed that there are four primary sources of information that are input, that come into us to act as the mechanisms to either increase or decrease our sense of self-efficacy. First, and perhaps this is the most important: Our own personal successes and failures change our self-efficacy through this process of reciprocal determinism that I've already talked about. In a sense, nothing succeeds like success. For example, if we constantly get high grades on a math exam, we come to believe that we have high math skills and we can take math exams with confidence.

Now the second mechanism or source is through observational learning, and we talked about that last time. In other words, we gain vicarious reinforcement. We see the successes and failures of other people who we perceive to be similar to ourselves and we think that these attributes that they have must also apply to ourselves. For example, if we see a person we identify as being successful at public speaking, you may think that you're a lot like this person and might have the same ability because you're a lot alike, and you're likely to imitate that person. So, we see others and see them rewarded or punished as vicarious reinforcement. We also see others and see what they're good at and what they're bad at; and, if we identify or see the similarities, we pick up on these things.

The third source is what others say about us. What others say influences how we think about ourselves. That seems obvious. If they say something good about us, or bad about us, we tend to be influenced by it. Also, it depends on whether they try to persuade us of the ability levels we have. For example, if the child's teachers and the child's peers constantly tell him he's stupid at math, or they persuade him to work harder because he's failing, he will likely change his sense of self-efficacy about math skills, to match what he's heard.

The fourth source of information that will change our self-efficacy is the emotional state of physiological pain and pleasure that we feel internally in the context of performing some task. We have feedback from our own experiences. For example, if while giving a public talk a person has really sweaty palms and a racing heart and feels light-headed and nauseous, the person tends to develop a lower level of self-efficacy about his public speaking abilities. He says, "Wow, under those conditions everything is falling apart." I think you can see that the idea of self-efficacy is a very important one because it will then influence where we go, the environments we'll pick and what challenges we'll take. What we think we can do will become what we can do.

There have been several other researchers that have developed theories of motivation that are very similar to Bandura's self-efficacy theory; and whenever I see a convergence of theorizing, a convergence of theoretical evidence coming from different people that are more or less working independently, I think that this is a good sign. This tends to strengthen, in my mind and others, the validity of this conceptualization. There must be something to this idea because several independent people are thinking about it and providing some evidence that it's working. So, at this time, I think it's very worthwhile to mention some of these other related theories. They were smaller theories, they didn't involve the entire field of development, but they were important. One that I think was extremely important was a theory that Robert White came up with in a classic paper written in 1959. He beat all the others to the punch, including Bandura.

He wrote this influential paper that argued that when humans have met their basic needs—such as being fed, having food, having water, having rest, being the right temperature, not being tired—when they've met these basic needs, they don't simply shut down like basic machines or like my dog. They don't function like lower animals—I'm going to drive you crazy with my lizard as my comparison—but when a lizard meets its basic need, it goes to sleep. It goes into a coma, almost. But when humans meet their basic needs, what happens? Think about it. You are not hungry, not thirsty, not too cold, not too hot, well-rested, feeling very comfortable. What

 ©2002 The Teaching Company Limited Partnership

do you do? You're ready for action! You want something to happen. And White said that we're very intrinsically motivated at these times to act on our world, to cause things to happen. Now in humans, at least in our culture and probably for a good share of human existence, these times are actually quite frequent. Most of the time we're not in some crisis of meeting the basic needs. So at these times, frequent times, when we're doing okay, what do we do? We seek out challenging tasks. We want stimulation. We want excitement. We want to avoid boredom.

Now, when we seek out challenges, ideally what we seek out is called *optimal challenges*. Those challenges that are not too boring, not too boring in a task, and not way above us, out of our range. An optimal challenge is going to push us to our limit if we're going to be successful at this task. There's a chance of failure with an optimal challenge, but there's also a chance that you can succeed. If you're playing tennis, an optimal challenge is picking out somebody who's about at your level, who it would be tough to beat. But, of course, you can beat that person once in a while. You don't want to play someone who's well above your level, and you don't want to play someone who's a beginner if you're somewhere in between. So you pick out these challenges, and when you're successful at meeting these challenges, you have this strong feeling or sense of efficacy that you had an effect; that you caused something to happen, that you effected the environment and you accomplished this. And, this sense of efficacy feels good; this is the motivation that makes us want to strive to seek this kind of feeling quite often.

In this process we're more likely to develop mastery and competence in our lives because we're seeking out the things that will push us to our limits and will help us to develop. So, you're more likely to develop flexible, different skills because of this motivation. Now, White argued that this mastery or competence motivation—he called it *mastery motivation* or *competence motivation*—was highly adaptive. It's because of this that humans remain flexible, that they remain ever-learning, they constantly try new tasks, they constantly try challenging tasks, and they don't wait for a task to be absolutely required to do it. For example, we take challenges at times when we're not required to perform something. In children, they do it in play all the time. They play because it can be stimulating and challenging and they work out a lot of issues and learn a lot through their play. We do challenging tasks when we don't have deadlines, when we aren't being evaluated. The kinds of things that often happen in our jobs don't necessarily push us to be challenged. We engage in hobbies. We do crossword puzzles. We do things just for the fun of it. And, these are the times where we'll take chances, take risks. Thus, we become more creative and more flexible. It's our human nature to do so.

I have to mention here that White also came from a Freudian background, as many of the other theorists that we've talked about. He was a psychoanalyst and he, like others, became disgruntled with the shortcomings of the Freudian psychoanalytic approach. And, in trying to talk about this motivation, why we do these sorts of things, he developed this view of mastery motivation to explain our creative, our playful and our risk-taking nature.

Susan Harter is another theorist who added to White's theory by giving examples of how one's history of successes and failures over time actually change a person's level of motivation to seek challenges or to avoid them. White came along and said, "We have this. It's built into the human nature." But Harter, like Bandura, talked about how it would change over time. She has several examples to show this, but basically her view is that over time, if we seek out a very challenging task and we're successful at it, again and again this happens, and also if we're rewarded by others for putting in an effort and trying to seek challenging tasks, eventually these things cycle back and increase our motivation to seek out mastery, and I would argue our self-efficacy. On the other hand, if most of the time we fail at challenging tasks, and we're actually punished for our initiatives again and again, this will cycle back and decrease our motivation to seek mastery and our self-efficacy. So, it's our conscious experience on one side or the other side that will change this motivation.

Martin Seligman was another person who developed a highly influential theory that's also related. His theory was a theory of *learned helplessness*. A person often learns to become helpless because of continuous experiences with failing at a task and not having the ability to effect a change in one's environment. Do these sound similar? White, Harter, Seligman and, of course, Bandura—I think they're related. In this learned helplessness case, in a sense, a person tends to give up if she thinks she's helpless and does not have

   ©2002 The Teaching Company Limited Partnership

any control. After a series of tasks that you can't solve, you can't try anymore. In experiments that Seligman did with both dogs and with humans, he found that you could put someone in a situation, give them a set of tasks that were really, unbeknownst to them, impossible to solve, and after a whole series of these tasks, then you would give the person a task that they, in fact, could solve, and they wouldn't even try. Another person who had been able to solve those tasks through working at them would try the new tasks. So his argument is that in our real life, we become helpless at times and that this in some ways relates to aging as well. Very often, older people believe they can't do something and they learn to be helpless—maybe because of failures and situations—and they quit trying to do the things that they can do in this theory.

Now, a student of Seligman's was Carol Dweck, and she developed a theory that's related to learned helplessness. It's a theory of how we come to believe what our basic skills and abilities are, what the sources are to which we attribute our abilities. Maybe she focused on people's conceptions of their intelligence, but it relates the same way. Dweck showed that when a person primarily has experiences in which she's made to believe that she can change an attribute or an ability because of her own efforts, she'll come to believe that this ability isn't in a fixed amount, it isn't a particular level; that effort determines the skill level that she can develop, it's not something you're born with. In this case, a person is likely to try harder after failures. Interesting. The effect of failures on someone who believes that effort makes a difference and you can change an ability, is to use those failures for feedback and to try harder and to accept challenges, take risks even though you might fail, it gives you a chance to develop those skills.

On the other hand, Dweck showed that when a person primarily has experiences in which he's been led to believe that an attribute or an ability has some fixed entity, that it's an amount within her, that it's inborn, then she comes to believe that she can't change this skill level. In this case, a person will be more likely to avoid challenging tasks, or tasks that might show her to be incompetent, and she'll give up in the face of challenges. She did research with children in schools and found that this was in fact the case. That if students believed that their intellectual level, for example, was what they were born with—intelligence is what you get at birth—then they didn't want to do tasks that might show them as stupid. They would do tasks that they knew they could do well at, but they didn't want others to see how stupid they were. If they believed that intelligence isn't some fixed entity, that intelligence is just something that you can get better and better at or worse and worse at depending on how you do, they were more likely to take the challenging task because they wanted to get better at it.

Boys, by the way, tend to blame teachers for their problems, and girls tend to blame themselves more in intellectual tasks on this ability, and it seems to be related to the way teachers treat them. In general, at least in the school years, even though boys and girls don't differ in abilities and even in the grades they get in the early school years, girls are treated as if they're really smart, and if they don't get something right, what's wrong? You should be able to do this. Boys are constantly told that they're lazy, not careful, and sloppy. They tend to blame the teachers for criticizing them, and they get the view that they can try harder and make a difference.

We need to now go to a review, an evaluation of Bandura's theory. You can see that in this part of it there are a lot of theories that converge and seem to relate together. Let me now talk about which parts of the theory Bandura contributed that are really good, and this is from the combined social learning theory and his self-efficacy theory. As with a lot of these theories, you have to keep in mind what they contribute and what was around before the person came up with the theory, and what's around today.

Before Bandura, learning theory did not take account of cognitive processes, nor did it account for the great importance of observational learning that we talked about last time. Now Bandura's theory is still mechanistic, it's grounded in behaviorist traditions of learning theory; but he added that cognitive focus, and he added—as we've seen with the self-efficacy theory—a focus on beliefs about attributions and expectancies. Bandura's theory has had a great impact on research in several areas: The development of aggression—we mentioned that—the development of phobias, how children, when observing others, learn to be afraid and not to be afraid, just by observing others. The lack of motivation to attempt tasks as adults when, in fact, they could do tasks—they come to believe that because of their efficacy they can't. He headed success on ways to deal with various kinds of problem behaviors and

   ©2002 The Teaching Company Limited Partnership

disorders. So, in an applied sense, his theory has become very successful. It has a great record.

Because he grounded the process of development in learning, he tended to equate development with learning. In his theory, it seems that all of development is simply what we've learned. Now, as a criticism, others would argue that because of that approach, he failed to explain some major reorganizations or structure in thinking or skills; he had a tendency to focus on the processes, not the stage-like changes or the structure. The processes he discussed are worthwhile—he talked about vicarious reinforcement, observational learning, and reciprocal determinism—but they function independently of the age of a person, and this approach has the tendency to treat children as miniature adults. They're less experienced, but they function the same way, with the same nature, and with the same internal processes that can be found in adults. Now in some ways, this is true; but because of this lack of focus on the unique ways of childhood, the way they change from birth to majority, a lot of people believe that social learning theory misses important aspects of development, and indeed of human nature. It falsely attributes some adult-like abilities to children that they don't possess at early ages.

In Bandura's terms, any process you do, any of these things we've talked about you could apply just as well to toddlers, school age kids, adolescents, adults, and older people. I'll leave it at that. But, as compensation, I have to say that his theory does do quite well with adulthood and aging—better than some of the other theories. We can ask again why an older person would believe that he had little ability to do something, and Bandura's theory will explain it, and Bandura's theory will explain how he can learn from others.

In our next lecture we're going to shift gears. We're going to talk about the fifth theory in our sequence, and that's Piaget's Theory of Cognitive Development.

Lecture Eighteen
Piaget's Cognitive-Developmental Theory

Scope:

This lecture introduces the most important theorist in the field of child development, Jean Piaget, and his place in the cognitive revolution in psychology. It describes Piaget's history and how he attempted to combine naturalist biology and philosophy to create a field called *genetic epistemology,* or how we come to know what we know. The lecture then discusses the basic developmental process of Piaget's theory. Schemes, patterns of knowing something, are the building blocks that are constantly changed and developed through two complementary processes: *assimilation*—everything we know must be processed through our existing schemes—and *accommodation*—we must adjust what we know to reality and new incoming information. *Equilibration* is the process of bringing assimilation and accommodation into equilibrium.

Outline

I. In our discussion of Bandura's theory, we got a hint of changes that would revolutionize the study of psychology in general, including the study of human development—a shift in focus to internal, cognitive processes. The shift brought about what is called the *cognitive revolution.* Jean Piaget was one of the foremost theorists to help bring about this revolution.

   A. From the 1920s through the 1940s in the United States, there was a fierce competition between Freudian theory and learning theory—and behaviorism—as ways of explaining psychological processes and change.

   1. By the 1950s, behaviorism dominated the study of child development, which essentially consisted of the study of learning.

   2. However, in the late 1950s and 1960s, theorists in several fields, including Bandura, began focusing on the important but neglected role that internal, cognitive processes played in explaining human learning.

   3. Although Piaget had been influencing European thinkers, he had had virtually no influence in the United States. Then, some of Piaget's writings in French were translated into English, and a few developmental

©2002 The Teaching Company Limited Partnership

theorists in the United States, in particular, John Flavell, began writing about his revolutionary theory of development. They introduced him to American researchers.

B. By the 1970s and 1980s, Piaget's theory completely dominated the study of child development, influencing almost all the questions and issues that were studied and the research methods that were used. Never in the study of development had there been such a complete paradigm shift, such a complete revolution in the collective worldview, essentially from a mechanistic approach to an organismic approach.

    1. Because of the cognitive revolution, learning theory dwindled in influence, just as Freud's theory had done earlier.

    2. Today, Piaget's influence has also abated, but just as Freud's theory became an implicit part of our thinking, so has Piaget's theory. Thus, most people who study development have internalized it into their views of human nature.

II. As with other theorists, Piaget's theory was directly influenced by his own development and history.

A. Jean Piaget was born in Switzerland in 1896, and died there in 1980.

    1. Even as a child, Piaget had a strong interest in biology, particularly Darwinian evolution. He was interested in how various species change through adaptation to varied environmental conditions. When he was 10 years old, he published his first scientific article about his observations of a sparrow.

    2. Because of the influence of an uncle who was a philosopher, when Piaget was in his adolescence, he began studying philosophy. He was particularly influenced by the field of *epistemology*, the study of knowledge and how we know what we know.

    3. Piaget more or less invented a new field he called *genetic epistemology*, the study of the origins of knowledge and how we develop what we know.

B. Piaget rejected the non-empirical armchair approach of philosophers and attempted to combine philosophy with the empirical, scientific approach of a naturalist in biology.

1. He received his Ph.D. in 1917, at the age of 21, from the University of Neuchâtel.

2. He then worked in Paris for a time on the development of intelligence tests, with the tests begun by Alfred Binet.

3. Although the purpose of the research was to develop norms and scoring for the test questions, Piaget became more interested in the errors children made and how their errors seemed to fit specific patterns at different ages. He discovered that children's thinking, though not on an adult level, was nevertheless organized and had a logic all its own.

C. In 1921, Piaget became the director of the Jean-Jacques Rousseau Institute at the University of Geneva, where he remained for the rest of his life.

1. It was no accident that this institute was named after Rousseau. No major theorist has so followed Rousseau's philosophy of child development to the extent that Piaget did.

2. Like Rousseau, Piaget believed that children who were allowed to follow their own course of development would develop in an optimal way.

3. He was the extreme organismic thinker, looking at the human as an organism that acted on the world and didn't just passively react to the environment, an organism that functioned as a structured whole, in which the whole is greater that the sum of the individual parts.

4. He believed that children went through a sequence of reorganizations of their mental structures or systems of processing information. Thus, Piaget found it easy to think of development in terms of stages, for which he was famous.

D. Piaget turned out to be one of the keenest observers of children's behavior we have had in the field. For some of his most important work, he kept detailed accounts of systematic observations of his own three children over a period of several years, harkening back to the baby biographer

©2002 The Teaching Company Limited Partnership

approach. Because of this, he discovered important points about child development that others had missed, though they had observed children for millennia.

E. Piaget did not accept the basic behaviorist traditions of thinking, which mainly came from American theorists.

    1. He believed that children should develop at their own rates and learn things for themselves—harkening back to Rousseau—whereas behaviorism, which placed no emphasis on age or stage differences, believed that we could speed up development and make it more efficient with the appropriate conditioning techniques.

    2. Piaget's answer to the American obsession with speeding up development was the following: "Anything you tell a child, you prevent him from discovering for himself." He believed that if a child developed more slowly, thinking things through on his own, in the long run, he would develop more adaptive, scientific, and logical abilities.

III. The foundation of Piaget's theory is dependent on a basic developmental process that he believed was at work throughout our lives. His idea for this process came from his early work in biology.

    A. Everything we know and understand is filtered through our current *frame of reference*. We construct our knowledge based on what we already know.

        1. Piaget called the basic unit of our understanding a *schema* or a *scheme*. A scheme can be defined as a pattern of knowing something, the structured way that we have stored in our minds of how we recognize, act on, and understand something. Schemes make up our frame of reference.

        2. Because we can't know anything without some frame or structure by which to process incoming information, we must be born with some schemes to get us started. Everything we know, thus, starts with the schemes we are born with.

        3. Three of the basic schemes we are born with are reflexive actions in dealing with the world: looking, grasping, and sucking schemes. A newborn's understanding of the world begins to emerge based on what she can look at, what she can grasp, and what she can suck. She does these automatically and reflexively.

4. However, we would stay completely static in our development without some process that allows us to expand and modify the schemes that we have and develop new schemes.

B. This development occurs through two complementary processes: *assimilation* and *accommodation*.

1. Remember, we only know what we can process through what we already know. This is the basic process of *assimilation*. We apply our current schemes to a new piece of information from the environment and incorporate the new information into our existing scheme.

2. It helps to think of the biological basis of this metaphor. If we eat something, we incorporate the new material into our body. We assimilate the food by making it part of ourselves.

3. A baby sucks what comes into his mouth. He knows a nipple by sucking it and by how it feels in his mouth. If he then has a finger placed in his mouth, he applies his sucking scheme to the finger. If he can suck it the same way, it becomes known as a suckable object.

4. An older child may have developed a scheme for a bird—a visual perception of feathery little things that fly around trees and land on the lawn. If he sees a large crow that hops on the lawn, then flies to a tree, he may apply his bird scheme to the crow and identify it as a bird, as well.

5. However, all new information from the environment requires that the person constantly modify his schemes because no two objects or situations are perfectly similar. One must adjust his mouth differently to suck a finger rather than a nipple. One must look for similarities between a sparrow and a crow in order to apply the bird scheme to both. Thus, assimilation requires generalization and, often, an overlooking of environmental differences.

 ©2002 The Teaching Company Limited Partnership

6. Though assimilation allows us to generalize and apply what we know to many individual instances, it tends to distort reality and not adapt to it. What else is needed?

C. The process of *accommodation* is necessary and complementary to assimilation.

   1. The process of *accommodation* is the process of adjusting or modifying our current schemes to be able to handle new incoming information or changes in an object. Thus, we adjust to reality rather than distorting reality.

   2. Accommodation allows us to modify existing schemes so that they can be applied to more varied instances.

   3. However, sometimes a new piece of information or new object is so different that we simply cannot deal with it with our existing schemes. Accommodation also allows us to create new schemes based on our current schemes. Thus, we are constantly developing new schemes.

   4. The baby in our example above may do fine applying her sucking scheme to various objects and modifying the scheme to handle the differences. However, one day she may run into a wall and try to suck it, but you can't suck a wall. She may accommodate by developing a new scheme, a licking scheme, because you can lick a wall.

   5. The older child in our example above may one day see a butterfly and apply her bird scheme, saying "bird." However, a butterfly acts differently in its flight pattern than a bird. The child's mother may say, "No, that's not a bird; it's a butterfly." The child will now accommodate by developing a new scheme for butterflies.

   6. Assimilation allows us to use what we know and understand already to make sense of the world and to generalize to new information. Accommodation allows us to modify what we know and expand our schemes so that we differentiate between different things in the world and adjust to reality rather than distorting it.

   7. The process results in the development of innumerable complicated and interconnected schemes that make up our mental structure, our understanding.

   8. For Piaget, this basic process was truly an interaction between the organism and the environment. It took into

account the child's active reaching out to understand the world and the world's influence on the child.

IV. Piaget's complementary processes of assimilation and accommodation comprise the *equilibration* process, which for Piaget, was the most important process in development.

    A. According to Piaget, by our nature as living organisms, we desire a sense of equilibrium; thus, we are constantly motivated to be able to fully assimilate and fully accommodate to objects and situations in our environment. When we can accomplish this, we reach a state of *equilibrium.*

        1. Piaget called the process of fully using assimilation and accommodation and bringing them into balance the *equilibration* process. This is the process by which we adapt to the world. This is the process of intelligence.

        2. Whenever we reach a new level of equilibrium, we cannot stay put for long because each new level of understanding opens up new problems and discoveries. Thus, the equilibration process is not static but dynamic. Our active nature and the constant influx of new challenges from the world keep us developing and adapting throughout our lives.

    B. When we can't fully assimilate a new object or situation or can't fully accommodate to it, we feel off balance and do not adapt well to reality. We may even feel emotionally upset. We are in a state of *disequilibrium* between assimilation and accommodation.

        1. If assimilation dominates and we do very little accommodating, we distort reality.

        2. For example, a child's mother said she was going to take him to the children's museum. He began to cry and said, "Please don't leave me at the Naughty Museum." What did he mean? He had a scheme for museums: We go to an art museum to see art; we go to a science museum to see science; therefore, we must go to a children's museum to see children. He was a child. His mother was going to leave him there, probably because he had been naughty. His assimilation of "going to the children's

©2002 The Teaching Company Limited Partnership

museum" to his limited museum scheme distorted reality.

3. If accommodation dominates and we do very little assimilating, we fail to understand what we are doing.

4. For example, a child thought she knew how to tie her shoes because she had observed and imitated her older brother. In fact, she performed all the similar body movements that her brother had. She bent down the same way, and she swished her shoelaces around the same way, but she tied no knots. Blind imitation is not adaptive to reality.

Supplementary Reading:

Miller, *Theories of Developmental Psychology*, 4th ed., chapter 1.

Phillips, *Piaget's Theory: A Primer*.

Piaget and Inhelder, *The Psychology of the Child*. (This is the best summary of Piaget's entire theory that he wrote; however, it is difficult to understand without already having some knowledge of the theory.)

Questions to Consider:

1. Review the previous discussion of the mechanistic and organismic approaches. In what ways do you see that Piaget's theory fits into the organismic approach?

2. What examples can you see in the behaviors and sayings of children and in the behaviors of adults that indicate their assimilation of new information to their existing schemes, often without full accommodation?

Lecture Eighteen
Piaget's Cognitive-Developmental Theory

Hello. In this lecture I'm going to give you an introduction to the fifth theory in our course, Piaget's Cognitive-Developmental Theory and then we'll continue to discuss his theory in the next three lectures, as well. I want to first discuss the context of the theories, the research that was going on in the United States when his theory came along. Secondly, I'll discuss Piaget's history in the context of his ideas. Then, we'll discuss his basic processes of development, the important ideas regarding schemes, assimilation and accommodation, and equilibration. In our discussion of Bandura's theory that we covered in the last two lectures, we got a hint of the changes that would revolutionize the study of psychology in general, including the study of human development. There was a shift in focus to internal, cognitive processes. The shift brought about what's called the cognitive revolution, and Jean Piaget was one of the foremost theorists to help bring about this revolution.

From the 1920s through the 1940s in the United States, there was this fierce competition in psychology between Freudian Theory and Learning Theory. Learning Theory, remember, came from behaviorism; and these were two approaches to explaining psychological processes and change. But by the 1950s, behaviorism dominated the study of child development. It essentially consisted of the study of learning: learning, development—exactly the same thing. However, in the late 1950s and the 1960s, theorists in several fields, including Bandura, were focusing on important but neglected aspects of development, or the role of internal cognitive processes and how these processes helped explain human learning. Although Piaget had been influencing European thinkers, his work had been written in French only; and so, during this time period, he had virtually no influence in the United States. Then, some of his writings were translated from French into English. A few developmental theorists in the United States, in particular John Flavell, began writing about his revolutionary theory of development, and this introduced him to American researchers, and it seemed to catch on right at a time, as I mentioned, when there was this cognitive revolution, when people were starting to look internally again and talk about how the mind worked.

©2002 The Teaching Company Limited Partnership

By the 1970s and the 1980s, Piaget's theory completely dominated the study of child development, influencing almost all the questions, the issues that were studied, and all of the research methods that were used. Never in the study of human development has there been such a complete paradigm shift with such a complete revolution in the collective worldview. Essentially, the shift was from a mechanistic approach to an organismic approach, as we've talked about. It was because of this cognitive revolution that learning theory dwindled in influence, just as Freud's theory had dwindled in influence earlier. Today, Piaget's theory has also dwindled in influence. But just as Freud's theory became an implicit part of our thinking, so has Piaget's. Thus, most people who study development today have internalized a lot of Piaget's ideas into their view of human nature and development. We can never go back; we have what he has given us. As with other theorists, Piaget's theory was also directly influenced by his own development in history. So, let me give you his background and how he taught his theory.

Jean Piaget was born in Switzerland in 1896, and he died there in 1980. Even as a child he had this strong interest in biology, particularly Darwinian evolution, as we know that influenced practically everyone in theory of development. He was particularly interested in how various species change through adaptation to the various environmental conditions. When he was 10 years old, he published his first scientific area. It was about observations of the sparrow, the adaptations of a sparrow. He was very precocious. But I have to tell you; I read that article and it wasn't much of an article— except that it was written by a 10 year old. It was sort of impressive.

When Piaget was in his adolescence he began to study philosophy because of the influence of an uncle who was a philosopher. So he switched from biology to philosophy. The field of epistemology— the study of knowledge, how we know what we know—particularly influenced him. Piaget more or less invented this new field that he called genetic epistemology. Think of genetics in a sense of Genesis. For him, genetic epistemology was the study of the origins of knowledge, how we develop what we know; however, he rejected this non-empirical approach philosophy of the philosophers, and he attempted to combine philosophy with an empirical scientific approach, the approach of a naturalist in biology. As a biologist, he really took the form of a naturalist. He received his Ph.D. in 1917, at the age of 21, from the University at Neuchâtel, and then he worked in Paris for a time on a developmental intelligence test.

He worked with a group that was working on intelligence tests, the group that was started by Alfred Binet and his work. Now all the purpose of this research was to develop norms and scoring for these test questions. Piaget got a little carried away, he got more interested in the errors that children made and how their errors seemed to fit specific patterns at different ages. Despite their craziness, he found method in what they said that was wrong, just as he found method in what they said that was correct. He discovered that children's thinking, even when it's not at the adult level, is nevertheless organized and has its own kind of logic. So, when they were giving questions on the test, he would follow up, he would say, "Why did you say that?" Or, "Why do you think that's true?" He would probe and try to get at the children's actual understanding of what they said; and this was carried on in the rest of his work.

In 1921, Piaget became the director in Geneva of the Jean-Jacques Rousseau Institute, connected with the University of Geneva, and he remained there for the rest of his life. Now, it was called the Jean-Jacques Rousseau Institute and it's no accident that this institute was named after Rousseau. Remember, our discussion earlier about Rousseau's philosophy and how it influenced people. No major theorist has followed Rousseau's philosophy of child development to the extent that Piaget did. Like Rousseau, he believed that children who were allowed to follow their own course of development would develop in an optimal way. He was an extreme organismic thinker, he looked on the human being as an organism that acted on the world and didn't just passively react to the environment. Humans were organisms that functioned as a structural whole in which the whole was equal to the sum of the parts.

He believed that children went through a sequence of developmental reorganizations of their mental structures, or a system of how they processed information; and so, for Piaget, it was easy to think of development in terms of stages, and he was famous for his stages that we will talk about later. Piaget also turned out to be one of the keenest observers of children's behavior that we've had in the field. Because of this, he discovered important points of child development that others missed. They observed children for millennia and then

©2002 The Teaching Company Limited Partnership

Piaget came along and found these things that we've subsequently found to be true.

When Einstein was still living in Switzerland, when he was doing his important work on the theories of relativity, he and Piaget became friends and they used to have discussions about issues about how you know about the universe, about time and space and other things. It's interesting that Piaget tested some kids on these concepts. He tested them on their understanding of knowledge. I think it's really interesting that Einstein said at one time, "Piaget's a genius." Coming from Einstein, that's pretty good.

For some of his most important work, he kept some detailed accounts of systematic observations of his own three children, and he did this over a period of years. It hearkens back to the "baby biographer" approach of doing research. Actually, we learned that his wife did a lot of those observations for him. Piaget did accept the basic behaviorist traditions of thinking, which were coming mainly from America—remember, it dominated thinking in American psychology. He believed that children should develop at their own rate and learn things for themselves, following Rousseau's philosophy. Whereas behaviorism placed no emphasis on age or stage differences and believed that we could speed up development and make it more efficient with the appropriate conditioning techniques or environmental situations, Piaget thought Americans were obsessed with speed. If something is good, let's do it faster. His answer to this American obsession of speeding up development was the following: "Anything you tell a child, you prevent him from discovering for himself." He believed that if a child developed more slowly, and he thought things through on his own, in the long run he'd develop more adaptive and scientific and logical abilities, rather than having people hand it out to him.

You could see this from an example of the way he'd talk to children. One of his children had asked him, "Why do clouds move in the sky?" Do you know what Piaget's answer was? "Why do you think?" And the kid would say something, and he'd question that, sort of in a Socratic method; and he'd keep pushing this way and asking the kid, but he'd never told the kid what he thought.

After giving this background, now let me tell you about his theory. And what I want to do is start with the foundation of this theory, which is dependent on a basic developmental process that he believed worked throughout our life. So, even though he talks about shifts and stages of development, this basic process is part of our human nature, and these ideas actually came from his early work in biology. He thought this was a basically animal kind of approach. Here it is: Everything we know, everything we understand, is filtered through our current frame of reference. We construct our knowledge based on what we already know. It's considered a constructionist approach. We can't know anything except by filtering through our current frame, our current structure. I want to give you an example of this. This is a quote by John Bransford, who is a cognitive psychologist and used this. I'm going to read a statement here. You try to figure out what I'm talking about, what this refers to:

> The procedure is actually quite simple. First, you arrange items into different groups. Of course, one pile might be sufficient depending on how much there is to do. If you have to go somewhere else due to the lack of facilities, that is the next step, otherwise, you're pretty well set. It is important not to overdo things. That is, it is better to do too few things than too many. In the short run, this may not seem important, but complications can easily arise. A mistake can be expensive as well. At first, the whole procedure may seem complicated. Soon, however, it will become another facet of life. It is difficult to foresee any end to the necessity of this task in the future. But then, one never can tell. After the procedure is completed, one arranges the materials into different groups again. Then, they can be put into their appropriate places. Eventually, they will be used once more and the whole cycle will be repeated. However, this is just a part of life.

What am I talking about? Does this make any sense whatsoever, or is this complete gibberish. Now, if I had told you that I'm going to read you a statement about washing clothes, about laundry, would it have made a difference? Let me start out again: "This procedure is actually quite simple. First, you arrange items into different groups. Of course one pile might be sufficient, depending on how much there is to do. If you have to go somewhere else due to the lack of facilities, that is the next step," and so on. You see, your frame of reference makes a difference; and this is a case that Piaget talked about. We understand things by what we already know, that's the

 ©2002 The Teaching Company Limited Partnership

way we get ahead, we adapt in the world. Piaget called this basic unit of understanding that we have, or the units of understanding, a schema, or a scheme. Now, a scheme can be defined—it's sort of vague, but I hope our examples make sense—a scheme can be defined as a pattern of knowing something. The structured way that we have stored in our mind of how we recognize and act on or understand something. Schemes make up our frame of reference because we can't know anything without some structure. We have to be born with some schemes in order to get a start at it. So, everything we know has to start with the schemes we're born with. We can't be complete blank slates or we would get nowhere in Piaget's view.

Three of the basic schemes that we're born with are really reflexive actions on how we deal with the world—Piaget talked about these a lot—they're looking, sucking and grasping schemes. So a newborn's understanding of the world begins to emerge based on what she can look at, what she can grasp and what she can suck, and she does these automatically and reflexively. They're very much action schemes. So what we call thinking starts with our actions on the world. However, we stay completely static in our development. We never really make much progress unless there's some process that allows us to expand and modify the schemes. We have to develop new schemes; grasping, looking and sucking don't get us too far. So, this development in Piaget's view seems to occur from two complementary processes. Both are important: assimilation and accommodation. He got these ideas from his biological background.

First, let's talk about assimilation. Remember, we can only process what we already know, and this is the basic process of assimilation. We apply our current schemes to the new piece of information from our environment, and we incorporate this new information into our existing scheme. It helps maybe to think about the biological metaphor, the basis of this. If we eat something, we incorporate the new material into our body. We assimilate the food, making it a part of ourselves. And so, this was the metaphor that Piaget used.

A baby sucks what comes into its mouth. He knows a nipple by sucking it and by how it feels in this mouth. If he then has a finger placed in his mouth, he applies his sucking scheme to the finger. If he can suck it the same way, it becomes known as a suckable object. What's a finger? A finger is this thing that feels a certain way when he sucks. That's what he starts with. An older child may have developed a scheme for a bird. It's a visual perception he has of this thing that flies around in trees, lands on the lawn. Now if he sees a large crow flop on the lawn and then fly into the tree, he may apply his bird scheme to the crow. He can identify it as a bird, as well, by assimilating it through his bird scheme. However, all new information in the environment requires a person to constantly modify schemes because no two objects or situations are perfectly similar. So we constantly have to change our mouth to suck different things like a finger or a nipple. We have to look for similarities between a crow and a sparrow in order to apply the bird scheme.

So, assimilation requires a generalization; and in generalizing from one thing to another, we often overlook environmental differences. This point is that assimilation, by allowing us to generalize to a lot of different things, tends to distort reality. It would not be too adaptive alone because we give up too much. We have to distort reality in order to be able to this. But what else is needed? Well, we're going to talk about the complementary process called accommodation. The process of accommodation is the process of adjusting or modifying your current schemes to be able to handle the new incoming information, the changes in the object. So we have to adjust to reality rather than just distorting reality. Accommodation then allows us to modify our existing schemes so they can be applied to more varied instances.

Just like for Freud, where everything was tied to sexual drives, for Piaget, almost everything is tied to intelligence and cognitive processes—even physical skills; he applies it to everything. Let me give you an example of one physical skill. A baseball player—let's say someone is playing shortstop and they're fielding grounders, they have a fielding scheme. You can call it a skill or a habit they have of how you pick up grounders. But for every new grounder that is unlike any other grounder in some ways, they have to accommodate to each new grounder and adjust. They apply or assimilate the grounder to their grounder fielding scheme. But they also have to adjust. Sometimes a piece of information or new object is so different though, that even though we try, we can't use our existing schemes; and accommodation also allows us to create new schemes based on the current schemes that we have. So we're constantly developing new schemes with this theory.

 ©2002 The Teaching Company Limited Partnership

So, in the example above of the baby who's sucking things, she's going merrily around. She sucks nipples, she sucks fingers, and she sucks some little toy. She's trying everything; she's assimilating everything and sort of modifying and adjusting. And eventually she runs into a wall and tries to suck the wall. But you can't suck a wall. You can't suck a wall to accommodate. In this case, she has to develop a new scheme. You can lick a wall. She might lick the wall; but it would be a new kind of scheme developed from the other one. In the other case of the older child who has this bird scheme, she's applying it to different birds and let's say one day she sees a butterfly and says, "Bird." But her mom says, "No. That's not a bird; that's a butterfly." She has to accommodate by developing a new scheme for butterflies because they act a little differently. So let me give you this summary now.

Assimilation allows us to use what we know and understand already, to make sense of the world, to generalize to new information. Accommodation allows us to modify what we know and to expand our schemes so that we differentiate between different things in the world and adjust to reality rather than distorting it. It's what some people call a *knowing circle*. Constantly, we have our schemes, we have objects or things from the world, and we're constantly in the cycle of assimilating the world to our schemes; and at the same time, adjusting or modifying our schemes because of information from the world.

According to Piaget, even though I've given you some very simple examples like sucking, this process results in the development of innumerable, complicated and interconnected schemes, and this makes up our mental structure, our understanding. By the time you get to be an adult, it's hard to think of individual schemes anymore. We have a very complicated structure now of thinking applied to the world. For Piaget, this process was truly an interaction between the organism and the environment, and they were constantly interacting. It took into account the child's active reaching out to understand the world, and the world's influence on the child.

Piaget's complementary processes, assimilation and accommodation, comprise what he called the *equilibration process*, fancy words for something that's really simple. Piaget thought that the equilibration process was the most important process in development. According to him, by our nature as living organisms, we desire a sense of equilibrium. We're constantly motivated to find equilibrium in different areas; and one of the areas that we want to find it is when we're motivated to fully assimilate information and also fully accommodate information that we bring in through our senses or from objects or situations in the environment. When we accomplish this, when there's a balance—but the balance really means full assimilation, full accommodation—then we reach a state of equilibrium. This is the equilibrium process. The process of equilibration is essentially bringing assimilation and accommodation into balance; and for Piaget, this is also the process of intelligence.

For Piaget, intelligence is not an amount; it's a process of adapting to the world. Whenever we reach a new level of equilibrium, we can't stay put for long because each new level of understanding opens up new problems, new discoveries; so it's a constant dynamic process, it's not static. Our active nature, and also the constant influx or new information and challenges from the world, keep us developing and adapting throughout our lives. When we can't fully assimilate and accommodate, we feel off balance and sometimes we actually feel emotionally upset. We're not very adaptive at those times. Let me give you one example.

I have some friends who had a little girl who loved art, like a lot of little kids do. She did a lot of drawing, but she also liked looking at art books. They decided that, as a treat, they would take her to the Guggenheim Museum in New York. Now some of you have been there, and this is sort of a strange museum if you think of a little girl going here for the first time. It goes around in circles; you usually go to the top and you walk around in a circle to come down, so you really don't get the sense of floors. Also, a lot of the paintings are placed off-center to the slope of the floor going down, but the paintings are horizontal to the ground; so it's a little off. Of course, it's a modern art museum, so a lot of the paintings that she saw were highly abstract. And part way through she clutched her mom's hand really tightly and then she started to cry and she just fell apart. She went to her knees in this tantrum, crying. Her mother was panicked and wondered what was wrong. Some other people rushed over, and when they got her calmed down, she said, "I keep looking at all these pictures and nobody will tell me what they mean."

So this kind of disequilibrium, if you will—I think in her case—threw her into an emotional panic. It can have that effect. If you

 ©2002 The Teaching Company Limited Partnership

think about it, when you don't quite understand something, when you can't get things in balance, sometimes it's very disturbing. What happens though when we don't have a balance? It's interesting to look at this. When assimilation dominates, and we do very little accommodating, we distort reality. Let me give you two examples. These are true stories.

There was a mother once with a preschool kid and she said in talking to friends, "Tomorrow is a holiday. I think I'm going to take my son to the children's museum. We'll go visit. He's never been there before." Her son was off with some other kids playing and being sort of noisy and there was this pause of quiet, and pretty soon he came out to his mother crying, and he said, "Mommy, please don't take me to the naughty museum." What did he mean, a naughty museum? Here's what I think. He had this scheme for museums. Now, when you go to an art museum, what do you see? Art. When you go to the science museum, you see science. And she was going to take him to the children's museum. What do you see at children's museums? Children. He was a child, so his mother was going to take him there to see children, but he was a child. Maybe she was going to leave him there as an exhibit. But why would my mom ever do that? Well, it's punishment. I've been naughty. By the way, this kid was naughty a lot. I knew him. His assimilation I think was, "I'm going to the children's museum to be left there." And it was interesting when he said it back and was upset. He said, "Don't take me to the naughty museum."

Now, let me give you another example. This was my son who once, like a lot of little kids when he was a preschooler of about four, asked about the facts of life. We get a lot of funny stories about kids and the facts of life, because—think about it—it's a fairly strange story. We had some friends who had a baby and he said, "Dad, where do babies come from?" And trying to be a good, modern parent, I tried to explain how they grow inside the mom and the mom goes to the hospital and the doctors help it to come out and all of this information. He said, "No. What I want to know is how they get in there." So I proceeded to explain, and I tried to explain the whole process. I talked about penises and vaginas and eggs and sperm and the whole schmeer, the whole story here, and he looked a little glazed over. I asked him if he had any questions and he said no. I tried to explain it so he'd understand it.

A few days later he was in the back seat of the car with his mom and her friend and her friend started to talk about how they had really tried to have a baby and it wasn't successful. She just couldn't get pregnant. They were thinking maybe they should adopt and they started talking about this. And he said, "Judy, I know how you can have a baby," and she said, "How?" He said, "First the dad goes to the refrigerator and gets out an egg and puts it on his penis and carries it in to the mom." Where did I go wrong in explaining this? Well, think of it in Piaget's terms. What happened here? As soon as I said the word "egg," he used his egg scheme to assimilate this story. And for his egg scheme, as for most kids, there is one concept, one scheme—chicken eggs. From then on, he had to adjust his story to this assimilation, to his egg scheme. So here's a piece of very practical advice from this course. If you're going to explain the facts of life to a little kid, either don't use the word egg; or, if you're going to use it, make it clear it's a very tiny little dot. You can't even see it. OK. You have to make sure you tell him it's not a chicken egg, to make any sense. That's assimilation that distorts reality.

What about the other case, where you have accommodation that dominates and you have very little assimilating? Well there was a girl once who thought she could tie her shoes, and she was imitating what her older brother did. In fact, when you watched her, she looked just like a person tying her shoes. She would take her shoes, put them on, swish around the laces and go like this, but there was no knot done, there was no tying. So often when we do blind imitation, we don't adapt to reality because we don't assimilate. We don't really understand what we're doing, we just blindly imitate in that way. These are two examples then of what happens when you don't bring things into equilibrium.

Now in our next lecture, we're going to continue with Piaget and talk about how equilibrium, the formation of equilibria then, leads to the formation of Piaget's different stages. Thank you.

©2002 The Teaching Company Limited Partnership

Lecture Nineteen
Piaget's Early Stages

Scope:

This lecture begins with a discussion of how each new major level of equilibrium reorganizes one's thinking. Piaget's sequence of four major stages describes how we get from infant to adult intelligence. The ages are not so important, but the invariant order of the stages is. The lecture describes stage one, the sensory-motor period, and how the baby starts life with reflexes and, by the end of infancy, develops emerging symbol use. The lecture concludes with a discussion of how preschoolers master symbolic skills in Piaget's second stage, the pre-operational period.

Outline

I. According to Piaget, we are constantly reaching new levels of understanding and forming new levels of equilibria. At times, however, so many new levels of understanding converge that we reach a major new equilibrium level. These new levels cause a major reorganization in the structure of our thinking.

    A. Piaget called these shifts to new levels *stages.*

        1. Think of a person climbing a mountain range as an analogy for development to a new stage of thinking. The person slowly but gradually makes progress up the steep grade. When she reaches the top, she can now see vistas that were not available to her before. She has a qualitatively different situation in front of her. She will see that she has yet other steep grades and challenges to meet, challenges she wasn't even aware of before she reached this particular level.

        2. Stages are defined as qualitative shifts in one's way of thinking, reorganizations of both one's understanding and one's mental tools and strategies to solve problems. They aren't simply quantitative additions to one's knowledge or skills.

        3. For example, in language development, one develops rules for how to form plurals and past tense; one does not simply add vocabulary. When a child says "my feets" or "I drinked the milk," we know that she has developed these rules and can use them in all her language.

4. Each stage is based on development in the previous stages. One cannot function at stage three, for example, without having the skills that emerged in stages one and two. In this way, the order or sequence of the stages is invariant.

5. Although Freud and Erikson considered the order of their stages to be invariant, their stages were more descriptive. Piaget's stages follow a logical necessity to the order; therefore, it is difficult to think of abilities at one of his stages being possible before the abilities at a previous stage have developed.

6. Although Piaget provided typical ages for his stages, his ages were not so important. Some children develop through the stages at a faster rate than other children.

7. Piaget believed that his stages were universal in two senses. First, he thought that all neurologically normal people, regardless of their cultures, would develop through the sequence of stages. Second, he thought that a person in a given stage would be in that stage for practically all of his or her developmental domains, whether in mathematical understanding, social skills, conservation skills, or other areas.

8. Because Piaget's primary goal was to describe the whole sequence of development in how humans get from the cognitive level they are born with to their adult level of thinking, he tried to explain how each stage grew out of the previous stages.

B. Based on his observations of children's abilities and reasoning at different ages, Piaget believed there were four major stages of cognitive development. He often called these major stages *periods.* Below is a brief overview of the four periods. The details and definitions will be covered later.

1. The first period is called the *sensory-motor period.* It begins at birth and lasts until about 18 to 24 months of age, during infancy. It starts out being based on the reflex schemes babies are born with and ends with children's development of symbol use.

 ©2002 The Teaching Company Limited Partnership

2. The second period is called the *pre-operational period.* It begins at about 18 to 24 months and lasts until about six to seven years of age, during the preschool years. It starts out based on basic symbolic skills that the child has developed and covers the period when he or she learns to master symbolic thinking.

3. The third period is called the *concrete-operational period.* It begins at about six to seven years and lasts until about 11 to 12 years of age, during the middle childhood years. It starts out with children's emerging ability to use multiple representations and cognitive operations and lasts until formal thinking emerges.

4. The fourth period is called the *formal-operational period.* It begins at about 11 to 12 years and lasts throughout adulthood. However, Piaget believed that this way of thinking was mastered during adolescence. Although adults continue to learn throughout their lives, Piaget saw no evidence for additional major reorganizations in thinking during adulthood. During this last period, people develop the ability to reason hypothetically and in highly abstract ways.

II. The *sensory-motor period* is aptly named. During this period, all that a child knows is based on the information that comes in through his senses and the motoric actions that he can perform.

A. At birth, the child gives no evidence of having symbolic skills or having an ability to evoke symbolic representations of objects or memories.

1. A *symbol* can be defined as one thing—an object, an idea, an image, or an action—that refers to or stands for something else, often called the *referent.*

2. The symbol can be differentiated from the referent. For example, the word *dog* is a symbol for the actual animal, whereas the dog's head is not a differentiated symbol for the entire dog. In pretend play, a stick may be a symbol for a car, or a person can conjure up a mental image of car to use as a symbol for a car.

3. We will return to a discussion of symbol use when discussing the next period. For now, it is crucial to realize that if a baby has no symbol use, then he must

live in the present dependent on his sensory input and his overt actions.

4. This does not mean that the child does not have memory, however. Children can recognize familiar objects or places by using their schemes. They also develop intentions and anticipations, when one thing signals that something else will follow. Thus, they develop an understanding of means-end causality in real three-dimensional space.

5. The major developmental goal during this period is for the child to learn how the real world works and develop the prerequisites for symbol use, which emerges during the second year of life.

B. Piaget divided up the sensory-motor period into six sub-stages.

1. First, children are born with reflexive schemes, such as sucking, looking, and grasping. Children come into the world using these schemes. The schemes are considered reflexive because the child does not have voluntary control or anticipate his actions.

2. Second, at the seven-week-shift in development, major portions of the cortex begin to fire, and this extra neural development seems to make possible shifts in the child's voluntary control of behavior. For example, the child can now decide to grasp an object or not or attempt to look at some object or face. The child shows intentions and the beginning of understanding means and ends.

3. Third, children develop a sense of means-end causality. For example, the child may grasp an object—the means—to bring it into his line of vision so that he can look at it—the end.

4. Fourth, children pay attention to variations in the end results of actions and what caused the variations. It is as if the child were playing with themes and variations in his explorations of the world.

5. Fifth, children systematically experiment with varying the means to test the end results. It is as if on a sensory-motor level, they have become young scientists. For example, one child learned that if he dropped food from his high chair tray—means—it would fall on the floor—

 ©2002 The Teaching Company Limited Partnership

end. He then, by accident, observed that the food fell in different places depending on where he dropped it. He then systematically varied the dropping of food and the force with which he threw it to watch what changes these actions would have. When his mother picked up the food, he discovered a new end using the same old means. He now could drop food—the same means—to get his mother to bend down and pick up food—new end—or to get her exasperated—yet a new end. He could also do these dropping experiments with toys and other objects. This is an example of a small sensory-motor scientist at work.

6. Sixth, usually between about 14 and 24 months, children make a transition into the next period. With all their experience with means and ends and causality and dealing with objects in the real world, they begin to show insight learning. That is, they perform the actions in their mind without actually going through sensory-motor trial-and-error learning. At the same time, they show budding symbol use. They begin using words and developing word order in their speech. They begin showing simple pretend play, such as pretending to drink from a cup, and they show a spurt in recall memory, in which they can think of things that are no longer present in their environment and without the aid of cues.

7. It now seems that neurological changes at this time in fact make possible the use of accompanying mental associations necessary for symbol use.

III. Symbol use is beginning, and with it, children have reached a new plateau or level of thinking. They are not tied to the here and now. They no longer require sensory input to think of things, nor do they need to act overtly on their environment to think about causality and how things work. This transition takes them into Piaget's second stage, the pre-operational period.

A. The major developmental task of this period seems to be for the child to perfect the ability to have anything stand for anything else.

1. For example, early on in a child's symbol use, she often needs external props that are highly similar to the

referent in order to symbolize the referent—a toy telephone is needed to stand for a real phone. Over time, the child can use props that are dissimilar and completely unrelated to the referent to symbolize it—a toy car can now stand for a telephone. Eventually, the child needs no external symbol at all but can merely imagine the referent. The symbol is completely internal and mental.

2. This mastery of symbolization is significant because it frees the child from the present environment. She can now think about anything, conjure up anything, talk about anything, and dwell on the past and the future, as well as the present.

3. Paradoxically, by freeing oneself from concrete reality, a person gains greater flexibility and adaptability to reality.

B. Despite children's accomplishments in mastery of symbols during the pre-operational period, Piaget's descriptions of this period often focus on the things that children cannot do, the errors they make. Understanding what children cannot do helps to define the transitions in development to the next stage—what they can do later on.

C. Preschool children can represent and imagine many things, but they tend to center their focus on only one thing or one aspect of a situation at a time.

1. Because of their lack of ability to *decenter*, or to consider more than one perspective or aspect at the same time, they often have problems with perspective-taking.

2. *Perspective-taking* is the ability to see a situation from more than one perspective and to compare them.

3. Piaget performed an experiment in which he had children look at a model of three mountains from each of the four sides of the model. Preschool children could pick out a picture of what their viewpoint looked like, but when they were asked to pick out what the mountains looked like from the viewpoint of someone looking at them from a different angle, they got confused and picked their own viewpoint again. Thus, they lacked perspective taking.

©2002 The Teaching Company Limited Partnership

4. Piaget said that this thinking in preschoolers was *egocentric thinking,* because children tended to center on their own viewpoint to the exclusion of other viewpoints. However, he later regretted using the term *egocentric* because he meant that children had a cognitive developmental deficit, not that they were selfish or egotistical.

Supplementary Reading:

Piaget, *The Origins of Intelligence in Children.* (This book, like all of Piaget's writing is difficult to read; however, in a recent poll of developmental psychologists, this book was voted as the most influential and classic writing published about child development in the 20th century. It gives a detailed account of the basic process and numerous examples of development during the sensory-motor period.)

Piaget and Inhelder, *The Psychology of the Child,* chapters 1 and 3 cover the sensory-motor and pre-operational periods. (Inhelder was one of Piaget's most important collaborators.)

Questions to Consider:

1. Do you think Piaget's equilibration process involving assimilation and accommodation can be anything more than a metaphor? Though this construct does make sense to many people, still many researchers question whether it can ever be empirically tested.

2. From your experience observing children, do you think of development in terms of set stages, or do you see development as much more gradual, without any qualitative shifts and spurts and plateaus?

Lecture Nineteen
Piaget's Early Stages

Hello. In the last lecture we introduced Piaget's theory and we discussed the basic process of equilibration between assimilation and accommodation. In this lecture, we'll begin with a discussion of how major equilibria defined Piaget's four major stages and then we'll discuss in more detail Piaget's first and second stages, the sensory motor period and the preoccupation period, and then we'll focus on the development of symbol use in the second stage.

According to Piaget, we're constantly reaching new levels of understanding and forming new levels of equilibria, and we mentioned how there's constantly this equilibrium formed between assimilation and accommodation. At times, however, there are so many new levels of understanding that converge that we reach a new major equilibrium that cuts across all the little pieces of information that we're trying to understand, and these new levels cause a major reorganization in the structure of thinking.

Piaget called these shifts to new levels, *stages*. Now let me give you an analogy. Think of a person climbing a mountain range as our analogy. The person slowly but gradually makes progress up a steep grade. When she reaches the top, she can now see vistas that were not available to her before. She has a qualitatively different situation in front of her than she did before. She'll see that she has yet other steep grades and challenges to meet, challenges she wasn't even aware of before she started this climb and before she reached this particular level. That's, in some way, the way Piaget looked at his stages. Stages are defined as qualitative shifts in one's way of thinking. A reorganization of both one's understanding and also the mental tools, the strategies we have to solve problems. Stages are not simply qualitative additions to one's knowledge or skill.

Let me give you an example from language development. Of course, kids add vocabulary, that's a quantitative addition; but early on, they start learning just by hearing things and gaining experience. They learn how to say things correctly. Like a child will say, "My feet, or my toys." Or, "I drank milk." But there comes a period of time that many of you have observed or know about when they start shifting to an incorrect form. While they said, "My feet" the first time, they'll now say, "My feets" or "I drinked milk." When we see this happen

 ©2002 The Teaching Company Limited Partnership

we realize that this person has developed rules—for example, the use of past tense on verbs—and now this person applies these rules in general to all situations, even cases where there are irregular forms and the person had it right before. You can't explain these rules as simple quantitative shifts or additions, you have to explain them as qualitative shifts, shifts in strategy, reorganizations. And, that was what was of most interest to Piaget, this reorganization of structure and how we think.

Also for Piaget, each stage is based on development in a previous stage. One can't function in stage three, for example, without having the skills that emerged in stages one and two. So in this way, in Piaget's stages, the order or the sequence of the stages is invariant. Now Freud and Erikson also had stages as you recall, and the order of their stages was invariant, but the stages were much more descriptive. Piaget's stages follow this logical necessity to the order. Whether you believe his stages are a good way of explaining development or not, when you look at the stages, it's difficult to think of the stages at one level being possible before the abilities of the previous stage having developed. There's a logical necessity and a hierarchy to these stages.

Piaget provided particular ages for these stages, and people get hung up and lost on the ages of the stages and whether they're correct or not. But, his ages were not so important to him. They gave the typical ages but he realized that some children develop through the stages at a faster rate than other children. The ages were just guidelines. Piaget believed then that it was just the order, the invariant order of the stages, and the logical progression was important. He also believed his stages were universal in two senses. First, he thought that all neurologically normal people, regardless of their culture, would develop through the sequence of stages. And second, more in the line of looking at the generality of stages, he thought that a person that was in any given stage would be in that stage for practically all of his or her development in all domains. So, whether we're observing mathematical understanding or social skills or conservation skills or whatever else we talked about, a person is in a particular stage once they've consolidated their skills. In that way, the stage is universal across all aspects of a human's life. We'll come back to this later, and whether this is a good idea or not.

Because Piaget's primary goal was to describe the whole sequence of development in how humans get to their cognitive level when they were born, to how they get to their level when they're adults, an adult level of thinking, he tried to explain how each stage grew out of the previous stage. And, based on his observations—because he was a keen observer of children, and his views of the reasoning of children at different ages—Piaget believed that there were four major stages of cognitive development. He didn't just pick these arbitrarily. This is how he saw the major cognitive shifts. He often called these major stages *periods*. So let me give you a brief overview of the four periods. We're going to talk about the details and the definitions later, as we go through.

His first period is called the *sensory-motor period*. It begins at birth and lasts until 18–24 months of age, give or take a few years—no, I'm just joking. Somewhere during infancy is this stage. It starts out being based on reflex schemes that babies are born with and it ends with children's development of symbol use. The second period is called the *pre-operational period*. It begins in about 18–24 months of age and lasts until six to seven years of age, so it's essentially a period of development during the preschool years, and it starts out based on the basic symbolic skills and then it covers a period when the child learns to master these symbolic skills, to be a symbolic thinker—a master symbolic thinker. The third period is called the *concrete-operational period*. It begins at about six to seven years and lasts until about 10–12 years, so this is occurring during middle childhood. It starts out with children's emerging use of multiple representations and cognitive operations—we'll define those later—and it lasts until formal thinking emerges. And the fourth and last period is called the *formal-operational period*. It begins at about 11–12 years; it lasts throughout adulthood.

However, Piaget believed that it was during adolescence that this way of thinking was mastered. Although adults continue to learn throughout their lives, and the processes apply, Piaget saw no evidence for additional major reorganizations in our thinking during adulthood. He thought that once we reached formal operations, this was the way we'd use our strategies. It was during this last period then, people develop the ability to reason hypothetically, and they became highly abstract in their ways of thinking. So now let me talk about the stages in more detail, and we're going to talk about the first two stages today, and then in the next lecture we'll go on to the

 ©2002 The Teaching Company Limited Partnership

subsequent stages. I'll have to mention at the beginning, I can't cover all that Piaget discovered. He had many findings that were important. But I'll try to cover highlights that I hope will make sense out of his sequence of stages.

Let's talk about the *sensory-motor period*. It's aptly named. It's during this period that all that a child knows is based on the information that comes in through the senses and the motoric actions that he can perform in the world and on things. It's sensory and it's motor. At birth, the child gives no evidence of having symbolic skills. Piaget argued this, but I think this is true. He doesn't have an ability to evoke symbolic representations of objects, or symbolic memories of objects. Now, a *symbol* can be defined as a thing—an object, an idea, an image or an action—that refers to or stands for something else. And when you have a symbol, often we would call the thing it refers to the *referent*. A symbol then stands for a referent; and the symbol can be differentiated from the referent. For example, the word *dog* in English is a symbol for the animal. But a dog's head is not truly differentiated as a symbol for the entire dog. A dog's head, if you see it, can make you think about a dog, but it's part of the dog. So in pretend play, a child may use a stick as a pretend car. Or, we may conjure up a mental image of a car, and this mental image in our mind is also a symbol for a car; it stands for a car. We're going to talk about symbol use later. But I need to give that at the beginning here because that is not what babies have when they come into the world. It's crucial to realize that if they have no symbol use, these little kids have to live in the present. They're dependent on their sensory input, and their overt actions, as I'd said. They're living in the here and now.

However, this doesn't mean that this child has no memory whatsoever. Children have memory; otherwise we argue that they couldn't learn anything. Memory shows that they learn. They recognize familiar objects and things. They use their schemes to assimilate objects. They also develop intentions and anticipations. They can use one thing to signal that something else will follow. They're learning about means and causality, about three-dimensional space. But when we talk about memory, it's usually what's called recognition memory. They see something, they can apply their scheme and they can recognize it. They're pretty poor at recall memory, just evolving something out of nothing and bringing it about.

The major developmental goal as Piaget saw it for this period for the child is to learn how the real world works. I mean by the real world, the physical world—how it works, how to deal with it, and how to master things in the real world. It means learning that objects are permanent in the real world, that they exist whether you see them or not, having enough experience to recognize that. Recognizing how three dimensional space works, that you can walk around things, for example, if there's a table in your way you can walk around it. You can get where you want to go. It seems simple for us, but babies have to learn all that kind of stuff. Having enough experience with the real world that the child develops the prerequisites, the experience, for symbol use which will emerge during the second year of life.

Now Piaget divided his sensory motor period into six sub-stages. I really don't think it's that important that a person keep every sub-stage exactly straight, but going through them generally will give you a sense that the sequence is happening in this development. First, children are born with some basic schemes to get them started. We mentioned that in the last lecture. They're born with these reflexive action schemes—sucking, looking, grasping. This is how they act on the world and know their world. They come into the world utilizing these schemes. They're like reflexes; they can't help themselves. They're reflexive because the child doesn't have any voluntary control, doesn't anticipate his actions. For example, on grasping, you put something into the child's hand and the child grasps it. It's not something like he has a choice. You put something in his mouth; he sucks it. This would be the first stage; we're born with this. We've already developed this prenatally, if you will.

At the second stage, what we've already talked about is called a seven-week shift. At some time around seven to eight weeks after birth, major portions of the cortex begin to fire, and there's an extra neural development and it makes possible developments in the cortex that weren't there before. Piaget didn't exactly know this when he came up with this, but what he said fits. A child shifts to being voluntary and showing voluntary control of behavior. For example, a child can now decide to grasp an object or not. It's voluntary. He can choose to look at an object or not, or suck an object or not. The reflexive automatic nature is lost and then everything becomes

©2002 The Teaching Company Limited Partnership

voluntary. The reflexive part seemed to be a way of just getting the kid started. The child starts to show intentions and the beginning of means-end understanding, that is, what things you do to create these kinds of results and how they're connected.

In the third stage in the sensory motor period, children develop this sense of means-end causality. For example, now they'll grasp an object, in this case it's the means, in order to bring it into their line of vision, so that they can look at it, the end. It seems to be this intentional case of doing one thing to bring about something else, and they start learning all the actions they take have results. They seem to be processing this, or learning what these connections are.

In the fourth sub-stage, children pay attention to different variations in the end results and to what cause these variations. In some ways, it's like a kid playing with theme and variations as he explores the world, and in the fifth stage, he takes this further. Children systematically experiment with varying the means in order to test the end results. The key word here is systematic. They seem to look like miniature scientists on a sensory motor level. Through trial and error, they seem to be more systematic as they're exploring the causality of the means-end relationships, more than they did in the random way before. Let me give you an example. This is one child, but you see it again and again in kids.

A child was sitting in a high chair and he had his tray in front of him and some food on the tray, and he accidentally dropped the food off, pushed it off. It fell to the floor—pretty cool. So, he did it again. And dropping the food to the floor became the end, pushing it off became his means, and he became really interested in this. So over and over again he pushed food off his tray. But then he observed, by accident I think, how it fell, and where it fell depended on where he dropped it, a pretty profound insight for this little kid, and then he proceeded systematically with the dropping of the food, and also with the force at which he threw it at different times, and he'd watch the changes in these actions—the changes that they'd have on where it fell, how fast it went down, the trajectory if you will. I'm reading a lot in, but this is what it looked like this kid was doing, this little experiment. He could now drop food, the same old means, to do different things. He could vary the way he dropped it—the means—to look at an effect in a systematic way. But his mom came along and bent down and started picking up some to the food, a new end. The same old means of dropping the food and mom picks it up and puts it back on the tray. So now he started doing it and shifted it to seeing what mom would do. Then mom got really exasperated with him. Ah, a new end! Drop it off and see if mom will get frustrated and upset. And he really looked like he was doing other experiments. He ended it with other objects. You put stuff on his tray, toys and other stuff; he would do the same things to see what happened. And one of the things he did was see how long he could keep people going, playing this game being part of his experiment. This is an example of a small sensory motorist at work.

The sixth sub-stage of the sensory motor period usually occurs somewhere between 14 and 24 months in kids. Children make a transition into the next period. It's sort of—the end of this stage is vague and becomes the next period also. With all of their experience with means and ends and with causality, with dealing with objects in the world, they begin to show insight learning. That is, they perform an action in their mind without actually going through all the sensory motor trial and error learning. They seem to show a budding symbol use. Piaget described a case where a child was trying to open a matchbox, one to those little wooden matchboxes with small, wooden matches in it. She couldn't get it open and then looked at it and with her mouth went—pop, pop—opened her mouth and looked at it again and reached in and opened it. You could say that child was still doing actions, but it's like the child was not just doing trial and error until she got it open, but the child was doing some insight learning, thinking about it. In this case, she was using sort of a prop, an action, an almost symbolic action to then go ahead and try to do this task.

They show then the beginning of symbol use, and it's not just trial and error learning anymore, they do it internally. One thing stands for something else; they think about these things. They begin to show this, of course, in language, the primary symbolic system that we use as humans. Not only do they use words that stand for other things, they develop a word order, beginning syntax in their speech. They begin showing simple pretend play. They'll pretend to drink from a cup or to sleep on something that stands for a pillow. They'll pretend to talk on a telephone as they've seen other people from their house do. There's a spurt in recall memory, they can now think of things that are no longer present in their environment without need of cues. They can go after something that's not there, act like they're

 ©2002 The Teaching Company Limited Partnership

searching for things that are not there. It now seems that there are neurological changes at this time that, in fact, make possible the use of these accompanying mental associations and symbol use. Piaget argued how it was previous experiences that led to this development, and that's probably true. But that's probably also in conjunction with maturation or neurological changes that make it possible.

So symbol use is beginning. If the children have reached this new plateau or level of thinking, they're not tied to the here and now any longer. They no longer require sensory input to think of things. Nor do they require the need to act overtly on their environment in order to think about it and to work through causality and see how things work. Do you see what a profound change that is? They're not tied to the here and now; they're no longer sensory motor. This transition then takes them into Piaget's second stage that he called the pre-operational period, and it was symbol use that provided the transition. You get the impression that the development of symbol use is a major breakthrough? I think I've mentioned it to you before—symbol use. Symbol use seems to be a big shift in the development in humans.

The task of the second period, this is during the preschool years, is really for the child to perfect the ability and to have anything stand for anything else. The master symbol-user can use anything for anything. He's really adept at bouncing around symbols and using them as part of a system, like a language system. This is what seems to be going on cognitively as the main task, as Piaget saw it. He called it the pre-operational period because it was before operations came in, and I'm going to talk about operations later and what that means. But let's focus on the mastery of symbol use.

For example, early on in a child's symbol use she will often need external props that are highly similar to the referent to use as a symbol. Later on, again she can use anything that stands for anything. Let me give you an example of this sequence of development that happens at the transition from the sensory motor period to the pre-operational period. This is some research I did with Elaine Jackowitz. We showed kids a sequence of objects and wanted to see how they would use these objects in a pretend play situation. In fact, we'd get them started by having somebody model some of these objects and then seeing if the kids would also do it this way. We presented them in a random order, not in the same order; and what we discovered was that kids didn't really blindly imitate what we did. If they understood something, they would use it in pretend play. They would do it as the model showed it. But if they didn't understand it, they wouldn't use it. They would look at you and bounce back to some earlier level and do something else.

Let me give you one case, and this was talking on a telephone, a very simple pretend task that a lot of kids will do. We started out with a real telephone receiver. We'd pick up the receiver and talk into it. Next, we'd use a pretend telephone, a little pretend telephone, it was the same shape, the same function and size. Could the child pick up the toy telephone and have a little pretend conversation? Then we made a shift. We used something that was similar, but a little different. We used a walkie-talkie that didn't look so much like a telephone receiver. We also used a banana that looks like a telephone receiver—of course it has a completely different function. Then we shifted further. We used a block of wood that was sort of ambiguous and nondescript. Could the kids use the block of wood and use it as a telephone? Then we used something that was tough; we used a toy car. Could a child use the toy car and talk into a toy car? And eventually we used what we thought might be the most extreme—no object at all. We just held up a toy telephone as if we were holding it in our hand and talked to an imaginary object.

Whatever order we presented these in, kids went through that order in the same order that I just gave that to you. Between 16 and 24 months, they first showed that it was very easy; all of them could talk into the real phone, and in fact, the telephone. Later on, as they got a little older, they got better and they could talk into the banana. But when they could talk into the banana, at first they still couldn't use the block or the toy car. Eventually, they could use the block and the toy car. And last of all, and most difficult, was the imaginary object. In fact, some of the kids at 24 months could do it, but it was so difficult that a lot of kids never got to that stage. One little girl, for example, when we talked with an imaginary object and it was her turn, she looked around for an object and there was no object present. She picked up a little piece of lint and held it up and talked into it. She needed some prop, some object to use.

My object is that some development of symbol use means that you distance the symbol from the referent, that you can use anything for anything, so that by the time the kid is four, certainly five, they can do it as easily as we can as adults. This frees the child from the present environment. She can now think about anything, conjure up anything, talk about anything, dwell on the past, and dwell on the future as well as the present. What a breakthrough! Paradoxically, by freeing one's self from concrete reality; a person gains greater flexibility and adaptability to reality.

Now, mastering entire symbol systems becomes a major developmental achievement for kids, and this takes kids then to the transition to the next stage. But, in addition to this kind of mastery, Piaget also talked about the errors that children would make, what they can't do as well as what they can do. And it's important, because sometimes when you look at errors, you can learn about what's going on in their heads. For example, even though they're developing symbol use, kids have a very difficult time representing things in multiple ways, looking at things from different viewpoints at the same time. Piaget called this *centration*, they center on one factor or one aspect of a situation, rather than *decenter* on multiple factors or aspects of a particular object or situation. Adults have, or older kids have decenteration ability, kids don't have decentration ability, if you want to look at it this way.

This leads to problems with *perspective-taking*. They have a perspective on things, other people have a perspective on things, but they have a very hard time coordinating these two, seeing that they both exist at the same time. Piaget did a classic study called the Three Mountain Task in which he laid out a model, like a papier-mâché mountain of three different mountains with a few little objects like a little cottage on one, and so forth. He had the kids look at this model and look around it from all perspectives. In fact, as they were on each side of the model, they could pick out a picture that looked like what they saw from that vantage point, and they could go around and find this. And then if you asked them, "How does this model of the three mountains look to you?" they could pick out the correct picture. But, if you put someone across at a different vantage point on a different side and said, "What does the model look like to this other person?" they would pick out—the little kids, the preschoolers—they would pick out their view again. They got confused and they would go back to their own viewpoint, rather than that of another person.

Piaget said that this is *egocentric thinking*; egocentric in a sense that they tended to prefer and focus on their viewpoint and not somebody else's. He later regretted that he used the word egocentric because egocentric had so many connotations for people as being something like selfishness or egotistical. He didn't mean that. He said, "*Egocentric* is a cognitive deficit that's just part of development. They can't look at it both ways."

There are a lot of cases of this lack of perspective-taking for kids. At one time, for example, one of my sons went to the dentist and got a little cheap plastic ring as a gift. He was very interested in it, and when we went home at night he was still playing with it. He went to bed; it was dark and I was in bed in the other room. He at least had enough perspective to realize that I was still awake, I guess. He yelled out, "Dad. Which finger does a ring go on?" It was dark and I was in another room. Being a bad Dad I was tired, I said, "The third finger. Go to sleep." There was this long pause and then he said, "Is this the right finger?" And I said, "Yes." Now if you count your fingers, one-two-three from any direction—he got confused that I could see his perspective. He had enough sense, enough perspective to realize that I might have the answer and could tell him, but he got confused when he put these things together, and kids often get confused in their perspectives.

That will set us up for what develops next in the next stage, and we'll talk about that next time.

Thank you.

©2002 The Teaching Company Limited Partnership

Lecture Twenty
Concrete Operations

Scope:

This lecture continues the discussion of Piaget's stages of development. It begins with a discussion of what preschoolers can and can't do, then looks at how the five-to-seven-year shift is a pivotal transition to Piaget's third stage, the concrete-operational period. During this shift, multiple representational skills emerge. The lecture describes what an *operation* is and why Piaget called the stage *concrete*. The lecture concludes with examples of children's developing concepts of conservation and kindness.

Outline

I. Looking at what preschoolers cannot do is a way to understand the five-to-seven-year shift, a pivotal transition to Piaget's concrete-operational period.

   A. Sometimes, preschoolers say poetic and humorous things because of their lack of perspective taking and their unique way of looking at one facet of a situation.

      1. In one example described by Chukovsky, a Russian author of children's stories, a mother was drying off her daughter after the girl's bath. The girl looked down at her naked body and, with the wonder and excitement of discovery, said, "I'm barefoot all over!"

      2. Although this was a delightful and poetic way of expressing something, it was based on a centering of only one aspect of her situation. She saw a lot of bare skin; she probably thought about when she had seen bare skin before—when she was barefoot—and she equated that one incident with what she saw now.

      3. The lack of perspective taking in this example is also an illustration of how a child might assimilate a new situation to an old scheme—one of being barefoot—without fully accommodating to the situation. Thus, the child distorts reality, albeit poetically.

B. Because of this same lack of ability to consider multiple perspectives or pieces of information, preschool children also have a difficult time understanding how someone else's mind works, how we come to believe what we believe.

   1. Researchers, such as John Flavell and Henry Wellman, have tracked the development of children's ability to understand how someone develops false beliefs or beliefs that vary from one's own.
   2. In one classic study, a child is shown a story about dolls in which a doll hides a ball in a drawer in his room. He then leaves, and his mother enters the room. The mother moves the ball from the drawer and puts it under the bed. Then the other person comes back into the room to get the ball. The experimenter asks the child where the boy will look for the ball and where he believes it will be. Three-year-olds say that the child will look under the bed where the mother put the ball and that the child believes the ball is there. Only at about five years of age do children consistently say that the child will look in the drawer for the ball and that he believes it is there because he doesn't know that his mother moved it.
   3. This development is not an all-or-none process. Children during this period gradually improve in these abilities. Even as adults, we often still show egocentric thinking and problems with perspective taking.

II. Because so many changes in thinking emerge during the transition from the preschool to the school years, many have come to call this time the *five-to-seven-year shift.* Sheldon White coined the term.

   A. What actually develops during this transition period?
   1. Many now believe that there is probably some neurological change in processing capacity that makes possible changes in cognition, though our knowledge about these neurological changes is not yet clear.
   2. Probably based on a combination of neurological changes, past experiences dealing with perspective-taking issues, and the emerging mastery of systematic symbol use, five- and six-year-olds develop the ability to represent a thing, a person, or a situation in multiple

©2002 The Teaching Company Limited Partnership

ways and to switch back and forth easily between these representations to compare them and to coordinate them. Thus, they develop *multiple representational ability*.

3. As an example, a child may now be able to understand how a person can be represented as having a false belief in something and, at the same time, be represented as wanting to tell the truth but being in error because of a lack of correct information. Likewise, another person may have a valid belief about something but also be represented as wanting to deceive the child and, thus, not give out the information the person actually believed to be true.

4. Multiple representational ability makes possible the ability to efficiently read others' intentions and truthfulness, to effectively deceive others, to use strategies to compete, to understand the needs of others, and to follow complex rules. The list goes on and on.

III. This shift in basic representational skill matches Piaget's observations and his belief that children enter a third stage, the *concrete-operational period*.

A. What's in a name? For Piaget, an *operation* is a *mental transformation* that a child can perform on some thing or idea that can also be reversed, or brought back to the original state by a complementary transformation.

1. The perfect example of an operation comes from basic mathematical operations. If we have four, then add three to it, we have performed a transformation on four to turn it into seven. Addition, therefore, is an operation. The transformation of four into seven can also be reversed with another transformation, that of subtracting three from seven to turn it back into four. Thus, subtraction is a reversible transformation of addition, just as division is a reversible transformation of multiplication.

2. In the case of the child hiding the ball in a drawer, there was an operation that transformed the situation, that is, her mother moved the ball to be under the bed. This operation can also be reversed by the transformation of moving the ball back to the drawer. Operations can function not just in mathematics, but also in nature, in social situations, in virtually all domains of our lives.

3. An important point to remember is that operations need not be physically performed. They can be done mentally, that is, symbolically.

4. Another important point is that operations are made possible because a child can simultaneously represent multiple aspects of a problem and compare them. The child can take account of how things are in State A before a transformation has occurred, how things are in State B after the transformation has occurred, and what the transformation is. This multiple representational ability makes reversible operations possible.

B. Why did Piaget call these operations *concrete*?

1. Some people mistakenly believe that what Piaget meant by *concrete operations* was that children had to perform them physically on real objects.

2. What he meant by *concrete* was that mental operations were possible as the child considered real-life situations, concrete instances of a problem, not hypothetical or highly theoretical problems.

3. For example, a seven-year-old child can understand how, if John is taller than Bonnie and Bonnie is taller than Peggy, then John is also taller than Peggy. A child can perform this type of inference by *seriating* the order of items—putting them in order to compare them. In this case, Bonnie is both shorter than someone and taller than someone. Once again, she is represented in two ways that can be compared. This is a concrete situation.

4. However, if we asked this same child to seriate a series of fractions with which he had had no experience or to define *seriation*, he would not have the capacity. *Concrete operations* means that children are limited to specific concrete instances for which they have had some related experience.

C. With the further mastery of operational thinking, children come to classify their world and learn about relations and causality through their own logic, not just based on what they have observed.

 ©2002 The Teaching Company Limited Partnership

1. They can understand that things aren't always as they appear. An object may appear red because of the lighting on it but indeed be white.
2. Associated with this operational ability comes the belief in necessary truth. Some things must be true because logic says they must be this way. A person's knowledge of transformations again tells him that certain transformations are not possible even if it appears that they are. For example, a magician is impressive because one knows that the trick cannot be magic, cannot be real. One cannot transform a scarf into a dove.

IV. We will discuss two specific examples of concrete-operational thinking, *conservation ability* and *conceptualization of kindness*.

   A. The concept of *conservation* refers to the ability a person has to understand what remains the same about an object or person when some things change. In other words, a person can conserve the identity of an object amid change.

     1. This ability is made possible because of reversible operations, which in turn, are made possible because of multiple representations.

     2. A perfect example comes from an experiment that Piaget first performed. If a preschool child sees two identical glasses that are filled to the same height with water, she will report that they both have an equal amount of water in them. However, if she sees one glass of water poured into a tall, thin beaker and sees the water rise to a higher level, she will say that that beaker now has more water in it. If she sees the water poured back into the original glass, she will say that the two glasses again have the same amount of water in them. She cannot take account of the multiple aspects of the transformation—pouring the water into a different-shaped glass—or keep in mind that the transformation is reversible. She is overwhelmed by appearances and does not conserve the basic amount of the water.

     3. If we repeat the same procedure but this time, with a school-aged child, we will observe a different outcome. This time, the child will report that the amount of water stays the same in both the short, wide glass and the tall,

thin glass. The child will be able to discuss the fact that we could pour the water back and it would be at the same level again, that no water was added or taken away, and the idea that the glass being thinner compensates for it being taller. This child, despite the appearances of the water in the glasses to the contrary, does conserve the basic amount of water.

4. Although we can train children to give the correct answers, their basic understanding of conservation under many different variations of this task on different materials—such as with masses of clay, with the number of things—shows the switch in understanding conservation that Piaget originally observed in children. Young children, at about three and four years, cannot conserve the amount or identity of things, while older children, at about five to seven years, can.

B. There are important implications of this conservation ability.

1. Problems in conservation appear in social relationships as well. One preschooler asked his father whether he would still be his father when he became a doctor. The child was quite concerned. In other words, how can one's identity be conserved in the face of changes in roles, appearance, or relationships?

2. Many young children have had problems dealing with the divorce of their parents in part because they are concerned with the conservation of the parent-child relationship when the spousal relationship has ended. Again, the question for children is what remains the same when some things change.

3. In one study performed by Susan Carey, a tube was surreptitiously connected to the glasses. In this way, the experimenter could change the water level to arbitrary amounts, as in a magic trick. Children who were found to not have the ability to conserve did not seemed surprised when the water levels did not end up where the children had predicted they would. On the other hand, children who did have the ability to conserve were upset and protested when the water levels did not end up where they had predicted they would. In other words, they had a necessary truth. Because of their

©2002 The Teaching Company Limited Partnership

understanding of conservation, they believed that certain results had to occur despite what appearances told them.

C. James Youniss completed an experiment that revealed another variation on the developing ability to perform concrete operations.

1. He asked children to define and describe what made a person kind. He gave each child concrete examples of social situations.

2. He found that preschoolers defined being kind in terms of *absolute behaviors*. For example, a person is kind if she shares her cookies with another child. A person is kind if he helps another person across the street.

3. However, school-aged children defined kindness in more *relative* terms. For example, a person is kind if her playmate doesn't have any cookies and is hungry, and she shares her cookies. A person is kind if another person wants to cross the street and can't walk on her own, and the first person helps her across the street.

4. The older children seemed to take account of a need or deficit—State A—that needed amending, and a transformation that could be performed that would bring about a better condition or end to the deficit—State B. In other words, giving someone who had too many cookies already or helping a person across the street who did not want to go were not considered acts of kindness. One had to take account of the full transformations, of meeting a need.

D. In conclusion, concrete-operational thinking makes possible many academic and cognitive accomplishments but also higher levels of adaptation in social situations, as well.

Supplementary Reading:

Inhelder and Piaget, *The Early Growth of Logic in the Child.*

Piaget and Inhelder, *The Psychology of the Child*, chapter 4.

Questions to Consider:

1. Do you think there is any connection between the cognitive shifts that children make between about five and seven years of age and the fact that most cultures that have formal education begin children's schooling at this age period?

2. Can you think of practical examples of children's confusions about the world that are based on their lack of ability to consider two viewpoints at the same time or their lack of ability to consider how a mental transformation can also be reversed?

©2002 The Teaching Company Limited Partnership

Lecture Twenty
Concrete Operations

Hello. Last time we talked about Piaget's sensory motor and pre-operational stages of development. Today we're going to continue the discussion of Piaget's stages of development. We left the child at end of the pre-operational period with the mastery of symbol use, and we also talked about what preschoolers could and could not do. Today, we'd like to continue that and talk about what they can't do as a way of understanding the five-to-seven-year shift. This shift is a pivotal transition to Piaget's third period, the concrete operational period. And then I'd like to discuss what he meant by an *operation*, this term and important concept for him that developed during this stage.

So, despite all of children's accomplishments and the mastery of symbols, we talked about some of the errors they had, the things they could not do during the pre-operational period. The problem they had of decentering and considering multiple perspectives at the same time, the problems in perspective-taking, the problems they had when they had to combine things and then showed a good deal of egocentric thinking. When we look at the errors that children make, it's a good way of then trying to make sense of what they can do in the next stage. Sometimes the preschoolers, particularly preschoolers, say poetic and humorous things. It's really because of their lack in perspective-taking, of their cognitive deficits that are common for them at this stage, but sometimes it's cute and sort of funny. Let me give you one example.

This actually came from Chukovsky, who was a Russian author of children's stories, and he told about this instance. A mother was drying off her preschool-aged daughter after the girl's bath, and as she was drying her with a towel, the girl looked down at her naked body and exclaimed with this excitement of discovery, "I'm barefoot all over!" Now this is a sort of a delightful, poetic way of expressing something, but it's based on the child's centering on only one aspect of her situation. It's very likely that she looked down and saw a lot of bare skin, probably thought about when she'd seen bare skin in the past, when she had looked down and saw her bare feet. She equated the one incident with the other, of what she saw now, and said this. A lack of perspective-taking, as in this example, is also an illustration of how a child might assimilate a new situation to an old scheme, one of being barefoot. I just want to point that out because we had talked about assimilation and accommodation before. In this case, the child didn't fully accommodate to the new aspects of the situation. So the child distorted reality, albeit in a poetic way.

Because of this same lack of ability, the lack of ability to consider multiple perspectives or pieces of information, preschool children also have a difficult time understanding how someone else's mind works, how we come to believe what we believe. Nowadays there's a whole area of research that we call Theory of Mind research. But what it really means is how little kids develop some naïve theory or conception of how their mind works and how other people's minds work. There are several researchers in this area. Two of them are John Flavell and Henry Wellman, and they've tracked the development of children's ability to understand how someone develops false beliefs or beliefs that vary from one's own. Two other people, Wimmer and Perner did a classic study in this area, and there have been many studies done along this same line, but let me give you this example.

In a situation, you put down a little kid to one side of you and an experimenter sets up a little story, often done with pictures or even more likely done with little dolls to act out the situation. And here's how the story goes. One doll, a person, comes into a room and hides a ball in a drawer in a cupboard and then leaves the room. Then another person comes into the room, another doll— let's say the mother—takes the ball out of the drawer and puts it under the bed and then she leaves. Then the other person comes back in to get the ball. Now, you ask the kid who's been watching this, "Where does the child go? Where does the child go to look for the ball?" What do you expect they're going to say? Well, three year olds almost always will say that the kid will look for the ball under the bed where the mom put it. It's only about at four or five years of age that kids will consistently say, "This little kid's going to go in and look for the ball in the drawer, because he still believes it's there. He doesn't know that the mom moved it." You see then, they have a problem in figuring out what they know vs. what someone else knows. It sounds like our perspective-taking problem. It's also a problem in trying to figure out how someone else thinks. It's called *false belief* because this little kid in the story could really believe that the ball's in the drawer, but it's a false belief because of lack of information.

 ©2002 The Teaching Company Limited Partnership

Now, development isn't an all-or-none process. Children develop gradually during this period of the preschool years and the school years; they improve in these abilities. I have to say in these abilities, even as adults, we show egocentric thinking—problems with perspective-taking, problems with coordinating things—especially, I think, when we're under stress and have too many things on our mind. It's not that little kids can't do it and we from then on can do it, but little kids are notoriously bad at these kinds of tasks and they get pretty good. So many changes in thinking emerge during the transition of the preschool years to the school years that many have come to call this period the *five-to-seven-year shift*. Sheldon White was the person who first coined this term. What actually develops during this transition period, the five-to-seven-year shift?

Well, many people now believe that there's probably some neurological changes, changes in processing capacity that make possible these changes in cognition. But we're still not clear what all of the neurological changes are. Probably, it's based on a combination of neurological changes and past experiences dealing with perspective-taking issues and this emerging mastery of symbolic systems and symbol use. The five to six year olds develop this ability to represent a person or thing or a situation in multiple ways at the same time, to switch back easily between these representations and to compare them and coordinate them. This is called the development of *multiple representational ability*, the ability to look at things in two ways at the same time, or more than two ways at the same time. Little kids, three year olds, even four year olds, have a very difficult time seeing the world in two perspectives; we've already mentioned that. In fact, they seem to have this belief that everything has to be only one way, that there's only one representation of the world. Even at times when they can shift to another representation, they just can't see that there could be two simultaneous representations.

I want to give you a quote that captures this from an unlikely source. This is from James Barry's Peter Pan. I'm now talking about Tinker Bell here. Tinker Bell, if you recall from the story, is very jealous of Wendy, and this is one of those cases where she tries to kill Wendy because of her jealousy:

> Tink was not all bad; or rather, she was all bad just now. But on the other hand, sometimes she was all good. Fairies have

to be one thing or the other, because being so small they unfortunately have room for one feeling only at a time. They are however, allowed to change, only it must be a complete change. At present, she was full of jealousy for Wendy.

It's interesting sometimes, that great truths about development are delightfully captured in children's literature by insightful authors—like James Barry in this case. Let me give you an example. A child may not be able to understand that a person can be represented as having a false belief in something and, at the same time, as one who can tell the truth, but being in error because of this lack of information can't tell the truth. Likewise though, another person can't have a valid belief about something, but also be represented as wanting to deceive the child and thus not giving out correct information even though what the person believed was true. Kids now are better at detecting what's true and what isn't true and whether the other person intended to deceive you, or in fact is making a mistake because of a lack of information.

Along with this wonderful ability also comes, unfortunately, the ability for children to perceive much better. Little preschoolers, even though they sometimes try, are lousy liars. They get to be the five-to-seven-year shift and kids are better at lying and deceiving because of this cognitive ability. They can use strategies to compete. So, in a competitive game or a sport they can figure out things to do to try to win or deceive another person. They can also understand the complex needs of someone else and complex rules. The list goes on and on. Of the numerous changes that can be made in children's thinking and in their ability and their social skills, as well as their academic skills, these basic changes, this multiple representation matches Piaget's observations and his belief that children enter a third stage that he called the *concrete operational period*. What's in a name?

The *concrete-operational period*: For Piaget, an *operation* is a *mental transformation* that a child can perform on something or an idea and that can also be reversed or brought back to the original state by a complementary transformation. Let me see if I can give you some examples of what I just said. A perfect example of an operation comes from basic mathematical operations. In fact, I think that's where Piaget got the word. If we have four in a mathematical problem and then we add three to it, we have performed a

 ©2002 The Teaching Company Limited Partnership

transformation on the four. We've turned it into seven. And, this transformation of four to seven can also be reversed by another transformation. We can subtract three from the seven and turn it back into four. It seems so obvious. In this case though, subtraction is a reversible transformation of addition, just like division is a reversible transformation of multiplication; and addition is considered a mathematical operation, as are subtraction and multiplication and division.

Let's go back to the case of the kid hiding the ball and try to figure out whether the kid understands this idea of false belief. If a child hides the ball in the drawer, that was an operation—that this kid transformed the situation—and then it's transformed subsequently by the mother moving the ball under the bed. And this operation can be reversed by the operation of moving the ball back from under the bed to inside the drawer. So, operations can, of course, function in mathematics, but they also function in nature, and Piaget pointed out that they function in social situations. They function in virtually all domains of our lives. Some people don't find it handy to think of children's thinking in terms of operations, but this is the way Piaget found it helpful and easy to think of these transformations that were being done.

Another important point to remember about operations is that they need not be physically performed; they can be done mentally or symbolically. Remember now as we go from this five-to-seven-year shift into the elementary school years, kids are master symbol users—that's what they've developed. Another point to remember is that these operations are made possible because the child can simultaneously represent multiple aspects of a problem and compare them. So the child can take account of the way things are in State A before a transformation has occurred, how things are in State B after a transformation has occurred, and also what the transformation is. This is a multiple representation ability. The idea of reversible operations means that you can consider it both ways. You can put it all together. Piaget called it the concrete operational period. That's operations. I hope that part's clear.

What is this word *concrete*? What did he mean? Some people have mistakenly thought that Piaget meant that *concrete operations* meant that children had to perform these operations physically on real objects; that's not what he meant. What he meant by *concrete* was that the mental operations—and they were mental and symbolic—but they were possible as a child considered real-life situations, concrete instances of a problem, and not hypothetical or theoretical problems. You can do things symbolically, but you're still dealing with real-world instances that you're representing.

For example, let's say that you have a seven-year-old child and that child can understand this problem. It's a transitive inference problem: If John is taller than Bonnie, and Bonnie taller than Peggy, then John is also taller than Peggy. A child can perform this inference by *seriating* the order of these types. You can put them in order and then compare them. In this case, Bonnie is both shorter than someone and also taller than someone. There's a multiple representation there. She can be represented in these two ways. But this is a concrete situation. If you asked the same child to seriate a series of fractions with which he had no experience, or to define *seriation*, he probably wouldn't have the capacity. So, in *concrete operations*, being concrete means that children are limited to specific instances for which they may have had some related experience.

With further mastery of operational thinking, children end up classifying the world. They learn about relations and causality through their own logic, not just based on what they have observed. Before, when they started out as babies and we talked about the sensory motor period, they learned through their sensory and motor experiences with the real world. Then they became symbolic. Now, in fact, they're learning through logic, they're not just tied to observations.

Let me give you another example of this. This is some work that was done by John Flavell on what he calls appearance vs. reality. He showed kids, preschoolers and older kids, different kinds of tasks. Let me give you an example of one of them.

He had a fish, a cutout of a clear or white fish on a piece of paper and he would ask kids, "What is this?" They'd say, "A fish." He'd ask, "What color is this?" They'd say, "White! No problem." "What color is it really and truly?" They'd say, "White." "What does it look like to your eyes?" "White." No matter how you'd ask the question, no problem. Then he'd show them a piece of clear plastic that was red. Transparent plastic. He'd say, "What is this?" "Plastic." "What color is it?" "Red." "Is it true, is it really red?" "Yes." He'd go through all of that. Then he'd put the red plastic over the fish and he'd say, "What color does this fish look like it is now? What does it look like to your eyes?" And they'd say, "Red." He'd say, "But what color is it really and truly, not what it looks like, but what color is it really and truly?" The three year olds would say, "Red," and four year olds were a little wishy-washy, sometimes they'd still say, "Red." By five, they've got it. "White. Really and truly it's white." "Well, when you pull this away, what color is it now?" "White." "When you put this on what color does it become?" "Red." "Well, is it really and truly red or does it just look like it's red?" "It's really and truly red."

He did some strange things like this. He had a fake rock. Have you ever seen one of these fake rocks that's really a sponge? He said, "What is this?" They'd say, "It's a rock." He'd say, "Feel it; it's a sponge." "Oh yeah, it's a sponge." "OK, but what does it look like?" "A sponge." Or they might see a rock. "But what is it really and truly?" They'd say, "a rock." They'd get confused. The three year olds consistently get confused between appearance and reality and they go one way or the other, but they say the same thing. Five year olds, they get it; and there are many kinds of related tasks that show this kind of progression. Some people think you're just confusing them with the words. Outside of saying to a kid, "Say this. This is the correct answer," he tried everything he could to simplify the task and to say it in the simplest ways, and they still made that mistake, these three year olds. It seems to be a problem again of this kind of multiple representations that they can't do it both ways; and yet, by five, they're into it, they have it. So again, this is one of the shifts that you see in how we understand our world. When I see that we can go with logic and not just the way that we observe things, this is one case of that. You can say, "Seeing is not always believing," for school age kids. But you can't really make that statement with three year olds.

This is also associated with another operation ability. This comes in the belief of *necessary truth*. Some people have called it necessary truth, and that is the idea that some things must be true because logic says that it's that way. A person's knowledge of transformation again says certain things have to be possible or certain things are not possible. Now in fact, magicians don't have very good audiences when they play to preschoolers, because a magician does a trick and the preschooler says, "Oh cool." Everything's magic, everything transforms. You do a magic trick for a school age kid or an older person and the excitement of the magician is to say, "How did he do that? That can't possibly be right." There's a trick. How did he do that? They sit around and try to figure it out. That's the excitement about it because I don't care what the magician did. That can't be true. That's called necessary truth.

I want to now discuss two specific examples of concrete operational thinking; one that Piaget talked about and one that was a development, an offshoot from Piaget's thinking. The first is *conservation ability* and the second is a *conceptualization of kindness* that kids have. Let's talk about conservation first. The concept of conservation refers to the ability a person has to understand what remains the same about an object or a person when some things change. In other words, a person can conserve the identity of the object amid changes, and this ability is made possible because of reversible operations, according to Piaget, and these in turn are made possible because of multiple representations.

Let me give you a perfect example in an experiment that Piaget first performed. It's been done in this form with many variations since. You first sit down a preschooler and you show him two identical glasses filled with water or some other liquid to the same height. You make sure first that this child says they're the same height—and trust me, if you do this with a child, usually they'll spend some time pouring back and forth to be precise, to make sure that they look exactly the same. You ask them, "Is there the same amount of water in each glass or is there a different amount?" They'll say, "There's the same amount." Then you take one of the glasses and pour that water into a tall, thin beaker—or you could go the other way and pour it into a flat plate, let's say you pour it into a tall beaker—and now the level is higher. And you say to this child who has watched you do this, "Now, is it the same amount of water in both glasses or does one have more?" Guess what, three year olds and four years old say, "This one has more," usually pointing to the tall one. And you'll say, "Why?" And they'll say, "Because it's taller." And you'll say, "But before they had the same amount, and now they have more?" And they'll say, "Yeah." "Well how could that be? Did I take any away?" "No." "How can it be?" " Because look at it, it's taller." You pour it back and they say it's the same amount again.

©2002 The Teaching Company Limited Partnership

A five, six or seven year old, somewhere in the shift, won't fall for this. They'll say, "No, it's the same amount." You'll say, "How can that be, it's taller?" They'll say, "It looks taller, but it's also skinnier," or they'll say, "Yeah, but you just poured it in. You didn't take anything away or add anything." Or they'll say—the reversible transformation—"You can pour it back and it will be the same amount again." So again, they can consider this representation of it in two ways at the same time and talk about the transformation of this liquid. Now you can do this with other kinds of liquid, as well. You can do this with other kinds of conservation tasks. You can do it with masses of clay or with numbers of things or with the shapes of things. You can also have conservation of people. It doesn't just refer to concrete things in the world.

So, for example, when I was in graduate school and I was working on my dissertation feverishly, my preschool son got worried because he'd heard what I was doing and he said to me, "Dad, when you become a doctor will you still be my father?" I of course said no—I didn't say no—I said, "Yes, why do you ask this?" The point is he had problems that when I changed, would I still be the same? Would I be conserved in my basic identity? It's a little bit different than the liquid problem, but it's still a conservation thing. Can he represent me in two ways at once?

He said at another time, "How come you call Grandpa, 'Dad'? How can he be your Dad and my Grandpa at the same time?" He's represented in two ways. So again, this kind of conservation of not only things in the world but even identities is something that school age kids have a pretty easy time dealing with, and preschoolers have a tough time with—even when you teach them the correct answer and give them experiences, which you can do. It doesn't generalize when they're young kids to new problems. After this age, it's easy. This is a problem sometime for kids. So, for example, when parents go through divorce, preschool kids often have a difficult time and a stress understanding it in this regard. They wonder if their parents get a divorce, will their parents still be their parents, because they get confused that the spousal roles may be the same as the parent-child roles. How can you get rid of one and still have the same person? And when kids get older, they don't have that confusion. In fact, older kids, even though they have problems with divorce, don't tend to blame themselves for it quite as much as the younger kids.

Let's go back to some other aspects of this. Susan Carey did some research on this area I talked about called necessary truth. I mentioned necessary truth previously. She took the old water experiment, the conservation of the water in different glasses, but surreptitiously, she put tubes into the bottom of these glasses so she could pump liquid in or out at any level she wanted. She could show you this thing and you'd pour it into a tall beaker and it would be the same level as before, it'd be shorter or anything like this. So it was like a magic trick, and the kids couldn't see this. Now interestingly, she would first do tasks to see which kids had this conservation ability and which kids didn't have the conservation ability. And then she did these tricks where she'd ask them what they predicted, and when she poured it in the tall, thin beaker it would be the same amount. Interestingly, the kids who didn't have conservation were not upset at all. That's the way it came out; that's the way it is. I see it. I was wrong, and whatever I predicted I didn't know what it would be. Kids that had conservation said, "That can't be right." She said, "Look, you just saw me do it." "That can't be right, you tricked me." And they'd look around for the trick. Necessary truth. Despite how things looked, things had to be a certain way because this was their logic telling them so.

Now let me shift to another issue—related I think—and it's this concept of kindness. James Youniss did this work, and it's in a very social domain, but I think it's related again to this concept of kindness; it's a variation. He asked children to define and describe what made a person a kind person, and he gave them some very concrete examples of different social situations, asked them are you kind in this situation? Are you not? Which ones would they be kind? Basically, he wanted to get their thinking, so it wasn't just asking them for straight yes or no answers, it was asking them to define it. In doing all of this work, with kids at different ages, he found that preschoolers, as a rule, defined being kind in terms of *absolute behaviors*. So, for example, a person is kind if she shares her cookies with another kid. A person is kind if he helps another person across the street. However, school age children defined kindness in more *relative* terms. For example, they would say, "A person's kind if her playmate doesn't have any cookies and is hungry and she has a lot and she shares them with the other person." Or, "A person's kind if another person wants to cross the street and she can't walk very well on her own. Then the first person helps her cross the street." In every

   ©2002 The Teaching Company Limited Partnership

case, the younger kids just talked about the act. That's what defined kindness, and the older kids talked about first there had to be a need or a deficit—call this State A—and then there had to be some way, call this a transformation if you will, of amending state A, this need or deficit, making it up and bringing about State B.

If the other kid has more cookies than you, giving cookies to the other kid isn't a kind act. If the other kid is stuffed, giving cookies to the other kid isn't a kind act. If the other kid's nauseous and about to throw up, giving cookies to the other kid is not a kind act. You see? There has to some need and deficit. In all of these cases, the older kids took account of it both ways, the younger kids didn't.

I could go on and on. There are so many examples of this ability that comes in with operational thinking. Let me just say in conclusion that this kind of thinking makes possible many academic and cognitive accomplishments. It also makes possible higher levels of adaptation in social situations; I hope I've given some of these.

Next time we're going to continue our discussion with Piaget's fourth and final stage, the formal operational period.

Thank you.

Lecture Twenty-One
Piaget's Last Stage

Scope:

This lecture begins with a description of Piaget's stage four, the formal-operational period, why it is called *formal*, and the ways in which it is a time of "idealistic" thinking. The lecture then gives examples of formal-operational logic, abstraction, and hypothetical thinking. The lecture concludes with a discussion of the problems with Piaget's theory and revisions that have been made. An example of the revisions can be given by using Robert Siegler's theory for how variation across tasks and domains is the rule in development and problem-solving strategies compete with each other for dominance.

Outline

I. In the last lecture, we left the child with the ability to reason logically and use multiple representations, but one major shortcoming in his concrete-operational level of development was that he could not deal with problems that were highly abstract and hypothetical. At about the time of puberty, children show a shift to a more abstract and theoretical level of thinking.

 A. Piaget called this transition his fourth and final stage, *the formal-operational period.* What did he mean by using that title?

    1. Pre-adolescents and adolescents still use mental *operations* to solve problems, but because of their experience with numerous specific problems and instances, they can now extract more general and all-encompassing strategies and concepts.

    2. *Abstract thinking* can be thought of as an *extraction* of general laws and principles from a set of specific instances of concrete problems in the real world. This level of abstraction is then no longer tied to any one concrete instance.

    3. Piaget called these operations *formal* to indicate that individuals could now deal with hypotheses or propositions in the abstract *form* of the proposition, regardless of the empirical evidence for the truth or

 ©2002 The Teaching Company Limited Partnership

falsehood of the proposition or the existence of any actual concrete instances. Think of the *form* in *formal*.

4. Because of this freedom from the concrete, adolescents could think about and apply strategies to hypothetical situations.

5. Piaget argued that adolescents became *idealistic* in their thinking. What he meant was that they could now deal with abstract *ideas*, rather than just concrete realities or representations of concrete realities. Think of the *idea* in *idealistic*.

B. Some concrete examples make these abstract ideas clearer.

1. Studies have been done of *propositional logic* and the rules that one uses to think logically using syllogisms. One basic abstract form is: "If p, then q." This form means, "If p exists, then q also exists." To determine whether this proposition is false, one need only find a case in which p exists, but q does not exist. If the proposition is correct, then one logical corollary is "If q does not exist, then we know that p also does not exist." However, if q does exist, then we can't know for sure whether p exists or not. If the first proposition is correct, "If p, then q," we can't have p without also having q, but we could have q without p.

2. For some who have experience with this kind of logic, this formal reasoning is easy, but for most of us, it is difficult to keep it straight. It is much easier, even for adults, to deal with concrete examples, rather than the abstract forms. Nevertheless, as adults with formal-operational thinking, we can learn to deal with these abstractions.

3. Let's switch to some concrete instances of "if p, then q." "If a person studies hard, then he will get good grades." This is a concrete instance of "if p studies hard, then q gets good grades." To disprove this proposition, I must find someone who studies hard—p—and, nevertheless, doesn't get good grades—not q. However, if the proposition is correct, then if I find someone who studies hard, I will know that he gets good grades. I will also know that if I find someone who does not get good grades, he did not study hard. But if I find someone who

gets good grades, do I know he studies hard? The answer is no because someone might get good grades for other reasons and still not study hard. We can't know for sure.

4. In this example, we have simply taken the general, abstract forms and applied them to a concrete instance.

5. Here is another concrete example: I said to an eight-year-old boy, "All men have hairy legs. I met a man. Did he have hairy legs?" The boy correctly answered, "Yes, because you said that all men have hairy legs." I then said, "I met a person with hairy legs. Was that person a man?" The boy again correctly answered, "Maybe not because some women might have hairy legs also." I then said to him, "All women have blue stripes down their backs. I saw a person with a blue-striped back. Was the person a man or a woman?" This time the boy said, "No one, because people don't have blue stripes down their backs."

6. The concrete-operational boy could handle some of the logic of these propositions when the instances were concrete and fit with his experiences of reality, but he couldn't handle hypothetical, non-realistic instances.

7. That ability is precisely what comes with formal-operational thinking. Mastery of this level of thinking at the end of adolescence or in young adulthood allows the person to deal with highly abstract forms of logic, forms found in mathematics, philosophy, science, hypothesis testing, and many other fields.

C. Another aspect of formal-operational thinking is the emerging ability to perform operations on operations.

1. A perfect example of these types of operations comes from mathematics. The child has already learned to perform simple mathematical operations, such as addition and subtraction. She may have even learned to deal

with some simple abstract forms, for example, using variables, such as a and b, to stand for fixed numbers. For example, $a + 24 = b$.

2. However, truly formal-operational thinking is shown when one can perform one operation on another or overlay one system onto another, as in: $2(a(b)/c + 24/c)$

 ©2002 The Teaching Company Limited Partnership

= 100. Examples of formal systems of mathematics that require formal-operational thinking are algebra and calculus.

3. In this case, people develop by building on what they already have mastered and combining skills.

4. Here are some philosophical and theoretical questions that formal-operational adolescents and young adults may now be able to consider: If evolution functions by genetic selectivity, then how might this account for the evolution of behaviors and personality traits? What if there really isn't a God? What if Hitler had never lived? What if I lived on an isolated island with 1000 inhabitants and had to start a new society?

5. Other abstract and philosophical questions that many teenagers apparently grapple with come from Erikson's fifth stage of identity development. What is there about me that forms my true identity, and what do I want to commit to in my life? It seems to be no accident that this level in Erikson's theory would match Piaget's level of formal operations.

II. Despite the value of Piaget's theory in changing our view of the sequence of development and generating much research, many developmentalists have pointed out weaknesses in his theory.

A. First, many argue that his basic process, which includes schemes, assimilation, accommodation, and equilibration, is merely metaphorical. It is impossible ever to disprove it.

1. However, this criticism can apply to many of the concepts of all the major theorists. To develop a general and major theory, one must go beyond the specific and concrete data.

2. Indeed, metaphors such as the processes of assimilation and accommodation have helped many researchers organize their thinking about development and guide their research.

B. Second, many recent studies have shown that Piaget often misjudged the ages at which children would show evidence for understanding a particular concept.

1. When researchers simplified the tasks, they found understanding of a particular concept in children at much younger ages than Piaget reported.
2. If one takes the view that development is not all or none but comes about gradually in steps over time, then these disagreements over age are not a serious criticism of the theory.
3. Many forget that Piaget stressed the invariant order of development, not the specific ages at which particular skills appear.

C. Third, many point out that with Piaget's focus on the development of logical thought, particularly in mathematics and scientific thinking, he ignored many other aspects of development.
   1. Specifically, Piaget said very little about the role and influence of social relationships and emotions in cognitive development. He also ignored development in several domains, particularly in the creative arts.
   2. Others have expanded Piaget's concepts to account for some of these gaps.
   3. And, once again, this criticism could be made of any developmental theory. No theorist has claimed to account for development in every domain or for every influential factor.

D. The fourth criticism is perhaps the most serious. Much recent research has now brought into serious question the universality of Piaget's stages, not so much in terms of cultural universality, but in terms of generality across all domains and contexts of development.
   1. In Piaget's conception, once a person has consolidated the skills and understanding of a particular stage, that person will be functioning cognitively in that stage regardless of the particular cognitive problem or domain of knowledge.
   2. For example, in Piaget's view, if a child has reached the period of concrete-operational thinking, then she can think in this manner when dealing with mathematics, science, social relationships, conservation problems, seriation problems, classifications, perspective taking,

©2002 The Teaching Company Limited Partnership

and so forth. She will be in the concrete-operational period.

3. It is true that Piaget recognized asynchronies or lags in level of development of understanding from one area to another or on one task versus another, but he thought these cases were minor and were the exceptions. Nowadays, these asynchronies are considered the rule in development.

4. Most current researchers can discuss how a child might use concrete-operational thinking on a particular problem, while the same child might use pre-operational thinking on another task and formal-operational thinking on a third task. Therefore, most researchers today do not think of a child being in only one stage.

5. Rather than having general stages, we now have sequences in the development of cognitive skills that are influenced by the child's level and experience in each specific domain and by the demands of each specific context and task.

III. The recent research of Robert Siegler illustrates some of the new conceptualizations of cognitive development that have modified and gone beyond Piaget's theory.

A. Unlike Piaget's model of general shifts in understanding at each stage, Siegler theorized that there is extreme variability at all times and all levels.

1. At any given age a child typically has several strategies or actions that she can use, and she will shift from one to another on different tasks.

2. Often, a new strategy or level of thinking happens once, then doesn't appear again for some time. The child may still use various strategies and simply add a new strategy to her repertoire.

3. Over time, however, more efficient and adaptive strategies may win out and be used predominantly until a new and better strategy is discovered.

4. Think of each strategy as having its own course of development over time. At any given time or age, a person may have several strategies available to use.

5. One should think of development not in terms of discrete stages but in terms of overlapping waves of skill or strategy development.

B. An example from Siegler's research comes from mathematics and concerns a child's initial development at counting and adding.

1. When children must add two numbers together, they usually begin by counting all the numbers, often using their fingers. For example, if they must add 2 + 6, they will count, "1, 2," then, "3, 4, 5, 6, 7, 8." We call this strategy the *count-all strategy*.

2. With time, children often discover a new strategy that is a much more efficient way of counting. They begin with the highest number, then count up the other numbers from there. For example, if they must add 2 + 6, they will start with "6," then count, "7, 8." This strategy is often called the *min strategy*.

3. Only with further experience will children shift to an even more efficient strategy, in which they memorize the sum for two numbers and quickly pull the sum out of memory. For example, they will now see 2 + 6 and say, based on their memory of the sum, "8." This is the *memorization strategy*.

4. In detailed observations of children over time, Siegler once again found that they showed great variability in which strategy they would use. Although the order of development was from count all to min to memorization, they would usually use all the strategies they had in their repertoire. Only gradually over time did the min strategy first win out over the count-all strategy and the memorization strategy win out over the min strategy.

5. Why would children ever return to using a less efficient strategy once they had discovered a better one? Siegler argues that we consolidate our mastery of new strategies or skills only gradually and with experience. We often fall back on older and more automatic strategies when we are tired or under stress or have too many simultaneous cognitive demands placed on us.

 ©2002 The Teaching Company Limited Partnership

6. With repeated use and mastery, a strategy becomes more automatic and requires less concentration and energy to use.

Supplementary Reading:

Piaget and Inhelder, *The Psychology of the Child*, chapter 5 and conclusion.

Siegler, *Emerging Minds: The Process of Change in Children's Thinking.*

Questions to Consider:

1. Despite the recent views of variation in development based on context, do you think there is any validity to Piaget's view of his stages being universal across virtually all individuals and across practically all domains of development?

2. Can you see examples in your life of Siegler's overlapping waves of skill development, in which a strategy for dealing with a problem eventually comes to dominate?

Lecture Twenty-One
Piaget's Last Stage

Hello. In the last lecture we left the child with the ability to reason logically and to use multiple representations. But one major shortcoming in his concrete operational level of development was that he couldn't deal with problems that were highly abstract and hypothetical. I say highly abstract; from birth on, we become more and more abstract, but at the level we normally think of abstract thinking—some of the problems I'm going to talk about today—some of these levels are beyond children and middle childhood. At about the time of puberty, children show a shift to a more abstract and theoretical level of thinking, and Piaget called this time period the *formal operational period*. This is his fourth and final stage. In this lecture we're going to discuss why this level is a period of formal, idealistic, abstract and hypothetical thinking, and then we'll evaluate Piaget's theory and discuss some approaches that have been used for revisions to this theoretical approach.

So to begin with, what did Piaget mean by using the title "formal operational." Just remember, the previous stage was concrete operational. Pre-adolescents and adolescents still use mental *operations*, as we talked about last time. But, because of their experience with numerous specific problems, in many instances they can now extract more general and all-encompassing strategies and concepts. *Abstract thinking* can be thought of as an abstraction of general laws and principles from a set of specific instances of very concrete real-world problems. The level of abstraction then is no longer tied to one concrete instance. For example, we talked about conservation as one of the skills and abilities that kids had—conservation of liquid quantity kids deal with, conservation or quantity of mass, conservation of numbers, conservation of personal identity and many other kinds of conservation which may be tried by a child—and after a lot of experience with these different cases, together, all of these cases give the child one general principle of conservation and the general principle might be what stays the same amid change. "This is the problem, look for these situations." This is the abstract form of conservation. So, when we went back to the previous stage, kids can do conservation, but I don't think that they can describe what it is and define it for you. They can do the concrete instances.

So Piaget called these operations *formal* to indicate that individuals could now deal with hypotheses or propositions in the abstract *form* of the proposition regardless of the specific instances and the empirical evidence or the truth or falsehood of a particular proposition. They were not tied to concrete instances anymore. Here's a good way to think about it. When you think about formal, think of the *form* in *formal*. People now can deal with the form of things, not just the content. And because of this freedom from the concrete, adolescents can now think about and apply strategy to hypothetical situations. Adolescents also become more *idealistic* in their thinking. There are different meanings for the word idealistic, but the way I think Piaget and people mean it when they talk about the formal operational period is that people can now deal with abstract *ideas*, again rather than the concrete realities or the representations of concrete realities. So, when you think of idealistic, think of the *idea* in *idealistic*. Now, there's some concrete examples that I want to give you that I think will make this abstract ideas clearer. Despite the fact that we might have abstract idealistic formal thinking, concrete examples always help.

There are a lot of studies of *propositional logic* and the rules that one uses to think logically, often using syllogisms. Let me give you the basic, very formal approach to this and then I'm going to give you some more concrete examples. But one basic abstract form is: "If p, then q." This form means: if p exists, then q also exists. Now to determine whether this proposition is false—the proposition "if p, then q"—one need only find one case in which p exists, but q does not exist to show that it's false. However, if the proposition is correct and we assume it's correct, then one logical corollary is: If q doesn't exist, then we know that p also does not exist. However, if q does exist, then we can't know for sure if p exists or not. If the first proposition is correct, "if p, then q," we can't have p without also having q, but we could have q without having p.

Now, has that lost you? For some who have experience with this kind of logic, this formal reasoning is easy and fun. But for most of us, like me, it's difficult to keep it straight, to deal with this kind of formal level. It's much easier, even for adults, to deal with the concrete examples rather than the abstract forms. Nevertheless, as adults, I want to point out that with formal operational thinking we can learn to deal with these abstractions. We have that ability if we practice it. Let me give you now a concrete instance of this "if p, then q" and see if this becomes clear.

If a person studies hard, then he will get good grades. In this concrete instance, "if a person studies hard" is p—if p—then "he will get good grades," that's q—if q. To disprove this proposition, I have to find someone who studies hard—remember, that's the p—and nevertheless doesn't get good grades—he doesn't have q. However, I'm going back to what I said before. If the proposition is correct and we assume it's correct, then if I find someone who studies hard I know that he gets good grades; and I also know if I find someone who doesn't get good grades that he didn't study hard. But, if I find someone who gets good grades—I said this, I know he studies hard—but if I find someone who gets good grades, do I know for sure if he studies hard? In this case, it's confusing for me too. I have q; do I know that p exists? He gets good grades. Does he study hard? And the answer is—I don't know. Because someone might get good grades for other reasons and still not study hard. We can't know for sure.

Now even there we can't keep it straight, but you can see how you can reason this way with one thing causing something else. In this case, this example, we've simply taken the general abstracts above and we tied them to a very concrete instance. Now the value of formal propositional logic is it doesn't matter what you put in, you could put wacky things in there that have no case or no connection to reality. You could even put in instances that aren't true and you can still use the logic. That's the hypothetical, the level that adolescents in thinking in a formal way can begin to deal.

Here's another example of using syllogisms. I actually did this; I talked to an eight-year-old boy and I was giving him little tests. I said to him first: "All men have hairy legs. I met a man. Did he have hairy legs?" The boy correctly answered, "Yes, because you said that all men have hairy legs." I then said, "I met a person with hairy legs. Was that person a man?" Remember, the opposite way? And the boy answered correctly again—but I'm not sure if it was for the right reason. He said, "Well, maybe not. It may be not because some women also might have hairy legs." I then said to him, "All women have blue stripes down their backs. I saw a person with a blue-striped back. Was the person a man or a woman?" And this time the boy

   ©2002 The Teaching Company Limited Partnership

said, "No one, because people don't have blue stripes down their backs."

So I think this very concrete operational boy could handle some the logic of these propositions when the instances were concrete and when they fit his experiences with reality. But when he couldn't handle the hypothetical, non-realistic instances, I don't think it's an all-or-none proposition for kids. But this was an example of the concrete level for handling things. Kids can be logical, but not when you throw them into the unrealistic or the hypothetical. That ability is what comes with formal operational thinking, or one of the main abilities. And mastery of this level of thinking comes really at the end of adolescence and in young adulthood. It starts at the beginning of adolescence and it allows a person to deal with highly abstract forms of logic, but these forms are also found in mathematics, in philosophy, in science and certainly in hypothesis testing, the way we do experimental work. This kind of logic is also found in other fields as well.

There's another aspect in formal operational thinking and that's the emerging ability to perform operations on operations. A perfect example comes from mathematics because operations originally for Piaget were taken from mathematics as prototypes, as an example. A child has already learned to perform simple mathematical operations like addition, subtraction, multiplication and division, and she may have even learned to deal with some simple, abstract forms such as using variables like a and b to stand for fixed numbers. So you could have the simplest form we start using in algebra: $a + 24 = b$, and a child could start dealing with that. However, truly formal operational thinking is shown when a person can perform one operation on another, or overlay one system onto another system. That's the complication that comes in later. It's difficult to talk you through this example; but for instance, you could have $2(a(b)/c + 24/c) = 100$. If that doesn't make sense, it's OK. But it's the kind of formula you would see in algebra, where you have an operation on an operation. Multiplication of a case where there's addition and division and variables mixed in with other fixed numbers. This it the kind of system you get in algebra and calculus and other mathematical systems. Those are formal operational mathematical systems. In this case, people develop by building on what they've already mastered, combining skills.

Here's some philosophical theoretical questions that I believe formal operation adolescents and young adults may now be able to consider; and, in fact, you see them considering these types of questions, but you don't see this so much in school age kids. If evolution functions by genetic selectivity, then how might this account for the evolution of behaviors and personality traits beyond just physical characteristics? That's a good question for you. If Hitler had never lived, what would be the implications, politically, and in the world today, where would we be? What if you lived on an isolated island with 1000 inhabitants and you had to start a new society?

Now, dealing with kinds of questions like this, I think, takes a systematic way of going through the logic and following through hypothetical situations. A younger child can ask what-if questions. A younger child could say, "What if I had a dog? What would that do; what would that mean?" But they have a difficult time with the complex and hypothetical questions like I mentioned, at least thinking through all the possible solutions or outcomes in a very systematic manner. You see, even in experimental work, kids will try different experiments. They look for causality. But until they get formal operations, they have a difficult time going through everything in a very systematic way, comparing one case to another case and looking at all outcomes.

Some of abstract and philosophical questions I think that teenagers grapple with come from Erikson's fifth stage of identity development that we talked about previously. What is it about me that forms my true identity, and what do I want to commit to in my life? That level of thinking about those questions, I think, show that it's no accident that in Erikson's theory, this kind of identity issue comes up at the same time that Piaget talks about formal operational thinking developing. There's a convergence here.

Now, despite the value of Piaget's theory in changing our view of the sequence of development and generating a lot of research and giving us an understanding of cognitive processes, there are several criticisms of his theory. Let me go through some of these. First, many researchers and theorists argue that his basic process— remember the basic process that included schemes, assimilation, accommodation and equilibration—that this basic process is merely metaphorical. It's impossible ever to disprove it because it's not specific in a way that you can empirically test it. That's true, I think;

 ©2002 The Teaching Company Limited Partnership

however, this criticism can apply to many of the concepts of all of the major theorists and theories that we've talked about. In order to develop a general and major theory, it seems to me now that a theorist has to go beyond the specific and concrete data. Indeed, metaphors such as the process of assimilation and accommodation have helped a lot of researchers organize their thinking about development and have helped them to guide their research. And in Piaget's theory, the idea of assimilation and accommodation has been taken by teachers and other people and helped to guide them in the way they design classrooms and curriculum. So, it's metaphorical, but that's not unusual in the big theories.

A second criticism is that there are many recent studies that show that Piaget often misjudged the ages at which children would show evidence of understanding of a particular concept or particular level. In general, people say Piaget put things at older ages than recent research has shown, whether it was understanding conservation or the ability to do perspective-taking or even certain formal operational tasks. When researchers have simplified the tasks, taking original tasks that Piaget used in his observations, and found ways to get rid of some of the fluff in the language and got the task down to the bare bones, they found understanding of a particular concept in children at much younger ages than Piaget had reported. However, if you take the view that development is almost never all-or-none, but it comes in gradually in steps—and I've mentioned that before as a view that tends to make sense—and, if these steps come in over time, then these disagreements over age are not a serious criticism of the theory, because what it really is showing is that if a task is presented at one level, it comes in at one age; if you simplify it and give it different context, it comes in at many a lower age, but it means a part of it's there. There's a germ of this understanding that's developing, not a full-blown mastery of a particular concept, but it is coming in gradually over time.

Also, a lot of people forget that Piaget stressed the invariant order of development in his stages, but not specific ages at which these stages appear. Because he mentioned ages, people assume that ages are absolutely a crucial part of his theory. But the ages were just guidelines for him. I don't think that he'd be thrown off if you found things happening at a different age, so long as you found the logic in the order still there.

There's a third criticism: many people point out that Piaget's focus on development of logical thought—particularly in mathematics and logic and scientific thinking—led him to ignore many other aspects of development. So, what I just presented in this lecture concerning operational thinking, people have argued is really sort of narrow in trying to explain everything that we do as adolescents and then on into adulthood. Specifically, Piaget said very little about the role and influence of social relationships. He said very little about emotions in cognitive development, and he also ignored development in several major domains. I think particularly of creative arts, where he really didn't identify issues and what goes on there.

My answer there is that others have expanded on Piaget's concepts, and they've filled in some of these gaps. So they've used Piaget's theory and then expanded into social domains and emotional domains. Once again, this criticism could be made of any of the developmental theories. There are no theorists that have claimed to account for development in every domain or for every influential factor. Each theorist has only so much that he or she can do in covering things.

There's a fourth criticism, and I think perhaps this is the most serious criticism of Piaget's work. There is a lot of recent research that's now brought into serious question this idea from Piaget that his stages are universal. I don't think it's so much a problem in terms of cultural universality, although we're not sure of that yet. There's been cross-cultural work. It shows, yes, that kids do go through his stages; it's not 100 percent clear if this accounts for all people everywhere. But the most important problem is the generality of his stages—a universality of all his stages across all domains and contexts of development for any given individual. Because, I mentioned for Piaget, he saw humans as developing gradually, but then into a stage; and, as the stage was consolidated, it overwhelmed and took over all areas of thinking. Once a person consolidated the skills and understanding at a particular level, then that person could function cognitively in that stage regardless of the particular cognitive domain of that knowledge.

For example: in Piaget's view, if the child has reached the period of concrete operational thinking, then she can think in this manner in her dealings with mathematics, science, social relationships, conservation problems, seriation problems, classification,

 ©2002 The Teaching Company Limited Partnership

perspective-taking, and so on. She's there. She's in concrete operations. Now it's true that Piaget mentioned asynchronies or lags in the level of development of understanding. By that I mean, he realized that you'd find in kids—he was a good observer—he would look at kids and see that they would be better or ahead of development in one area and they'd lag behind in another area. Everything didn't come in lock-step synchrony; there was this asynchrony for lags and development. He saw that; he realized that that was there. He thought it was probably due to contextual differences and environmental differences. But he thought these cases were minor; he thought those were the exceptions.

Nowadays, with a lot of research on cognitive development, these asynchronies or lags are considered to be the rule of development. So most people nowadays say, "That is the way all development happens. Expect it, because that's just the normal way thins are." Most current researchers now discuss how a child might use concrete operational thinking on a particular problem while that same child might use pre-operational thinking on another task and formal operational thinking on a third task. Therefore, most researchers today do not think of a child being in only one stage. Rather than having general stages, we now have sequences and cognitive skills that are influenced by the child's level of experience in each specific domain and by the demands of each specific task or context. So you might have a lot of lines or courses of development depending on context and task.

Now, there are a lot of researchers out there that people have actually given the name of "Neo-Piagetians." Remember the neo-Freudians? Well, now Piaget has reached that high level that we can now have Neo-Piagetians. People are greatly influenced by his theory and are doing new stuff and really changing things. There's some recent research done by a cognitive developmental psychologist named Robert Siegler that I think illustrates some of these new conceptualizations of cognitive development. I think his work has modified and gone beyond Piaget's theory and is quite interesting and I think quite good. Let me tell you a little bit about Siegler's work now to show you an example where things are going. Unlike Piaget's model of general stage shifts and understanding, Siegler theorized that there is extreme variability at all times, in all levels. I just set you up by talking about this variation. So, he believed that at any given age, a child typically has several different strategies or actions that she can use, and she'll shift from one to another of these different strategies on a task. Often, a new strategy or a new level of thinking happens once and then doesn't appear again for some time. So rather than thinking, "Oh! The child now gets it. The child now understands some new level of thinking," now the child is going along and shows some new level of thinking or some new strategy and doesn't use it again for weeks, then it comes back in. So, the child keeps using various strategies and simply adds a new strategy to the repertoire of all these different strategies that it can use. Over time though, more efficient and adaptive strategies seem to win out and become the predominant or the modal way that the child deals with a particular task, and they stay in vogue for the child until a new and better strategy is discovered. But, there are always variations.

So, think of each strategy as having it's own course of development over time, and at any given time, or any given age, a person may use several of these strategies and have them available. So think of development, not in terms of discrete stages, but overlapping ways of skills or strategies. If you could really pinpoint a time, and look accurately at what a child is doing, you might see that that child at this time is sometimes using strategy 1, sometimes strategy 2, sometimes strategy 3, and you could trace the development of each of these ways.

Now let me give you a concrete example from a study that Siegler did, and this study comes from mathematics and concerns a child's initial development and learning of how to count and how to add. We're talking about preschool kids into early school years here, but mostly preschool kids. When children have to add two numbers together, usually they begin by counting all the numbers together. Often they use their fingers. For example, if a child has to add $2 + 6$, they will count sometimes on their fingers, 1,2,3,4,5,6....7,8, and they'll have eight. So they're counting all the numbers starting from one and going up. We call this strategy, the *count-all strategy*. You start with some number and you count everything.

But over time, children very often discover a new strategy, and it's very often an efficient way of counting. What they end up doing is beginning with the highest number and then they count up from there the other numbers. So, for example, they still have to add $2 + 6$. The first thing they realize is that 6 is a big number; 2 is sort of small. I'll

 ©2002 The Teaching Company Limited Partnership

just start 6...7,8. Easy. A much more efficient way to count, and people call this the *min strategy*.

It's only with further experience that they'll shift to an even more efficient strategy in which they memorize the sum of two numbers and they quickly pull the sum out of their memory. So I'll say, "what's 2 + 6?" And they'll pull this out of their memory and say, "8," because they've memorized it. Call this the *memorization strategy*. So we have the count-all strategy, the min strategy and the memorization strategy.

In very detailed observations of children over time, looking at everything they did, Siegler found that they showed great variability in which strategy they'd use. Although the order of development seemed to be from count-all to min to memorization, they usually used all the strategies that they had in their repertoire and only gradually over time did the min strategy first win out over the count-all strategy, and then later the memorization strategy won out over the min strategy. But at any given point in time, you might see a kid counting everything at some times, doing min strategy sometimes and a little later starting to memorize things sometimes. Even after they'd memorized things, they'd bounce back to the min strategy.

Now why would children ever return to a less efficient strategy once they'd learned a better one? Siegler argued that we consolidate our mastery of a new strategy or skills, only gradually, and only with a lot of experience using it. So, we often fall back to older and more automatic strategies when we're tired, when we're under stress, when we have too many simultaneous cognitive demands placed on us. But, as we repeatedly use and master a new strategy, it becomes more automatic and it requires less concentration and energy to use. Does that ever happen to you as an adult? Well, I'll bet it does. Sometimes—I have to confess here—I switch back to the min strategy. Let's say I have an equation, 52 + 3. I go, "53, 54, 55," because it's so simple and it takes no thought and it's automatic. It's a simple way of doing things, but it's mindless at this level. So very often when we have automatic skills we switch back to what would be considered a less efficient skill, but it's not less efficient for us if we've already made it automatic and we use less energy. This was a good discovery by Siegler, I believe, on a way that we constantly develop and learn to use these strategies.

In our next lecture, we're going to discuss the last theory in our course, Vygotsky's Cognitive-Mediation Theory. I think it provides a nice complement to Piaget's theory and we'll discuss how that happens.

Thank you.

 ©2002 The Teaching Company Limited Partnership

Lecture Twenty-Two
Vygotsky's Cognitive-Mediation Theory

Scope:

This lecture introduces the sixth and last major theory: Lev Vygotsky's Cognitive-Mediation Theory. It begins with a description of Vygotsky's history. Although he died in 1934, and was practically unknown to Western thinkers until recently, his theoretical influence on development and education is constantly increasing. As a Russian theorist, he believed that Marxism, with its focus on the value of tools and society, could provide a foundation for a better theory of psychological development. The lecture compares the metaphor for the developing child based on Piaget's theory—the child as lone scientist—with the metaphor for the developing child based on Vygotsky's theory—the child as apprentice. The lecture describes how psychological tools, such as language, come from other people but is made a part of one's own thinking. Thus, development occurs when we incorporate tools for thinking from our society.

Outline

I. One of the criticisms of Piaget's theory that we noted in the last lecture was that he took virtually no account of the influence of society and social interactions in explaining the processes of development. In contrast, Vygotsky's *cognitive-mediation theory* focuses primarily on how social interactions influence cognitive development. Although all of Vygotsky's work was completed before social learning theory and the cognitive revolution came about, his theory is currently increasing in influence on developmental researchers and educators.

II. To understand why we have had this "sleeper effect," we must understand Vygotsky's history.

  A. Lev S. Vygotsky was born in 1896, the same year that Piaget was born, near Minsk, Russia, and died in Russia in 1934, at the relatively young age of thirty-seven. He had tuberculosis and was quite sick for a good share of his life.

   1. Vygotsky was born into a middle-class Jewish family. Like Piaget, he was precocious and intellectual at a young age. In particular, he read Western philosophy.

2. Because of the discrimination against Jews in Russia at the time and the quota system limiting the number of Jewish college students, Vygotsky thought he would not be able to attend college. But on a lottery, he was able to attend Moscow University, and graduated in 1917.

3. Vygotsky thought that the Bolshevik Revolution would put an end to discrimination against Jews in Russia, and he fully welcomed it. He was strongly influenced by Hegel's and Marx's philosophies, which stressed the importance of society and the value of work in helping humans rise to something better.

4. He believed that the Marxist view, in which technology and tools transform society and help humans to evolve socially, could be the foundation for a new Marxist theory of human development that would better account for human functioning than what he had read up until that time.

5. Part of this social view of development was a *dialectic* view of change. In dialectic reasoning, one begins with a *thesis* or argument. An *antithesis* is presented to challenge the thesis. And, by the combination of thesis and antithesis, a person constructs a *synthesis*, a new level of argument or understanding. Indeed, this combination has already been seen in complementary and often conflicting processes found in other theories, such as Erikson's constant interplay between seeking connectedness and independence and Piaget's interplay between assimilation and accommodation.

6. For Vygotsky, the dialectic was between the individual and others. In synthesis, they combined to move development to higher levels of thinking and functioning. These principles became the foundation for Vygotsky's theory.

B. Once Vygotsky settled on psychology as his primary field of interest, he worked as an academic in Moscow.

1. His first publication was on the psychology of art. He also wrote about language development, intelligence testing, and principles of education.

©2002 The Teaching Company Limited Partnership

2. He knew he was sickly and probably would not live to old age, and he worked feverishly as if he had a short time to complete his life's work.

3. Unfortunately, even though he may have been the supreme Marxist theorist on human development, at the end of his life, his work was banned in the Soviet Union. Although the reasons aren't clear and could have included the fact that he was Jewish, it seems that his greatest "sin" was that he integrated so much Western philosophy and so many Western ideas into his theories.

4. Because of the ban, Vygotsky was able to publish little work in his own lifetime. Most of what we have comes from posthumous publications and the writings of his students.

5. We had virtually none of Vygotsky's work in English until the 1970s. With the collapse of the Soviet Union, there has been an increased interchange between American and Russian scholars that has provided even more details and insight into Vygotsky's thinking.

III. Vygotsky's theory provides a good comparison with, and complement to, Piaget's theory.

A. In many ways, a metaphor for Piaget's conceptualization is the child as a lone scientist. The child, on his own and through his own actions, discovers how the world works and applies his reasoning to various problems and challenges presented by the world.

B. In contrast, a metaphor for Vygotsky's conceptualization is the child as apprentice. The child actively learns skills and symbolic processing by his interactions with an adult mentor and incorporates what the adult provides to him in knowledge and cognitive tools.

1. In traditional learning theory and social learning theory, society is thought to influence and shape the child, but in Vygotsky's theory, the child is a part of society and a *collaborator* in his learning with adult mentors. He isn't simply a passive recipient of conditioning and socialization.

2. In reality, both Piaget's and Vygotsky's theories account for the way children develop. Thus, we might consider them as important complements of each other.

IV. Why is Vygotsky's theory entitled *cognitive mediation*?

    A. First, Vygotsky believed we share lower mental functions with other animals. What differentiates us is that we go beyond other animals because of the mental or psychological tools we acquire to help us think. Remember, based on Marxist philosophy, Vygotsky believed that tools mediated progression.

        1. The way we acquire psychological tools is from our culture and the previous learning of our species.

        2. As with learning theory, at first, outside stimuli elicit responses from an individual. However, when we acquire a psychological tool, such as language, the tool *mediates* between the outside stimuli and the responses. Our psychological tools create intentionality, comparisons, and higher-order planning. Thus, we are no longer at the mercy of outside stimuli, as are lower animals.

        3. Culture is handed down to us through our society, which is handed down to us through adults in our society, such as our parents. What was in the culture is incorporated into our own cognitive processes as the psychological tools that we use. Vygotsky said, "What was inter-mental becomes intra-mental."

        4. For Vygotsky, we can't function on an adult level without the culture of which we are a part bringing us along and providing what is necessary. This conceptualization acknowledges a deeper level of social interaction than the simple social influence and conditioning envisioned by learning theory. As Vygotsky once said, "A colt is already a horse; a human baby is only a candidate to become a human being."

    B. What are these psychological tools that came from the culture and are so necessary for our development of higher cognitive processes?

        1. The tools are symbolic.

 ©2002 The Teaching Company Limited Partnership

2. The same symbol systems we have already encountered in our discussion of Piaget are our primary tools for thinking: language, symbolic play, art, writing.

3. This description may sound similar to Piaget's description, except for two aspects that Vygotsky emphasized. First, the symbol systems come to us from others rather than from within ourselves. Second, the symbol systems are not just used in our thinking but completely reorganize our thinking.

C. *Language* is the most important psychological tool. Vygotsky described the process by which children internalize language as a personal tool.

1. First, others in the culture provide the child with a particular language and set of symbols.

2. As the child masters the use of the language, she begins using language not just to communicate to others but as *egocentric speech.* She talks to herself, usually out loud.

3. Then, with more experience, the child is able to eliminate the overt speech and internalize her egocentric speech. Vygotsky called this *inner speech.* The child is still talking to herself but only mentally.

4. Eventually, this inner speech becomes the mediating tool for the child's thinking. She begins using automatic and truncated speech to think, to plan, to direct herself. It is no longer speech for communication; it is now a personal psychological tool that changes all her thought processes. It came from others, but it now is part of the child's mind.

5. Although language is the primary tool, other symbolic tools become internalized as well, such as mathematical thinking and visual thinking.

6. We can point to many examples in both children and adults of egocentric speech. In one example, a preschooler's mother told him to go to his room and put on his pants and shirt. From the other room, the adults heard the child say, "Label in the back, label in the back." They realized that the child was repeating the instructions for putting on shirts and pants that his mother had provided to him. He was giving himself directions.

7. In another example, a person is driving and attempting to follow directions to someone's house. She realizes that she is thinking to herself, "Go two lights, then turn left. Look for the red house." When we consider how we think, we often use these symbolic devices derived from inner speech to guide our thinking, planning, and actions.

V. Vygotsky also believed that society, through adults, helps children regulate themselves at first until they have internalized the mediators so that they can regulate themselves without adult aid.

A. This process of internalization from others does not carry the connotations of conditioning or behavior modification being effective whether the child cooperates or not. In Vygotsky's conceptualization, children mentally cooperate in this joint regulation.

B. Piaget also had a view—albeit a different one—of egocentric speech.
1. For Piaget, a child in egocentric speech exhibited a lack of perspective taking.
2. Egocentric speech, in Piaget's view, is when you talk about something to another person without making sense to that other person.
3. In Vygotsky's view, egocentric speech is talking to yourself.

C. Vygotsky and Piaget also held differing views about pretend play.
1. Piaget saw pretend play—symbolic play—as an immature process and predominantly assimilation that distorted reality. The value of pretend play is to give the child a way to "act out" situations she doesn't understand.
2. Vygotsky viewed pretend play as the area where a child performs at the best level of his abilities. Play is a safe place to try things.

D. Our next lecture will discuss this adult-child co-construction process and how it influences current educational decisions.

Supplementary Reading:

Miller, *Theories of Developmental Psychology*, 4th ed., chapter 7.

©2002 The Teaching Company Limited Partnership

Kozulin, *Vygotsky's Psychology: A Biography of Ideas*. (This recent book provides an overview and biography of Vygotsky by a Russian psychologist who has been familiar with his work and its influence in Russia.)

Vygotsky, *Mind in Society: The Development of Higher Psychological Processes.*

Questions to Consider:

1. Do you believe that your thinking is primarily controlled by symbolic skills that you originally acquired from others, in particular, language? Does this approach adequately account for most of our thinking?

2. In your mind, how would you combine Piaget and Vygotsky's theories to provide a more valid account of real-life development?

Lecture Twenty-Two
Vygotsky's Cognitive-Mediation Theory

Hello. In this lecture, we'll discuss the sixth and last of our major theories of human development, Lev Vygotsky's Cognitive-Mediation Theory. We'll discuss his history and how it provided the context for his theory, just as each theorist's history influenced each theory. We'll then describe his idea of the incorporation of psychological tools from others, and the basic premise that what is "inter-mental becomes intra-mental." That's one of his quotes; we'll get back to that.

Now, one of the criticisms of Piaget's theory that we noted in the last lecture was that he took virtually no account of the influence of society and social interactions in explaining processes of development. Piaget did try to explain how we think about others, how we learn to deal with others, but he didn't really talk about how others influenced us. In contrast, Vygotsky's *Cognitive-Mediation Theory* focuses primarily on how social interactions influence cognitive development. Although all of Vygotsky's work was completed before social learning theory ever came along and also before there was a cognitive revolution, his theory currently influences developmental researchers and educators in a great way. It seems to fit in with a lot of ways that we're thinking about development today.

To understand why we had this sleeper effect, if you will, in the influence of his theory, we have to understand Vygotsky's history. Lev Vygotsky was born in 1896; interestingly, the same year that Piaget was born. He was born near Minsk, Russia and died in Russia in 1934, at the relatively young age of 38 years. He had tuberculosis and had been quite sick for a good share of his life. Vygotsky was born into a middle class Jewish family, and like Piaget he was quite precocious as a young child. He was quite intellectual. In particular, he read a lot of Western philosophy. In fact, he read some of the early work of Piaget. But because of the discrimination against Jews in Russia at that time, he had some problems getting into the education system. He was very much worried because they had a quota system limiting the number of Jewish college students. But Vygotsky, although he thought he couldn't attend college, was lucky and won a lottery and was able to attend Moscow University. He

©2002 The Teaching Company Limited Partnership

graduated in 1917. Again, interestingly, it was the same year that Piaget received his Ph.D.

From this background, Vygotsky thought that the Bolshevik Revolution would put an end to the discrimination against Jews and other minority groups in Russia. He fully welcomed it, and he had been strongly influenced by Hegel and Marxist philosophies. These philosophies stressed the importance of society and the value of work in helping humans rise to something better. He believed that this Marxist view, which included a view that technology and tools transform society and help humans to evolve socially, he thought this view could be a foundation for a new Marxist theory of human development, a theory that would be better in accounting for human functioning than what he had read up to that time.

Part of this social view of development was a *dialectic* view of change. In dialectic reasoning one begins with a *thesis*, an argument, and the *antithesis* is presented to challenge the thesis, and then by a combination of thesis and antithesis, a person constructs a *synthesis* or a new level of argument, a new level of understanding. This combination by the way, we've already seen in the complementary and often conflicting processes that we find in other theories— Erikson constantly talked about the interplay between seeking connectedness and independence, and Piaget had interplay between assimilation and accommodation. But for Vygotsky, the dialectic was between the individual and others, and in the synthesis, they combined to move development to a higher level of functioning and thinking. These principles became the foundation for Vygotsky's theory.

Once Vygotsky settled on psychology as his primary field of interest—because he tried out different things and had experience with education in various areas—once he settled on psychology, he worked as an academic in Moscow most of the time. His first publication was on the psychology of art, but he wrote about language development and intellectual testing and principles of education. He knew he was sickly. He knew he had tuberculosis and he probably wouldn't live to an old age, and it seemed like he worked very feverishly, as if he had a very short time to complete his life's work. Unfortunately though, even though he probably was the supreme Marxist theorist in human development, at the end of his life his work was banned in the Soviet Union. Although the reasons aren't clear, and they may have included the fact that he was Jewish, it seems like his greatest "sin" was that he included so much Western philosophy and ideas integrated and mixed into his theories.

Because of this ban though, Vygotsky was able to publish very little work in his own lifetime, and most of what we have comes from posthumous publications and also the writings of a few students. In fact, he didn't have a strong influence on a wide following, but he had a few dedicated students who paid attention to what he was doing and carried on his work. They carried on his work, for the most part, in the Soviet Union. We had virtually none of his work in English until the 1970s. With the collapse of the Soviet Union, there's been an increase in interchange between American and Russian scholars in human development, and this has provided us with many more details and insights into Vygotsky's thinking.

I think this explains the sleeper effect. So, though he died some time ago before the other people were coming along with much of their theorizing, his influence has come about nowadays, primarily in the '80s and '90s. And Vygotsky's theory provides a good comparison and a complement to Piaget's theory. Let me see if I can make this comparison. In many ways, a metaphor for Piaget's conceptualization is that the child is a lone scientist. Here's this child out on his own, and through his own actions discovers how the world works and applies his reasoning to various problems and challenges presented by the world. What a great lone scientist there. In contrast, the metaphor for Vygotsky's conceptualization is the child is an apprentice. So, this child actively learns skills and symbolic processing by his interactions with an adult mentor, and he incorporates what the adult provides to him in knowledge and in cognitive tools. So in both cases, the child is developing cognitively. But for Piaget, the child is the supreme active discoverer, out discovering things on his own. For Vygotsky, the other person, the apprenticeship to other adults was extremely necessary.

If you recall, Piaget even said that everything you tell a child you prevent that child from discovering for himself. The view was that children would get further if they discover everything on their own. That wasn't Vygotsky's view. Also, in traditional learning theory and in social learning theory, society is thought of as an influence on children's development. Society influences and shapes the child. So is Vygotsky like a learning theorist?

In Vygotsky's theory, the child is a part of society, a *collaborator* with his adult mentors. He isn't simply a passive recipient of conditioning or of socialization; he is interacting and cooperating with the adults or the mentors to learn. So there's a subtle difference here. He's not Piaget with the lone scientist. He's not the social learning people or the learning people where the child is influenced by others socializing that child. The child then, as an apprentice, is working with the adults to develop cognitive thinking.

In reality, Piaget and Vygotsky's theories account for the way children develop. Both of them do. And we might consider them then as important complements to each other, rather than saying that one's right and one's wrong. They're looking at different ways that children learn, that both occur.

Why do we call Vygotsky's theory *cognitive-mediation*? Well, first, Vygotsky believed we share lower mental functions with other animals. What differentiates us is that we go beyond other animals because of the mental or psychological tools that we acquire to help us think. Now remember, based on a Marxist philosophy, he believed *tools mediated progression*, and "tools" became the hot word for him and he tried to use the idea of tools as used by Marxism in the way of talking about internal or psychological or cognitive tools. Tools made the difference between humans and other animals. The way we acquire a psychological tool is from our culture, and that means from the previous learning of our species. You see, with learning theory, the outside stimuli elicit responses in the individual. But with Vygotsky, when we acquire a psychological tool such as language— his main psychological tool—the tool now is a part of our understanding; it becomes our way of thinking. The tool mediates between the outside stimuli and the responses. So in learning theory, stimulus leads to response. As humans now, stimulus leads to our mediation, our internal cognitive processing because of our psychological tools to responses. Our psychological tools then create intentionality and comparisons and higher order planning, and no longer are we at the mercy of outside stimuli, as lower animals are.

I heard someone once describe it this way, if I can explain it. He said that once he was trying to do something in the bathroom, to fix something, replace a light, it was up high, and he climbed upon the sink and was hanging on the door that was open to reach what he was trying to do. As he reached, the door started to close, his weight was on the door, he had his fingers on top of the door and it started to close on his hands. He reached to another part of the door and this forced it to close even more. It was just a reaction to sort of save himself. So far, just like an animal. But, as it started to close faster and faster from his weight, he thought through the situation. He thought, now if I keep going like this, my hands are going to get caught in the door. If I shift my weight from the sink and reach over here, I can pull back and then the door won't close anymore, and some way he could make this adjustment.

The point is, he wasn't just responding as an animal would, he was thinking through or mediating the situation. For him it was almost like he was talking through the alternatives that he had. He had to do it very quickly to save his hand—as an example of mediation.

Going back to Vygotsky, culture is handed down to us through our society, and our society is handed down to us through the adults and our society, mainly our parents. So, what was in our culture is incorporated into our own cognitive processes as psychological tools we use. Vygotsky said, as I mentioned already, "What was inter-mental becomes intra-mental." What was outside now between individuals becomes a part of us.

For Vygotsky, we can't function on an adult level without culture because we bring all of these things in from our culture, and the culture—this previous learning that we have—is necessary to bring us to an adult level. This conceptualization, I think, provides a deeper level of social interaction than the simple social influence and conditioning that's envisioned by learning theory. Another way of looking at it is what Vygotsky once said, "A colt is already a horse, but a human baby is only a candidate to become a human being." So for Vygotsky, you didn't really truly become human until you developed cognition from your culture.

What are these psychological tools that came from our culture and are so necessary for our development? The higher cognitive processes? It goes back to something we've already mentioned again and again—that tools are symbolic. Tools seem to be one of those big watersheds in human development. The same symbol systems that we've already encountered in our discussions of Piaget and of others are the primary tools for thinking. For example, language for Vygotsky—it makes sense—is the most important psychological tool. But you also have symbolic play or pretend play; you have art, writing, each of these different kinds of symbol systems. *Language* is a verbal symbol system. Symbolic play is an inactive, acting symbol system. Art and writing are graphic symbol systems. But they're all ways of using symbols.

This description may sound similar to Piaget's description except for two aspects that Vygotsky emphasized. First, the symbol systems come *to* us from others rather than *within* ourselves. In Piaget's view we sort of create our symbols and are able to use them. Second, the systems are not just used in our thinking. Piaget said that language is a symbol system; it's very helpful for thinking. But for Vygotsky, it goes further. We don't just use it in our thinking; it completely reorganizes our thinking, takes over our thinking. It's the symbolic mediator or tool that changes everything. So language is the most important tool. Vygotsky described this process by which children internalize language as a personal tool. First, others in the culture obviously provide the child with a particular language and set of symbols. That's absolutely necessary. Others have to have the language and give it to the child. Then, as the child masters the language, she begins using the language not just to communicate to others—that's the purpose of language—but she starts using the language in *egocentric speech*. She talks to herself, usually out loud. So you could argue that for Vygotsky, the definition of egocentric speech is talking to yourself, not to communicate with others, but just to talk to yourself. So here's an example.

A kid is playing with some toys, playing with Star Wars let's say, and the child says; "Now this person comes to the space ship. He's scared. He walks up to Darth Vader. Now I'm this person." Have you ever heard kids talk like that? They sort of switch in their play from dialogue to narrating the story to stagehands to giving directions to the characters, and often they're doing it out loud. This is egocentric speech. Then, with more experience, the child is able to eliminate the overt speech and internalize the egocentric speech. Or, it becomes partially internalized. So sometimes for adults, and certainly as children, we talk out loud, but don't say the whole thing. Like, "Darn, now I have to do this. Darn, go here." You just say little pieces, and children start doing this thing also. So, Vygotsky's view here is what was outside the speech that the child learned from the culture, these symbols, the child practices and guides herself through speaking to herself and it starts to become internal. The child is still talking to herself, but now it's only mental.

Eventually, this *inner speech* becomes the mediating tool for the child's thinking. So she begins using automatic and truncated speech to think, to plan, to direct herself. It's no longer speech for communication where it started; it's now a personal psychological tool that changes all her though processes. It came from others, but now it's part of the child's mind. Although language is this primary tool, other tools become internalized as well. So, mathematical thinking can become internalized, visual thinking can become internalized. And there are many examples in both children and adults of egocentric speech. In one example—and I was present when this happened, we were with some friends—and this preschooler's mother told him to go to his room and put on his pants and shirt. We were going to go somewhere, and he was a little kid, about two and a half or three, just getting used to trying to get dressed on his own, and we were in the other room waiting and we heard this little kid in the other room say, "Label in the back. Label in the back. Label in the back." We realized that he was repeating the instructions for how to put on his shirt and his pants that his mother provided to him. He was giving himself directions, and he's giving these directions out loud. And it occurred to me that I'm an old guy, I put on my shirt maybe 10 or 20 times in my life, and I still say to myself—but it's now truncated, it's inside—I say to myself, "label in the back." I can sometimes give myself instructions when I'm trying to figure out things like this.

I've given this example before, but here's another one. You, as an adult, are driving down the road and trying to follow some directions. It's not automatic where you're going, you haven't been there often, but you have directions. And as you go along you think to yourself, "Go two lights. Then turn left and look for the red house." And you give yourself these directions. So when you consider how you think, very often you use symbolic devices that are derived from inner speech to guide your thinking, your planning, and your actions. And the argument is that even when we're learning new things, we're thinking through ideas and alternatives, we're using inner speech. But it becomes so inner, and so automatic, that we may not realize we're using this speech. That was Vygotsky's view.

 ©2002 The Teaching Company Limited Partnership

This process of internalization from others doesn't carry the connotations of conditioning or behavior modification that learning theory does. In conditioning and behavior modification, even though a child cooperates and goes easier, the idea is of a more passive person that's being conditioned—whether the person cooperates or not. But in Vygotsky's conceptualization, the child is an active processor, the child is cooperating in this joint regulation, and the child is doing it.

Now, Piaget had a view of egocentric speech as well. In fact, Vygotsky probably stole the term egocentric speech from Piaget, from some of Piaget's early writings. But Piaget had a different view of it. They disagree. For Piaget, a child in egocentric speech was really being egocentric. It was a lack of perspective-taking. The child was in some ways talking past another person, not taking account of what the other person knew vs. what the child himself knew. So, egocentric speech is where you talk about things and you're not making any sense to the other person. It's egocentric; you're taking only your viewpoint. In Vygotsky's view, egocentric speech is talking to yourself. Let me give you an example of Piaget's egocentric speech.

At one time for a short time one summer, we had a family live next to us who were from Switzerland. In fact, interestingly, the man and his family was a student of Piaget's, had received his Ph.D. with Piaget and was a professor. They were living there and he had little kids, preschool kids, and we got together for the first time. His kids spoke only French, and our kids spoke only English, and I watched them interact. They were watching TV and playing with some toys. It was strange. If we had turned off the sound, it looked as though they knew what each other were speaking about. One person was speaking French, one kid; the other person was speaking English, and they were just talking about toys and talking about TV and going on. And I know that they didn't understand what the other was saying, but they just kept talking. In Piaget's view, that's egocentric speech. One kid says, "It was my birthday yesterday, I got a lot of presents," and the other one said, "We're going to McDonald's after we leave here." And one said, "I really love Darth Vader and the Star Wars toys," and the other one said, "I'm going to get chicken nuggets." That's egocentric speech, whether it's in the same language or not.

I'll give you another example. There was a child at show and tell in preschool. It was in autumn and he had brought in a large leaf and he was telling the kids about the leaf. He said, "I got this leaf out by the garage. It came from the big tree and fell down from the big tree." And I was watching the kids and they were all nodding. And he said, "I got it with my friend, Kevin" and another kid looks confused and said, "I'm Kevin." And that's how the conversation went. They're nodding. He hasn't taken account that they don't know which tree he means or which garage. He doesn't say that he got it by "a large tree that's by my garage." He said, "I went out and got this leaf by my garage from the big tree with Kevin." That's egocentric speech. He's failed to explain things. It makes sense of what he knows and what they don't know.

I bring that up only to say that both Piaget and Vygotsky were probably right. They used egocentric speech in reality to describe different processes. In one case, Piaget is talking about this lack of perspective-taking, it's speech sort of passing each other, not taking account of knowledge. In the other case, Vygotsky is talking about how we end up talking to ourselves and how it becomes internalized and becomes inner speech. But they're two processes that probably both exist.

Let me point out another comparison between Vygotsky's view and Piaget's view. And this is the two views they had of pretend play or symbolic play. For Piaget, pretend play, symbolic play was an immature process. It developed after kids had symbol use, and it was predominantly assimilation. It distorted reality. And he was right. So for example, when a child simply takes a block of wood and pretends it's a car and drives it along—vroom, vroom—he's distorting reality because a block of wood really isn't a car; it isn't too much like a car. He's not paying attention to the features and the characteristics of the block of wood as a block of wood, he's thinking car. He's assimilating in a sense that he's using his car scheme and applying that to the block of wood in pretend play. But he's not accommodating; he's not putting it all into balance. And so, in pretend play, whether we play the role of another person or we use an object as a substitute for some other object, we use props and change the situation. We distort reality. And, as Piaget looked at that—because he was already hung up because of his theory on how assimilation and accommodation should be in balance to really have adaptive thinking and understanding—he was led I think, or maybe even biased to look at play as being an immature and maybe a second-rate process. It occurs because kids really aren't very good at putting assimilation and accommodation together when they first start out using symbols.

However, Piaget did first see a value to play. He could see that, because kids distort reality, because they assimilate so much, they didn't have to worry about all the demands from reality. If you don't have to worry about it, in some ways, if you can distort it in that way, you can act out things that are your own problems. He actually borrowed from Freud here and talked about how, in play, it is almost like we have a projective test and we can almost do therapy on ourselves. We can act out situations where we had problems or where we didn't understand stuff, and we can act it out again and again to try to understand it. So he saw some value again in play, you see?

In fact, there was a case once where some little kids saw a film about childbirth, a very graphic film as preschoolers. Probably they weren't ready for it. They didn't seem to be upset. They were sort of surprised, but they weren't upset. The adults asked them if they had any questions and they said, "No." A few days later they'd taken some of their action figures and pulled the arms and legs off the figures and had one figure with the legs spread apart and then were going through birth. They were trying to put the dolls back together and acting out birth. And they did it again and again, trying to act this out, almost like they were trying to understand what was happening.

For Piaget though, play drops out around the school years when operational thinking comes in, and we now have a much more efficient process that's more adaptive. Vygotsky though looked at play and he had the view that it wasn't a second-rate process; it isn't a problem of adjusting to reality. Play, in fact, is the area where a child performs at his very best level, at the highest level of his skills, at the upper edge of his abilities. He can practice things that he doesn't practice otherwise. Now, for some of the same reasons, play doesn't require that the child do something for an external reason. It isn't real. You don't have to worry about failing or about the risks involved. If you pretend to be chased by a tiger, there's no chance that a real tiger is going to catch you and eat you, to be extreme. You don't have to worry about things, so it makes play a nice safe place to try things out. But it's because of this safety, because of the chance of having others help you along and the culture helps you along that, in Vygotsky's terms, you can do things at your highest level.

So, for example, children can practice being patient or being mature or acting like parents and acting out the roles of taking care of a child, things that they couldn't possibly do in real life. But in play, they can practice these roles and get better at them or at least see how it feels. They can try out handling different serious emotions in play. One child was hiding out from some dangerous monsters and everybody had to be extremely quiet in their hiding places. He had to go to the bathroom very badly. It was extremely uncomfortable for him, but he stayed in his place for a long time quietly, something he would never do in his real life. He did it well beyond his abilities because he was in play, and the support from others in the contest gave him his chance.

So for Piaget, play was a second-rate process that worked for a while until something better came along. For Vygotsky, play was the leading edge. Here's another comparison of the differences between their theories, and we're going to explain how that fits in in our next lecture when we talk about adult-child co-construction and some of the other important contributions by Vygotsky.

Thank you.

    ©2002 The Teaching Company Limited Partnership

Lecture Twenty-Three
Vygotsky's Zone of Proximal Development

Scope:

This lecture discusses Vygotsky's important argument that a person's level of development is not a point on a developmental course but a range or zone. This *zone of proximal development* shifts over time. The lecture then discusses the concept of *scaffolding* in the zone, which is provided by other people. Examples of scaffolding are given: how an adult and a child co-construct the child's narrative memory and how pretend play helps bring about development at the next highest level. The lecture concludes with a discussion of how this important concept applies to education.

Outline

I. One of the most important contributions of Vygotsky's theory has been the concept of the *zone of proximal development.*

   A. In the previous developmental theories we have studied, one assumption is that children progress along a given course of development toward some end point of mature and adaptive functioning. This is most easily seen in stage theories, such as those of Freud, Erikson, and Piaget. Thus, at any given time, a child is thought to be at some distinct point along the course of development.

   B. For Vygotsky, there was no single point of development. Instead, an individual's level of development varies across some fuzzy range along the course of development, some zone.

   1. According to Vygotsky, the zone that covers an individual's current developmental level stretches from the level at which the child has already completely mastered lower level skills and knowledge to the level at the upper limit of the individual's capacity, where the child can use a skill or know something only in the best of circumstances.

   2. The lower level of the zone is called the *actual level* of development; everything below this level has already been mastered—the past. The upper level of the zone is called the *potential level* of development; everything above this level, or outside this level, is as yet unachievable by the person and beyond his or her limits—the future. Everything between these two levels is in the zone and is potentially achievable by the person—the present.

3. This area is called the zone of proximal development because this range covers the problems, challenges, and tasks that are *proximal*, or next to, the person's last fully developed level.

C. Why did Vygotsky propose a zone rather than a distinct point in the course of development?

1. As Vygotsky observed, whether or not a person can perform a task or successfully solve a problem depends on many environmental factors. It depends on whether a problem is worded clearly, whether the problem or task is a simple version or a complicated version, whether someone else is helping the person, and whether aids or cues are given.

2. Some tasks are not very challenging because they are highly similar to what the person already knows. Other tasks are more challenging because they are complicated and require the person to perform without any help.

3. As an example, some fathers and sons were building birdhouses together. For the youngest boys, the fathers read the directions, explained the use of the tools, did most of the measuring, sawed the wood pieces, nailed the pieces together, and did much of the painting. For boys a little more experienced, the fathers told the children what to do at each step, sawed the wood, and let the boys do the rest. For the oldest boys, the fathers simply watched and gave suggestions from time to time. Each instance appeared at a different level in a child's zone of developing construction skills.

4. In another example, a kindergarten girl was learning to read with her mother. At first, they chose books that had large pictures and only one or two words on each page. The words were simple and were often repeated. The mother said the word first, and the child would then repeat it. Later, after the child had mastered the easiest books, the mother would have the girl guess the word,

©2002 The Teaching Company Limited Partnership

and then try to sound it out, but the mother would help with part of the sound. After more time, they chose books with more complicated sentences, and the mother let the girl do more sounding out and reading without the mother's intervention. Eventually, they chose books with mostly writing and very few pictures. The girl either recognized or sounded out most of the words without the mother's help. Finally, the girl read books without the mother even being present. Each instance showed a different level in the child's zone of reading development.

5. In each of these examples, at what point would one be able to say, "The child has now developed that skill [that is, making a birdhouse or being able to read]"? There is no single point at which the child had developed the skill, but didn't have it before. Thus, Vygotsky argued for calling the entire zone the individual's level of development rather than one single point.

II. How does a person progress through his or her zone of proximal development?

A. First, as the person develops new skills at a high level of mastery, both her actual level and her potential level increase. In other words, with mastery, the entire zone moves along the developmental course. The zone is dynamic and never static.

B. Second, Vygotsky never meant that a child had only one universal zone of development that spanned all tasks and domains. Each different domain, such as wood construction or reading, was likely to have its own dynamic zone.

C. Third, one would expect to find individual differences in a person's zones of development.

1. In a given domain, one child's zone might be farther along than another child's zone.

2. One child might progress faster through the zone than another child does.

3. The span of the zone from the actual to the potential level might be wider for one child than for another.

D. What was the mechanism of development?

1. Because of the instructions, cues, and assistance given by someone else, a child is able to handle more challenging problems and eventually learns to handle the problems without the help of others. Once again, society and adults cooperate with the child in providing tools for development.
2. As mentioned in the last lecture, this help from someone else is then internalized and becomes part of the child's own repertoire.

E. Jerome Bruner coined the term *scaffolding* to refer to this cooperative help from others and the environment
   1. Physical scaffolding supports a building project at the level where current building is going on. As the building progresses, the scaffolding needs to be placed higher to keep up with the level of construction on the building. It is no longer required for the levels of the building that are already in place. This is the metaphor for all kinds of developmental tasks.
   2. Adults add scaffolding at the edge of development but remove it when some levels have already been mastered. In addition, scaffolding makes no sense if placed above the level where the developmental work is occurring.
   3. In the construction example given above, the fathers, in effect, provided scaffolding to their sons' construction of birdhouses. They systematically removed the scaffolding when no longer needed—that is, for tasks that the children could do on their own. In the reading example, the mother provided scaffolding to her daughter's reading by helping and giving cues right at the edge of the daughter's abilities. She also removed help as the daughter could do tasks on her own, and she added higher-level tasks, such as books with more words and fewer pictures, which again, required more help from the mother.
   4. One can see that the process of scaffolding is a dynamic one that constantly shifts levels.
   5. Scaffolding is not effective if the adults provide help well beyond the child's zone of proximal development at levels not yet available for mastery or below the child's

 ©2002 The Teaching Company Limited Partnership

zone of proximal development at levels that the child has already mastered.

III. Here are two more examples of the scaffolding process in a child's zone of development.

   A. Robyn Fivush and others completed research on the *co-construction* of narrative memory in children.

     1. In observations of children being asked to tell about something that happened, the parent and the child usually co-construct the narrative account. In other words, the parent provides cues as to what happened and helps the child recall events. These events then become more permanently encoded in the child's memory.

     2. Within this process, it is impossible to say what the child remembers and what comes from the parent.

     3. However, young children would not remember most sequences of events without the initial aid of the parent recalling the event with them.

   B. Vygotsky believed that during *social pretend play*—that is, symbolic play that children carry out with someone else—the play context provides "scaffolding" for the child's development through her zone.

     1. Play first requires that a child concentrate more on the meanings of what she is doing, the referents, than on the actual objects or actions that are used. Pretend play helps children distance the symbol from the referent.

     2. When the child pretends to be in another role carrying out actions appropriate to that role, she is performing actions that are often well above her zone in real life. For example, when a girl pretends to be a mother and take care of a sick baby, she is trying out responsibilities and stretching herself beyond what she really can do.

     3. Other players also push a child to stay within the "rules" of the play game and act according to the roles and plot. For example, a child may be frightened, but if she is pretending to be a superhero, she must act at not being frightened. Thus, social pretend play teaches children emotional control and discipline at the edge of their abilities.

4. For all these reasons, play, according to Vygotsky, demonstrates the leading edge of development and creates a zone of proximal development for the child.

5. In contrast, most other theorists, including Freud, Erikson, and Piaget, looked at play as a reflection of what the child already knew or believed, not the cutting edge of her development.

IV. The concept of a zone of proximal development, with its attendant scaffolding from adults and society, demonstrates a different conception of the relation between learning and development for Vygotsky than for other theorists.

A. For learning theorists and social learning theorists, learning is equated with development. Because differences in potential based on age are not considered, the process of learning new skills or knowledge and development are virtually indistinguishable. The focus is on the environment influencing the child.

B. For Piaget, development comes from within and comes before learning. It makes possible learning of individual skills and knowledge. The focus is on the child's normal course and rate of development when he is left on his own.

C. For Vygotsky, learning happens as a person masters new skills, aided by other people at the advanced edge of his zone of development. Learning comes first and brings about development. The focus is on cooperative scaffolding in learning.

V. The ideas of a zone of proximal development, scaffolding, and the recent research on co-construction of various skills have had a large impact on educators.

A. Teachers use the idea of adjusting instruction to the students' current zone of proximal development.

1. This approach to education requires that teachers focus on individual student levels to determine what will be challenging and accessible to students.

2. A good teacher is someone who can determine the appropriate help that a student needs to gain mastery of a task such as the number of examples and the amount of

©2002 The Teaching Company Limited Partnership

practice. A good teacher must also know when to withdraw help and scaffolding so as not to bore students.

3. Good teaching usually means that the teacher must begin with what the student already knows but ensure that new and challenging information is also presented.

B. This approach does have limitations and weaknesses, however.

1. Like other theoretical conceptions we have discussed, the zone of proximal development, as well as the idea of scaffolding, are metaphors that are not easily tested or disproved. Their value seems to be in the way they can organize and guide a teacher's or researcher's thinking, but they are rather imprecise.

2. In applying these concepts to classrooms, it is logistically difficult to see how a teacher could possibly assess any one child's actual levels of development across several domains, let alone do it for the entire classroom. Some compromises to individual instruction are often required.

VI. In conclusion, the main theoretical constructs and the emphasis provided by Vygotsky seem to be a healthy addition to other theories, but the ideas may be limited in their applicability. The most important results so far have been in conceptualizations of education and teaching and in a new emphasis on the context of development, especially across cultures.

Supplementary Reading:

Rogoff, *Apprenticeship in Thinking: Cognitive Development in Social Context.*

Berk and Winsler, *Scaffolding Children's Learning: Vygotsky and Early Childhood Education.*

Questions to Consider:

1. What examples of scaffolding can you think of in the learning and development of adults? Do the concepts of a zone of proximal development and scaffolding still apply to adults?

2. How do you think Piaget and Vygotsky would differ in their conceptualizations of intelligence? Do you think that, in terms of Vygotsky's theory, intelligence might mean that a person can progress through the zone of development at a faster rate than average and need fewer cues or aids and less scaffolding to do so?

©2002 The Teaching Company Limited Partnership

Lecture Twenty-Three
Vygotsky's Zone of Proximal Development

Hello. In the last lecture we introduced Vygotsky's theory and today we'll conclude our discussion of his theory. One of the most important contributions of Vygotsky's theory has been the concept of the *zone of proximal development*. I'll explain that concept and then discuss an attendant concept of *scaffolding*. Then we'll discuss the process of co-construction that follows under this view of scaffolding, and we'll conclude this discussion with how these concepts, these ideas, apply to education.

In the previous developmental theories that we studied, there was one assumption in all of them, and that was that children progress along some given course of development, towards some endpoint of mature and adaptive functioning. So, even if you take the view that development occurs throughout the lifespan, one of the primary endpoints that people look at is children make it to adulthood. And, at the adult mature level, we take that as a goal, if you will—at least an automatic goal in development—and we try to pinpoint where a child is along this path. This is most easily seen in stage theories, such as those of Erikson and Piaget. At any given time then, the child is thought to be at some distinct point along this course of development, and we're not always good at figuring out exactly where it is, but in theory, if we were perfect in our knowledge of development, we could find it.

For Vygotsky, there wasn't a single point of development. Instead, an individual's level of development varies across some fuzzy range in this course, some zone. According to Vygotsky, the zone that covers an individual's current developmental level stretches from the level at which the child has already completely mastered skills, the lower level skills, and then stretches to the other end, the upper limit of the individual's capacity, where that child can only use a skill or know something only in the very best of circumstances. The lower level of the zone is called the *actual level* of development. And in Vygotsky's terms, everything below this level has already been mastered; that's the past. That's what happened in the past. The upper level in the zone is called the *potential level* of development, and everything above this level, or outside of this level, is not yet achievable by the person; it's beyond his limits. That's the future.

And, by the way, everything beyond that isn't possible, even if you really try hard to teach kids something. So, if you really try hard to teach a two year old to drive a car, it's beyond his level. He can't do it for various reasons, some of them physical. Everything between these two levels is in the zone and is potentially achievable by the person. This is the present. So this zone that the child is working in at a particular time. I'm trying to draw this out with my hands, but think of it as this course, this line of development, and you have some zone along this line. The actual level is down at the lower end, everything below that the kid has already mastered and is really good at. The potential level is up at the upper end, everything above that is beyond the child, and this is the zone the child is currently working on. Across the time, this zone moves, it moves ahead in development. But it's the entire zone that moves. This area's called the zone of proximal development. Proximal, because this range covers the problems and challenges and tasks that are proximal or next to the person's last fully developed level.

So why did Vygotsky propose a zone, rather than a distinct point in the course of development? As Vygotsky observed, whether or not a person can perform a task or successfully solve a problem depends on many, many environmental factors. It depends on whether a problem is worded clearly, whether the problem or task is a simple version or a complicated version, whether someone else is helping the person to do the task, whether there are aids or cues given to do a task. These things seem so obvious, but sometimes they're forgotten by Western and American psychologists and developmentalists as they tested kids. You see, some tests aren't very challenging because they're very similar or highly similar to what a person already knows. Other tasks are more challenging because they're simply more complicated or they require a person to perform without any help.

For example, you're a student taking an exam, a final exam for a course. If the exam is simply recall and says, "Tell me what this is, this concept," that's a lot more difficult than—at least in theory—a multiple choice exam that says, "What is the definition of this," and it gives you several choices and you have to choose. You already have cues, you already have something in front of you that you have to recognize. You see? So for most people, just pulling something out of your head with no help is more difficult. You can make exams more difficult or easier, even to test the same kind of information.

©2002 The Teaching Company Limited Partnership

Let me give you an example in terms of children. Remember, for Vygotsky we're always talking about cooperative development; we're not talking about this lone kid developing. We're talking about the kid developing in terms of having someone to help or mentor or be an apprentice to this person. Here is a true example of some fathers and sons that, as a group, were building birdhouses together that they were going to then display in some situation. And the kids were at different ages, but all school age kids, and they had different levels of abilities, as did the fathers, by the way.

There were kits. There were directions on how to build the birdhouse. For the youngest boys, the fathers read the directions, explained the use of the tools, did most of the measuring, sawed the wood pieces, nailed the wood pieces together; they did most of the painting. So you saw some cases where they talked to the kids, they let the kids do a few things—hammer, paint—but the fathers did a heck of a lot of the work, and they were working together on it. But for boys a little more experienced, the fathers told the children how to do each step and would let the children do most of it. However, I noticed in this group that the fathers sawed the wood. They were afraid to let the kids get a hold of these saws. They let the boys do most of the other stuff. For the oldest boys, the kids that seemed to have the most experience, the fathers simply sat and watched. They gave suggestions from time to time, but for the most part they sat back and the boys did it.

In each instance there was an appearance of help that seemed to be at a different level in the child's zone of developing construction skills. So, the level of help varied depending on how advanced and how good these kids were. Now in fact, you could have taken any level of help and picked out any boy and given this help to this boy, and the ones where the fathers did it all would have been at a very easy level—in fact, it might have been below the child, below the zone—and help where the fathers just sat back and did almost nothing and made suggestions might have made the task extremely challenging to some boys. Maybe they could have done it, but it would have been tough.

Let me give you another example. A kindergarten girl was learning to read with her mother. At first, they together chose the books they were going to read, and the books they chose first were one's with large pictures and only one or two words on each page. You know the types of books. The words were simple and they were often repeated. So, it would say, "Go, go, go." And the next page would say, "We go" or something like that. When they read these books, the mother would usually say the word first, and then the girl would repeat the word. Later, after the child mastered these easiest books, often through simply memorizing them or learning what words went with which pictures, they then looked for books that were a little more difficult. There were a few more words; the words were harder, and the mother tried to get the girl to guess at what the words were, and then tried to sound them out from the letters. But the mother would help with part of the sound. Maybe the girl would get the first letter of each word, the sound. The mother would say, "C-Can." And after a while, they chose more books that had more complicated sentences and the mother let the girl do more of the sounding out, and reading without the mother's intervention. Eventually, they chose books that were mostly writing with very few pictures and the girl would either recognize each word or sound them out without the mother's help. Finally the girl read books without the mother even being present.

This should be a typical kind of sequence in learning to read. At each instance though, this mother and this child showed a different level within the child's zone of reading development, and you realize that some things that the mother did with the child made the task really easy, and some things that the mother did made the task extremely challenging. So at any particular level of the child's reading, the mother could choose to do things or present a situation that was tough for the kid or very easy for the kid. But it was all within the zone of what the child was working on at that particular time in her life.

In each of these examples, at what point would you be able to say, "This child has now developed that skill. This child now knows how to build birdhouses." When did that come in? Or, "This girl can now read." When do we say that? See, there's no single point at which the child has developed the skill and didn't have it before. So that's why Vygotsky argued that to call it a particular point is misleading; it's impossible to find. It's a whole zone. It's better to say—where's the child at in development? Within this zone; that's where the child is at. And it will depend on the context and on the task. It won't be a single point. And it goes back to this view that we never have an all or none development. Development is always a little less, a little more, a gradual development until you get something in. When we learn to read, it's not all or none. When we learn certain mathematical concepts, it's not all or none. When we learn to swim, it's not all or none.

So how does a person progress now through this zone of proximal development? First, as a person develops new skills at some high level of mastery, then both her actual level and her potential level increase, so think of this line of development again, and as you develop new skills, your actual level comes up. But as your actual level comes up, what you've already mastered, so does your potential level. The zone moves up. So with mastery, the entire zone moves along the course. See, this zone is always dynamic; it's never static. As you're developing and as you're learning, the zone is constantly coming along as well. Second, Vygotsky never meant that a child only had one universal zone of development that spanned all tasks and all domains. Each different domain, for example, construction of birdhouses, or reading, or something else was likely to have its own dynamic zone. You couldn't just say, "This is the zone the kid's in."

Third, we would expect to find individual differences in a person's zones of development, individual differences across the zones of that person, and certainly, individual differences with some other child. So, in any given domain, a child's zone might be further along than another child's zone. One child's reading might be over here, and another child's might be over there. That seems obvious. One child also might progress faster than another child, so the zone moves along faster than some other child. And the span of the zone, from the actual to the potential level, might be wider or narrower for one child. Maybe this child can work within a wide zone and another child works in a narrow zone. It's all very theoretical at this point. Zones may expand in how wide they are, or narrow. This is the theoretical part. It's a good way of thinking about it. It's very imprecise when you're trying to do measurements of specific zones for a person.

But, for Vygotsky, what was the mechanism of development? Because of instructions, cues and assistance given by someone else, a child is able to handle more and more challenging problems and eventually the child learns to handle problems and eventually a child learns to handle problems without the help of others. So once again—remember what we said last time—once again society and adults cooperate with the child in providing the tools for development. As we mentioned in the last lecture, help from someone else is then internalized, and becomes part of the child's own repertoire. So the zone is where this help is provided, what has already been developed. Now the child has internalized it and can do it without help.

Jerome Bruner was a developmental theorist and researcher who coined the term *scaffolding* to refer to this cooperative help from others and also from the environment. It's a nice term, I think. It sort of captures what we mean. If you think of physical scaffolding in the construction business—in building—scaffolding, although it really doesn't hold up the building, it certainly holds up the work that's in progress. The scaffolding supports the building project at the level where the current building is going on. So, beginning with the building, you build the scaffolding sort of low. As the building progresses and is built, the scaffolding needs to be changed, it needs to be placed higher up to keep the level of the construction of the building. It's no longer required on the lower level, and in fact, you can take stuff away from the lower levels and keep building it up to the higher levels.

So this is the metaphor for all kinds of developmental tasks. Scaffolding also really does support what's going on in development at the time. I think of a very simple but very physical example of scaffolding. You want to take a picture of your new baby because she's so cute, and she's only about four months of age and she really can't sit up on her own. So you put her on the sofa; you put her with some things and you prop her up with pillows to take the picture. That's *really* physical scaffolding, to have those pillows there. You don't put them there once she can sit on her own. You take that scaffolding away. So adults add scaffolding at the higher edge of development, but they remove it after some levels have already been mastered. And in addition, scaffolding makes no sense if you're putting it at a level beyond the developmental work that's occurring. If you put it up too high, it's just crazy.

So, in the birdhouse construction example that we gave, the fathers, in effect, provided scaffolding to their sons' construction of the birdhouse. They systematically removed the scaffolding when it was no longer needed. That is, for the tasks that the children could do on

 ©2002 The Teaching Company Limited Partnership

their own. In the reading example, the mother also provided scaffolding to her daughter's reading by helping, giving cues that were right at the edge of her daughter's abilities. She also removed help as her daughter could do the task on her own, and she added higher level tasks, like more words, fewer pictures, which again required help from the mother. You see how that works? Now, I'd say they did this correctly, assuming they were good scaffolders. So one can see that the process of scaffolding is this dynamic process, they're constantly shifting levels, and I just mentioned that the adults in the culture, in the society, could be good scaffolders or lousy scaffolders, because they have to be in touch with the zone for a particular domain of development, and for a particular child. Again, scaffolding is not effective if the adults provide help well beyond the child's zone at levels that that child can't master, even with all the help, or below the child's zone at proximal development at levels the child has already mastered.

Let me give you a few more examples of this scaffolding process and of a child's zone of development. This research comes from different people, but one of the primary researchers here is named Robyn Fivush and she and others have completed research on the *co-construction* of narrative memory in children. The idea here, the buzzword, is "co-construction." Let me give you an example and then I'll explain that. In observations of children where the children were asked to tell about something that happened, she discovered this: In this sort of natural situation where you have the mother and child talk, she finds that typically a parent and a child usually "co-construct the narrative account." In other words, the parent provides cues to what happened and helps the child to recall events. The events then become more permanently encoded into the child's memory.

So co-construction goes something like this—and she found this, by the way, you can see this easily if you look at parents and children in how they talk—you come home and mom's been to the zoo with her little daughter this day. Her daughter's maybe two-and-a-half or three. They come home and the mom says to dad, "We had a great day at the zoo, didn't we?" And the girl says, "Yeah." So the mother says, "Why don't you tell dad what we did at the zoo?" And the girl just stands there, sort of in a stupor, and doesn't say anything. And the mom says, "Come on. Do you remember what we did at the zoo?" The kid doesn't say much. And the mother says, "Do you remember when we saw the elephants? Do you remember when we saw the elephants?" The girl nods. The mother says, "What did the elephants do?" And she says, "Swish around." "Oh yeah, you saw them swish their trunks around. Did they eat something?" And the girl says, "Yes." The mom says, "What did they eat?" "Hay." And then the girl says, "And they threw it on their backs." And the mom says, "Yeah they threw it on their backs to keep the sun off. And then what did the elephants do." And the girl says, "Drank." "Did they drink water?" And the girl says, "Yes, with their trunks. And we saw bears." "Yeah, we saw bears, too. And what did they do?" And the girl says, "The bears slept." And mom says, "Yeah, they didn't do too much, did they?" The girl says, "No. They didn't do very much at all."

And then they go on like this and you say, "Then what happened?" And she says, "We got popcorn." "Oh yeah, we got popcorn to eat." And the girl says, "And lemonade." "Yeah, we got lemonade to eat." And the girl says, "I got a shirt." You see how the conversation goes? So within this process it's impossible to say what the child remembers and what comes from the parent. If afterwards you ask whether this child remembers the trip to the zoo, does she have some narrative memory, does she recount it? Well, young children would not remember most sequences of events that happened in their lives without the initial aid of the parent recalling the event with them. It doesn't happen without the child and the parent co-constructing the memory. But, just as this case I gave you, as the parent adds cues and tries to draw it out of the children, the children will then see the associations and as they say one thing, they'll remember something else and bring part of it about. Eventually, they'll actually say more and more and they'll get pretty good. They not only improve their memory, they learn how to tell stories, how to tell about narratives of what happens. OK?

A lot of people have argued that when you have these early memories from childhood, do you really remember it or, in fact, do you just remember it because people tell you that it happened, your parents tell you it happened? Did you ever hear that before? That's an old idea. And then maybe some way, after they've told you enough times, you think you actually remember it. This kind of co-construction research, the view of a Vygotskyan approach, is, in fact; it is you remembering it, but only in conjunction with somebody else also telling you. It's not all the other person; it's not you. Things come from our cooperation in learning, and incorporating things.

That's interesting, how you can use this kind of co-construction. Robyn Fivush also did some research on narratives and people talking to their kids. She discovered a way of looking at how we learn gender differences, how boys and girls maybe feel things and talk about things differently. And this is a little different than the standard case of "oh, we just condition." We reward girls for doing "girl things" and we reward boys for doing "boy things" and they have to learn what's appropriate. In this case, it wasn't that way. It was more co-construction. She discovered in taping and watching a lot of discussions of mothers with their children that the mom would talk about emotions; and the moms wouldn't even know that they were doing this. But with the girls, they would talk about more emotions than they would with the boys.

So, if the girl fell down and skinned her knee, they'd say, "Oh. You got hurt. Does that really hurt?" And they'd say, "Yeah." And the mother would say, "How did that happen?" And they'd talk about it and the girl would say, "It hurts. I'm crying, I'm sad." And the mom would say, "Oh, you really feel sad; I know how that feels." And they'd go on and they'd talk about it. And they'd elicit it and they'd bring it out in the child. So, it was more talking about sadness and feeling happy than feeling scared. And for the boys, they just didn't talk about emotions. "Oh, you feel down and got hurt. Let's see if we can clean that up." And they got on with it. Except for anger— mothers would talk more about anger with their sons than they would with their daughters. But the other emotions, they talked more with the girls. And, surprise, surprise, boys will talk about anger and seem to feel it, but they seem to be thwarted in talking about or feeling fear or sadness, or at least expressing it. In some ways there are differences that you can see, and maybe it comes in some part from the way we co-construct our narrative and the way we express these things. It isn't like a parent saying, "Don't talk about those things!" She never says that to her son. It's just this co-construction of the narrative, an account of what's going on.

Let me go back to another case, this is pretend play again. I know that in the last lecture we talked about Vygotsky's view of play vs. Piaget's view of pretend play. Let me go back now and put Vygotsky's view of play in the context of the zone of proximal development and scaffolding within that zone. Vygotsky believed that in *social pretend play*—that is, symbolic play which the child carries out in conjunction with somebody else in a social context—the play itself provides the scaffolding for the child's development through that child's zone. And it's the social scaffolding that often becomes very important. Play first requires that the child first concentrate on the meanings of what she's doing. The reference/referents for the various objects, and doesn't just focus on the objects. In other words, symbol use develops. You can distance the symbol from the referent.

But, when the child pretends to be in a particular role, or carrying out an action that's appropriate to that role, she's often, as we'd mentioned, performing actions that are well above her zone in real life. For example, a girl might pretend to be a mother and take care of a sick baby. She's trying out responsibilities and stretching herself beyond what she can really do. And other players will often push a child to stay within the rules of the game and how to do it. So for example, a child may really be frightened because the child's playing a superhero and maybe it gets out of control and the child really does have some fear. But the child has to act at *not* being frightened. So, social pretend play often teaches children how to act with responsibility, how to respond in certain situations, and emotional control. Discipline at the edges of their abilities.

Play then, for Vygotsky, was scaffolding within the zone. It meant you could go higher and make some tasks easier than they would be without this help. Play for Vygotsky demonstrated the leading edge of development. It created this zone for the child. It led to where the child was going. For most other theorists—Freud, Erikson and Piaget—they looked at play as a reflection of what the child already knew or believed, but not as the cutting edge of that child's development.

Now, there's also a difference in the way we look at learning. For Vygotsky, learning leads development. We learn through this cooperative process, this scaffolding process. So for Vygotsky, learning is the highest level we can get. Learning then brings along our development. For learning theorists and for social learning theorists such as Bandura, learning is equated with development. They're one and the same thing. They really don't look at development as a separate process than learning, because their focus is on the environment influencing the child. For Piaget, development comes from within and it comes before learning. It makes learning possible, and you learn all kinds of individual things, but it's because you've already developed some way of thinking, some mental structure. Do you see the difference? Learning comes first for Vygotsky. It's the same thing as development for the learning theorists. For Piaget, development comes first and now you can use that to learn all kinds of things. Maybe it's just a different way of looking at things, but in fact it might also give you a way of teaching and looking at the world.

Vygotsky's research had a great influence on education. Teachers really picked up on this and they still do today. The idea of scaffolding, the idea of co-construction had a big impact on teachers. Teachers use this idea of adjusting instructions to the current zone of proximal development for their student in a particular domain or class. But you realize when you take this approach, it requires that teachers focus on individual student levels to determine what's a challenge, what's accessible to students. A good teacher is someone who can determine the appropriate help to give a student at an appropriate level on a task, with the right amount of examples. A good teacher must also know when to withdraw help and scaffolding so you don't bore students, and this is true at any level of teaching, whether you're preschool or high school or even in adult classes. So good teaching means the teacher has to begin with what the student already knows and then take the student with the scaffolding to new challenges beyond.

This approach though has weaknesses, both for education and in general for Vygotsky's approach. This zone of proximal development and the idea of scaffolding is great, but it's still a metaphor like so many other concepts that we've encountered. And a metaphor is not easily proved or tested or disproved. The value seems to be the way it organizes and guides our thinking and teachers thinking to look at things. It's also logistically difficult for a teacher or anyone else to possibly assess where a child's actual levels are and potential levels, and figure out the precision of these zones that are constantly changing. So, it's a good way to guide your approach to education, or your approach to development. It's hard to be very precise about it.

In conclusion, the main theoretical constructs, that is, the emphasis that Vygotsky provided, seemed to be very helpful additions to other theories; but the ideas might be a little limited in their applicability. The most important result seems to be conceptualizations have influenced education and teaching.

Next time, we're going to have our concluding lecture and see if we can put together some of the ideas and integration of various theories.

Thank you.

Lecture Twenty-Four
Conclusions—Our Nature and Development

Scope:

This concluding lecture begins with the well-known metaphor of the blind men and the elephant, and uses the metaphor to discuss how different theories might give us a partial understanding of human nature and development, or a false understanding. The lecture discusses whether we can integrate these major theories. An example of a comparison and integration of three theories is described: the case of gender-role development from Freudian, social learning, and cognitive-developmental theories. The lecture ends with a reprise: Where does the student now stand regarding major issues of human development?

Outline

I. A well-known metaphor is appropriate to use as a model for how we might compare and integrate the six theories that we have discussed in this course.

    A. In this story, there were six blind men who approached an elephant to discover what kind of creature an elephant was.

        1. The first man happened to fall against the elephant's side. He declared, "The elephant is like a wall."

        2. The second man ran into the tusk and, after feeling it, explained, "The elephant is like a spear."

        3. The third man grabbed onto the trunk and said, "The elephant is like a snake."

        4. The fourth man held onto the elephant's leg and exclaimed, "The elephant is like a tree."

        5. The fifth man chanced to touch the elephant's ear and said, "The elephant is like a fan."

        6. The sixth man grasped the elephant's swinging tail and said, "The elephant is like a rope."

        7. Because of the personal experiences of each man, each came up with a different conception. Although all were partly right, they were all wrong.

    B. Like the blind men and the elephant, does each of our six theories give us a partial understanding of human nature and development or, worse, a false and biased understanding?

1. The answer probably depends on what one does with each of these theories. One can use one theory only with the belief that that particular theory is the best explanation for human development, or one can realize that each theorist was biased by personal experiences and focus and dealt only with a piece of the whole picture.
2. Thus, each theory must be used with a view of the context in which it was developed and the purpose for which it was developed.

C. Freud's theory dealt primarily with unconscious conflicts and emotionally charged issues that formed one's personality.
  1. He contributed an awareness of the importance of the unconscious and talked about multiple, often unconscious, motivations.
  2. His approach was biased by trying to explain everything through sexual drives.

D. Erikson's theory dealt primarily with the development of identity and the joint issue of connectedness and independence.
  1. He contributed a good guide to the issues people face throughout their life spans and the sequence of focus on these issues.
  2. He was biased by his own struggles with identity confusion as he grew up and his attempts to reconcile his theory with Freud's stages.

E. Bowlby and Ainsworth's theory dealt primarily with the development of close relationships and their functions.
  1. Their theory has generated many new findings about how attachments form and how relationships affect subsequent behaviors.
  2. Bowlby, however, saw development as being mainly instinctual; Ainsworth saw development as tied to whether parents were good or bad or consistent.

F. Bandura's theory dealt primarily with how we learn through observation and how our self-efficacy influences our development.

 ©2002 The Teaching Company Limited Partnership

1. His theory has generated many applications, for example, in treating phobias or dealing with aggression in youth.
2. He did not focus much on the importance of childhood or on the developmental processes that occur at different ages.

G. Piaget's theory dealt primarily with how we change our cognitive skills over time and how we develop intelligent thought processes.
   1. His theory generated thousands of studies, probably more than any other theory, which have led to a wealth of knowledge about how children develop.
   2. He seemed to be biased toward logical mathematical operations, thus shortchanging more social and emotional domains. His stages may also have been too rigid.

H. Vygotsky's theory dealt primarily with how we interact with adults to incorporate important symbolic tools from them and how adults aid in our development.
   1. He influenced the way we look at cooperation and how we approach education.
   2. His theory was somewhat narrow in what it covered and lacked precision in its processes.

I. We should be able to combine and integrate the theories to organize our thinking regarding different aspects and domains of development.
   1. For example, we can use Erikson's theory to talk about major issues that we face, combined with Bowlby and Ainsworth's theory to discuss the process whereby trust and connectedness develop as a foundation for autonomy and independence.
   2. As another example, we can use Piaget's theory to provide a structure for understanding how we approach new information from the environment and the general sequence of shifts we make in our thinking, combined with Vygotsky's theory to add insight into how others help us gradually become more independent in problem solving.

3. However, there are also some contradictions among theories and some aspects that are based on opposing worldviews. It is probably impossible to integrate everything, just as it is impossible to believe that any one theory is completely correct.

II. One final example, the explanation of gender-role development, provides a good comparison of three of the theories.

   A. During the preschool and early elementary school years, children develop a firm conception of what is masculine and feminine behavior and how the role of each sex functions and differs from the other sex's role.
      1. In the field of development, *sex* refers to the actual physical differences between male and female. *Gender* refers to the attendant roles, behaviors, and attributes that go along with any particular sex.
      2. These conceptions are called *gender roles* and are believed to originate not only in our biology but also in the beliefs of our culture.
      3. Not only do children develop an understanding of gender roles, but they also incorporate them into their own identities.
      4. Three of our theories have attempted to explain how this development occurs and what the motivation is for children to develop these strong gender conceptions. The theories are Freudian psychodynamic theory, Bandura's social learning theory, and Piaget's cognitive-developmental theory as interpreted and used by Lawrence Kohlberg.
      5. Each sequence below is presented as if a preschool boy can state what he is thinking and feeling, even his unconscious thoughts and desires.

   B. According to psychoanalytic theory, the following sequence occurs. It is based on one's Oedipal desires and their resolution. The development of gender-role identity is initiated from within the child based on his own desires.
      1. I want my mother as a love object.
      2. To get her, I must be like my father.
      3. Therefore, I want to be a male like my father and do masculine things.

 ©2002 The Teaching Company Limited Partnership

C. According to social learning theory, the following sequence occurs. It is based on one's expectancies and beliefs about reinforcement contingencies. The development of gender-role identity is initiated from the environment socializing the child.

1. I want reinforcement.
2. I have observed others and realize that I get reinforcement when I do masculine things.
3. Therefore, I want to be a male and act like males act.

D. According to cognitive-developmental theory, the following sequence occurs. It is based on one's categorization of things in the world, including social relationships. The development of gender-role identity is initiated from within oneself; the child seeks it out.

1. I have discovered that I am a male and will stay a male.
2. I want to be a competent male.
3. Therefore, when I do masculine things, I am competent.

E. Empirical evidence does not provide much support for the psychoanalytic explanation. However, there has been much empirical evidence for both the social learning and the cognitive-developmental accounts.

1. The social learning account focuses on what comes from the environment.
2. The cognitive-developmental account focuses on what comes from within and how we socialize ourselves. It assumes that a child needs a prerequisite understanding of his own sex and identity before gender roles can be learned.
3. Most researchers today see some combination of these two accounts as the best explanation.

III. As a final assessment, we will return to some questions we asked in the first lecture concerning where the students stand on some major issues of development. Students should see if they have had any changes in their thinking. Students should recognize certain themes in each question, themes that cannot be proven or disproved but which guide one's theoretical leanings. For each statement, choose the alternative that best matches your belief.

A. Children are:

1. Creatures whose basically negative or selfish impulses must be controlled.
2. Neither inherently good nor inherently bad.
3. Creatures who are born with many positive and few negative tendencies.
4. This question addresses our conception of the basic nature of humans. The first alternative came from early conceptions but also matches Freud's theory. The second alternative matches Locke's philosophy and that of other theorists, such as Bandura. The third alternative matches Rousseau's philosophy and that of Piaget's theory.

B. People are basically:
1. Active beings who play a major role in determining their own abilities and traits.
2. Passive beings whose characteristics are molded by either environmental or biological factors.
3. This question addresses our basic worldview of an active organismic versus a passive, mechanistic approach to human nature. The first alternative matches Piaget's theory, and the second alternative matches Bandura's theory.

C. When we compare the development of different individuals, we see:
1. Mainly similarities; people develop along universal paths and experience similar changes at similar ages.
2. Mainly differences; people undergo different sequences of changes and have widely different timetables of development.
3. This question again addresses the issue of an organismic approach that focuses on universal norms of development versus a mechanistic approach that focuses on individual differences. The first alternative matches Piaget's theory, and the second alternative matches Bandura's theory.

D. Biological influences and environmental influences are thought to contribute to development. Overall:
1. Biological factors contribute more than environmental factors.
2. Biological and environmental factors are equally important.

 ©2002 The Teaching Company Limited Partnership

3. Environmental factors contribute more than biological factors.
4. This question addresses the relative influence of nature versus nurture. All theorists believe that both factors are important, but Bowlby's theory focuses more on biology, and Bandura's theory focuses more on environment.

IV. As a final question, can we apply these theories to development in adulthood and old age?

    A. Although most aspects of these six major theories dealt with development during childhood and adolescence, they each provide explanations for developmental processes and models that are part of our basic human nature. Thus, these processes and ideas should be found at all age levels.

    B. In the case of human development, we do indeed see a little child in the adult and the fully developed human adult in the little child.

Supplementary Reading:

Miller, *Theories of Developmental Psychology*, 4th ed., chapters 8–9.

Hwang, Lamb, and Sigel, eds., *Images of Childhood*. (This book of readings reveals some insightful differences in theoretical backgrounds as people view children differently in other cultures.)

Kagan, *Three Seductive Ideas*. (A foremost developmental psychologist questions some of the basic tenets that have provided foundations for some of our theories.)

Questions to Consider:

1. Using the criteria provided in the first lecture, how would you evaluate each of the six theories as to whether it makes a good theory? Of particular interest is the last criterion, "Is the theory self-satisfying?"

2. Where are the major gaps as you see them in explanations of development? Where might you want to see and expect to see new theories emerging?

Lecture Twenty-Four
Conclusions—Our Nature and Development

Hello. In this concluding lecture, we will discuss how different theories may give us partial understandings about human nature, and we'll discuss possibilities for integrating these theories. We'll conclude with a reprise, an assessment of where you stand as the student regarding some of the major issues of human development.

Let me begin with a well-known story. A well-known story that I think is appropriate to use as a model for how we might compare and integrate the six theories that we've discussed in this course. In this story there were six blind men who approached an elephant to discover what kind of creature the elephant was. The first man happened to fall against the elephant's side, and he declared, "Ah, this elephant, this kind of animal is like a wall." And the second man ran into the elephant's tusk and after feeling it he said, "Ouch. The elephant is like a spear." The third man grabbed the elephant's trunk, and as it swung around he said, "The elephant is like a snake. The elephant's a kind of snake." And the fourth man held onto the elephant's leg and exclaimed, "The elephant is like a tree." The fifth man chanced to touch the elephant's ear, and as he held it he said, "The elephant is like a fan." And the sixth man grasped the elephant's swinging tail and said, "Oh. The elephant's like a rope."

Now because of the personal experiences of each man, each one came up with a conception of this animal, the elephant; and, although they were all partly right, they were all wrong. So, like the blind men and the elephant, does each of our six theories and the theorists behind them give us a partial understanding of human development, or worse, a very false biased understanding? Well, the answer probably depends on what you or what a person does with each of these theories. If you use one theory only, with the belief that a particular theory is the best explanation for human development, then you will have one view and I think it will be a very biased and false view. But if you realize that each theorist was biased by personal experiences, and the focus they had in their dealings were with only one piece of the whole picture, then you may be appropriate in using a theory appropriately. You see, each theory must be used with the view of the context in which it was developed, and also the purpose for which it was developed. Let me review these very briefly.

 ©2002 The Teaching Company Limited Partnership

We started out with Freud's theory. Freud's theory dealt primarily with unconscious conflicts and emotionally charged issues that formed one's personality. He contributed an awareness of the importance of unconscious, a very strong contribution from him that we often forget that he contributed because it's become such an implicit part of our thinking today. He also talked about multiple motivations, often unconscious motivations. We often want things, but we want different things at the same time. He was biased, however, by a desire to explain certain kinds of psychopathologies and to develop a type of therapy to strengthen his theory. He tried to squeeze everything through sexual drives—as I saw it—and it biased his approach to explaining this motivation.

The second theory, Erikson's theory, dealt primarily with the development of identity and the development of the joint issues of connectedness and independence. He contributed, in my opinion, a very nice guide to the issues we face throughout the lifespan and the sequence, the focus that we have on these various issues. But, he was biased by his own struggles of identity confusion as he grew up, and he seemed to need to reconcile his theory with Freud's stages. If he had broken away, and didn't have that initial conception, maybe he would have developed other approaches to looking at his concepts.

The third theory was the theory that was given to us by John Bowlby and Mary Ainsworth. Their theory dealt primarily with the development of close relationships and the functions of close relationships of this reciprocal attachment system that develops. Their theory seems to have worked in that it has generated a lot of research, and from that research a lot of new findings about how attachments form and how relationships affect subsequent behaviors and development. It has very solid applications. As we mentioned, it's already been used to change around the way we handle children going into the hospital, the way we handle necessary separations of children from their parents, and the way we handle foster care. But Bowlby saw development as somewhat instinctual; almost more than was needed. Ainsworth saw development as primarily tied to whether the parents were good or bad, and consistent as parents. Maybe more of than was needed. But theory doesn't explain a wide range of development. But rather than saying that's a major criticism, it was never intended to explain everything about development.

Bandura's theory dealt primarily with how we learn through observation, how we learn by imitating others, and how our self-efficacy—our beliefs about what we can accomplish and what we can effect in the environment—influences our development, what we will try, what we will expect will happen. This combined theory has been very effective in generating a lot of applied programs for treating phobias and having people learn not to be fearful, for looking at people who give up trying and how to help them to have a different sense of self-efficacy and learn that they can accomplish certain things. It's also given us models of dealing with aggression in our youth, and the incidents in our youth that make people become aggressive. But Bandura didn't focus very much on the importance of childhood per se, or on the developmental issues and processes that occur at different ages.

Piaget's theory dealt primarily with how we change our cognitive skills over time and how we develop intelligent thought processes. His theory, probably more than any other, generated thousands, literally thousands of studies. Because of that, we have a lot of knowledge about the normal course of development of children, what they can do at different ages and how they develop. We have information that we never had before from Piaget. But he seemed to be biased towards a kind of logical thinking of mathematics called operations, and this for him was the highest form of intelligence. And even though that might have been helpful, he's short-changed more social, emotional and creative domains of development. Also, it seems to me and to others that his stages may have been much too rigid in the way he looked at them.

The sixth theorist and the last theorist, Vygotsky, and his theory dealt primarily with how we interact with adults to incorporate important symbolic tools for them and then how the adults aid us in our development. He influenced the way we looked at effective cooperation, in helping children to learn, how we approach education. But his theory was somewhat narrow in what it covered. It only covered some aspects of development; it didn't even try to cover everything. And the precision of his processes is lacking. His theory helps us have an approach to education and to development; but not so much to lie out a very specific way of assessing a child's level of development.

 ©2002 The Teaching Company Limited Partnership

We should be able to combine and integrate these theories, to organize our thinking regarding the different aspects and domains of development. I can't do all of that integrating for you. I think maybe you can do that as you look at these theories, but let me give you some examples. In one instance, we can use Erikson's theories to talk about the major issues that we face, combined with Bowlby and Ainsworth's theories to discuss the processes whereby trust and connectedness develop as a foundation for subsequent autonomy and independence. Looking at that early development, both Erikson and Bowlby combined could give us a good view of how we put this together. Let me give you another example.

We could use Piaget's theory to provide some structure for how we approach new information from the environment and the general sequences of shifts that we make in our thinking. But we could combine that with Vygotsky's theory to add some insight into how others help us to actually, gradually become more independent in our problem solving. Put these together—there's no reason why these two theories in this regard are in conflict. They should be able to go together.

However, there are contradictions between theories and some aspects because, in many cases, these theories are based on opposing worldviews. If you recall, we talked about a mechanistic worldview and an organismic worldview. It's probably impossible to integrate everything, just like it's impossible to believe that any one theory is completely correct.

Let me give you now one example of an explanation of some aspect of development that was actually provided by three of these different theories, as a way of comparing them. In some ways you can integrate these approaches; but in some ways, they're contradictory. This is an explanation of gender role development. This is a good comparison. Let me start out with giving you a background for gender role development. During the preschool and early elementary years, children develop this firm conception of what it is to be masculine and what it is to be feminine and the attendant/intended masculine and feminine behaviors that go with these gender roles, and how the role of each sex functions and differs from the sex's roles.

Let me take a break for a minute and just tell you how people currently use sex and gender. Even though these words are used interchangeably—at least in the field of development—people have tried to use the word sex to refer to the actual differences between the two sexes. So my sex is male, and your sex may be female. Sex refers to anatomical differences and everything that is absolute or physically real. Gender is then used to refer to the attendant roles, and behaviors and attributes that go along with any particular sex. So, my gender may be masculine, and my sex may be male; but my sex may be masculine in the sense that my gender includes a lot of things—preferences, attitudes, the way I behave, other things that I've learned. Except in some rare cases, I really can't change my sex. It's tough to change gender as well, but I at least have learned my gender—in theory.

Now, by the time you look at this tape, this lecture, those conceptions might have changed. People are always using these words interchangeably and trying to figure out how to use them. I'll try to use them in this way. These conceptions are called gender roles, and they're believed to originate not only in our biology, but in the beliefs of our culture. They come from both. Everybody knows that, but some people are very passionate in their extreme beliefs that either biology matters most or environment matters most, especially in specific cultural values that we get from our environment. And these—either the biology or the environment—really determine for the most part the specific gender roles that develop. Some argue that development of a gender role is normal and valuable for subsequent development and functioning. They think it's good. Others believe that we'd be better off, and we'd have more optimal development of children, if we could be freed from all gender roles, from separate gender roles. We could all be alike, and they would even strive for that. Some believe that's a possible accomplishment, others believe that condition is impossible, you'll never get there.

You may have noticed this intense personal concern and debate in some people, and you certainly see it in some developmentalists, and in parents and educators. But one thing everyone agrees on is that not only do children develop an understanding of gender roles, but they also incorporate these gender roles into their own identity. The gender role becomes important for identity. In fact, some researchers have shown that if you give kids a lot of different conceptions, you give them choices of how they classify themselves, do they identify

 ©2002 The Teaching Company Limited Partnership

with this or that—you give them age differences, ethnic differences or racial differences, you give them sex differences—sex wins out for most kids. Sex is a core construct of who we are and our identities, and comes in fairly soon, by the later preschool years. As I mentioned, three of our theories attempt to explain how this development occurs and what the motivation is for children to develop these strong gender conceptions that we all know are there. The theories are Freud's Psychodynamic Theory, Bandura's Social-Learning Theory and Piaget's Cognitive-Development Theory, although Piaget's Cognitive-Development Theory is shown as it was interpreted and used by Lawrence Kohlberg, not by Piaget himself.

So, each of these sequences that I'm going to give you in this example is presented as if a preschool boy can state what he's thinking and feeling, even the unconscious thoughts and desires. Each case is set up like a sort of syllogism, if you will, or a way that a child goes through his reasoning to come to a conclusion. Remember, this is the way that they think these gender roles develop, but it's not that a child would actually be conscious of it and be able to talk about it this way.

So first let's start with Freud's theory. According to psychoanalysts, this is the following sequence that occurs, and it's based on one's Oedipal desires and the resolution of these desires. The development of gender role identity is initiated from within the child, based on his or her own desires. So remember, I'm taking the boy's viewpoint now. He starts out saying, "I want my mother as a love object. To get her, I must be like my father, and therefore, I want to be a male like my father and do masculine things." You see, it comes from the desires for the mom and how you resolve that with the dad and you learn to be masculine.

Let me give you the next one. This is social learning theory and this is the sequence that occurs. It's based on one's expectancies. Remember Bandura's theory? The beliefs one has about reinforced contingencies, what will be reinforced. The development of gender role identity is initiated from the environment socializing the child. But of course, the child has to believe and learn to believe what can be possible. This starts out with the boy thinking, "I want reinforcement." In other words, I want good things to happen. "And I've observed others and I realize I get reinforcement when I do masculine things, because they get reinforcement when they do masculine things. Therefore, I want to be a male and act like males act." You see, it starts from wanting reinforcement, seeing how it's done in society. It comes from outside, in.

This is the last theory. This is according to cognitive-developmental theory from Larry Kohlberg; this is the sequence that occurs. It's based on one's categorization of things in the world, including social relationships. The development of this gender identity is initiated from within one's self. In this case the child does it to himself and seeks it out. It starts out this way. The boy thinks, "I have discovered that I am a male, and I'm going to stay a male. Well, if I'm a male, I want to be a competent male. Therefore, when I do masculine things, I'm competent." A different approach.

Now the empirical evidence that we know so far doesn't really provide much support for the psychoanalytic explanation that children who resolve their Oedipal conflict appropriately identify stronger gender role development. However, there's been a lot of empirical evidence that supports both the social learning view and a cognitive developmental account of this. You see the social learning account focuses on what comes from the environment; the cognitive-developmental account focuses on what comes from within and how we socialize ourselves. It assumes that a child needs a prerequisite understanding of his own sex and identity before the gender roles can even be learned. In fact, this is shown to be somewhat true. Kids have the sense of sex conservation even in the preschool years. That is, they learn first that we have labels, that we call some people boys and some people girls or some people women and some people men, and they learn to be able to identify—pretty easily—who's called what. They also learned that once you have this identification, once you have this label, you could stay in that label, and there's a period of time that they're a little confused about that.

So often kids will say, "When I grow up…" A boy will say, "When I grow up I want to be a mommy." And someone will say, "You can't be a mommy." And he'll say, "Why not?" "Because you have to be a girl to be a mommy." And he says, "Well, then I'll be a girl, and be a mommy." They think that sexes are sort of interchangeable. You do what you want when you grow up. But they learn fairly quickly that that's not possible because people tell them and they also observe that there's conservation of sex across changes. For example, a boy's mom has long hair and goes out and gets a haircut. She comes home with very short hair and that kid goes crazy. He's upset because it's a conservation problem. Is that still his mother? Can he still see the identity of his mother? If he learns that, yes, she's still mom, he might learn things like moms can wear pants or dresses. They can change styles and mothers are still women. And men can change styles and do different things and they're still men. You stay the same. Once they've learned this then in that cognitive-developmental approach, then they say, "I am this, and now I have to start paying attention to people that are in this role." So most researchers today in some way combine these two accounts as the best explanation.

Let me give you one more story about this. Recently, we had a visit from my oldest son—who is an adult, a young adult who is living away from home—and we went on a hike. And one of my youngest sons—my younger two sons, they both adore him and when they're with him, because they don't get to see him too often, they pay a lot of attention, and they love being with him, and I observed them on this hike; it was very interesting—so one of the younger ones, looking up to his younger brother, walked along and ended up doing everything the older son did, everything his brother did. When the brother walked up on some rocks a particular way, the other one would walk up that way. When the older one took off his shirt and tucked it into his belt, the younger one took off his shirt and tucked it into his belt. When the older one went up to an area to look out, the younger one went up there. When the older one ordered something in a restaurant, the younger one ordered the same thing at the restaurant. So far you can say that this is imitation, and this is imitation based on maybe this view, this social-learning view of vicarious reinforcement.

They also talked to each other, but I also discovered something else. It wasn't just imitation, it was something that I call co-construction of their roles, from Vygotsky's theory. Not only was the younger one imitating the older one, but together they were sort of working out what you do. So very often they'd talk about it; the younger one would say, "What do you like?" What happens here? The older one would say things like, "Don't do that. Don't you like this?" And together they sort of co-constructed what I call masculine roles. So the older one was a role model for the younger one in terms of gender roles. But it was a combination. It wasn't blind imitation only from outside, in; it was also a co-construction, a combination. That's just an example of maybe how you can put these kinds of things together.

As a final assessment, I want to return to some questions that we asked in the very first lecture. This was a test I gave you concerning where you stood as a student on various major issues of development. You should see if you had any changes in your thinking. You should recognize that certain of the themes in the questions, things that might now be more familiar now that we've talked about the different theories. And you might recognize that these issues or the answers really can't be proven or disproven, but they guide one's theoretical lenience. We'll see if you think the same way or not. Now, I'm going to ask these as multiple choice questions, so for each question you have some alternatives. Choose on a gut level what you think best matches your beliefs. The first question is:

Children are:

1. Creatures whose basically negative or selfish impulses must be controlled.

2. Neither inherently good nor inherently bad.

3. Creatures who are born with many positive and very few negative tendencies.

This question addresses our conception of the basic nature of humans. The first alternative came from our early conceptions of this person born evil and born with a lot of negative characteristics. But you may recognize that in many ways it matches Freud's theory. Not completely. The theory that looked at these internal conflicts, this selfishness, these problems that people had and then had to cope with and then work out. The second alternative matches Locke's theory; that is, of people being born neutral and more or less blank, ready to be molded. It also matches other theories from the learning theory tradition and more of Bandura's approach. And the third alternative matches Rousseau's philosophy that people are born good and left to their own devices will develop optimally. And this matches Piaget's theory of the normative optimal development of children.

Let me give you now the second question. People are basically:

1. Active beings who play a major role in determining their own abilities and traits.

2. Passive beings whose characteristics are molded by either environmental or biological factors.

You may recognize now that this question addresses our basic worldview of either an active, organismic approach to humans, or a passive, mechanistic approach to humans. The first alternative matches Piaget's theory. We're active in that we seek out and initiate our own development. The second alternative matches Bandura's theory of observational learning, though Bandura changed a little bit with his self-efficacy theory. Let me give you the next question. When we compare development of different individuals we see:

1. Mainly similarities. People develop along universal paths and experience similar changes at similar ages.

2. Mainly differences. People undergo different sequences of changes and have widely different timetables of development.

This question again addresses an issue of the organismic approach that focuses on universal norms of development vs. a mechanistic approach that focuses on individual differences. Now the first alternative matches Piaget's theory. The second alternative better matches Bandura's theory. Where does Vygotsky's theory fit in here? Vygotsky really stressed individual differences, but he certainly had a view of the normative development of these cases. Here's the fourth question:

Biological influences and environmental influences are thought to contribute to development, both. The question is though, overall:

1. Biological factors contribute more than environmental factors.

2. Biological and environmental factors are equally important.

3. Environmental factors contribute more than biological factors.

This question addresses the relative influence of nature vs. nurture, or biology vs. an environment. All the theorists believe that both factors are important. But part of Bowlby's theory focused more on biology, even though Ainsworth who combined her theory with Bowlby focused on environmental factors from the parents. Bandura's theory focused more on environment.

Have you changed your basic conceptions regarding these issues from the beginning of this course? Have you changed some of them or have you possibly found any way to see human development and human nature from multiple perspectives as they relate to these questions? If you can't see it from only one way, that's good too.

As a final question you could ask about these theories: Can we apply these theories when they talked about child development to development in adulthood and old age? Although most of these theories, these six theories, dealt with development during childhood and adolescence, they each provide explanations for processes and models that are part of our basic human nature. Thus, these processes and ideas should be found at all levels. As an example, the conflicts often unconscious, or only semi-conscious that drive us, the motivations to want conflicting things, some of our motivations being very selfish, some of them more realistic, some of them idealistic. Does this sound like Freud's theory?

This stuff seems to play out for everyone at all ages, and I think that Freud would have agreed that this is part of our human nature. I believe we do deal with issues of identity in our commitments to various courses of development, and we certainly see this in children and particularly in adolescents during their identity crisis. But we certainly see it in middle age, we see it in older adults, we deal with who we are and our commitments at different times in our lives. We constantly deal with our attachments to others in our close relationships. It comes out again and again of what this means.

So let me just say in our final conclusion about this, is that this is our human nature, this combination that I think these theorists have picked up. In the case of human development, we indeed do see the little child in the adult, and the fully developed human adult in the little child. We're the same, just as we're different. Thank you.

Timeline

1600s–1700s ....In Europe and America, no interest in child study and a lack of concern for children. Children are treated as miniature adults.

1690 ....John Locke publishes an important essay on human understanding; argues that children are born neutral.

1762 ....Jean-Jacques Rousseau publishes *Emile*; argues that children are born good and should not be corrupted by society.

1787 ....Tiedemann publishes the first *baby biography*.

1856 ....Sigmund Freud is born.

1877 ....Charles Darwin publishes his child observations.

1882 ....Preyer publishes the first textbook on child development.

1896 ....Jean Piaget and Lev Vygotsky are born.

1902 ....Erik Erikson is born.

1907 ....John Bowlby is born.

1913 ....Mary Ainsworth is born.

1920s ....John Watson becomes "the father of behaviorism."

1925 ....Albert Bandura is born.

1934 ....Vygotsky dies.

1939 ....Freud dies.

1920s–1940s ....Arnold Gesell writes about his maturational stage theory; Freud's theory competes with behaviorism for dominance in child

	development; ethologists (Tinbergen, von Frisch, and Lorenz) do comparative animal research in Europe.
1950s–1960s	Behaviorism and learning theory dominate in child development.
1956	Ainsworth begins studies with the *strange situation*.
1959	Robert White publishes his theory of mastery motivation.
1960s	Bandura publishes his first studies on imitation and aggression.
1963	Erikson publishes *Childhood and Society*, laying out his eight stages.
1969	Bowlby publishes the first book of his trilogy on attachment theory.
1970s	Vygotsky's writings are first published in English.
1970s–1980s	Piaget's theory dominates child development.
1980	Piaget dies.
1980s	Bandura develops his self-efficacy theory.
1990	Bowlby dies.
1990s	Vygotsky's influence on development in context and on education becomes prevalent; Robert Siegler does research on developing cognitive strategies.
1999	Ainsworth dies.

Glossary

Accommodation: The process of adjusting or modifying one's scheme to fit an object or situation in the environment.

Assimilation: The process of applying one's scheme to an object or situation in the environment so that the object is incorporated into the scheme.

Behaviorism: A theoretical approach associated with learning theory in which overt behavior is the object of study. Covert cognitive processes are not considered a part of psychological study. Rather, the conditions that lead from stimulus to response are the focus.

Co-construction: Two people (usually a child and an adult) together solve a problem or perform a task (usually with the adult scaffolding the child).

Cognition: The mental processes of thinking, which include representation, imagination, and problem solving.

Conservation: The ability to understand what qualities (and quantities) of a thing remain the same (or are conserved) amid changes in other qualities.

Defense mechanisms: Freud's term for processes that the person unconsciously uses to control the conflict among basic primary drives, the demands of the superego, and the demands of reality. Though they are often maladaptive, these defenses protect the self from being conscious of all the conflicts and pressures.

Ego: Freud's term for the realistic, conscious, rational, problem-solving functions of the individual that develop out of the id to deal with reality.

Egocentric speech: Talking to oneself, often to guide one, rather than to communicate with others.

Equilibration: Piaget's term for the process of bringing assimilation and accommodation into an equilibrium.

Ethology: The study of animal behavior for the purpose of learning about complex, instinctual, and adaptive processes. The theory was begun by Konrad Lorenz and others.

Fixation: In Freud's theory, some libidinal energy is fixed on the pleasures and focus of a particular stage of development. Thus, one retains some behaviors and desires associated with that focus (e.g., oral fixations).

Human development: The sequence of steps and the processes that bring about change and reorganization in humans from conception through the entire life cycle.

Id: Freud's term for the unconscious, irrational, amoral, basic animal functions and needs of the individual.

Identity crisis: Erikson's concept of the emotional turmoil one goes through in trying to understand and resolve conflicts and confusions of who one is and what one can commit to. This term more specifically applies to Erikson's fifth stage, which occurs during adolescence.

Innate releasing mechanism: In ethology theory, an automatic behavior or characteristic that instinctually acts as a cue to other individuals to feel a certain way and respond a certain way. For example, babyish features act as innate releasing mechanisms to elicit feelings and responses of nurturance and the desire to be close to the individual with the features.

Internal working model: Bowlby's term for an internal representation that a person develops for an attached person and the relationship with that person. An individual uses this representation for comfort and to guide behavior in subsequent relationships.

Learning theory: A theoretical approach associated with behaviorism in which the focus is on the study of how individuals learn habits and contingencies between means and ends. Learning theory generally deals with the principles of reinforcement that lead to effective conditioning of behavioral responses.

Libido: Freud's term for the psychic (psychological) energy he believed powered all the cognitive and emotional processes. It was generally channeled through two instinctual drives: *Eros*, which motivates one to seek sex, pleasure, and survival, and *Thanatos*, which motivates one to seek death, aggression, and competition.

Mechanistic worldview: An approach to human development in which a machine is the model for humans. Humans are seen as passive responders to the world.

Observational learning: Learning by observing a model's actions, then encoding the behavior and imitating the model.

Oedipus complex: Freud's theoretical construct of a conflict involving the child's desire for the exclusive affection of the opposite-sex parent and the ensuing (imaginary) competition with the same-sex parent. Its resolution comes through identification with the same-sex parent.

Operation: Piaget's concept for a mental transformation that a person performs on something, which can be reversed.

Organismic worldview: An approach to human development in which a complete organism is the model for humans. Humans are seen as active initiators of action and change.

Primary process thinking: Freud's term for the most primitive level of thinking, associated with the basic needs of the id.

Reciprocal determinism: The circular effect of the environment's determining one's behavior and the person effecting a change in the environment.

Reinforcement: A term from learning theory for a result of some behavior that is rewarding and causes the frequency of the behavior to increase in the future.

Scaffolding: The process of someone "propping up" or aiding an individual to help him or her understand something or perform a task.

Scheme: Piaget's term for a pattern of knowing something.

Scientific theory: A systematic explanation that unifies various observed phenomena and facts. A theory often consists of metaphors, models, or formulas.

Secondary process thinking: Freud's term for rational, problem-solving cognitive processes that develop along with the ego.

Self-efficacy: The belief that one can cause some specific effects on one's environment.

Strange situation: A widely used research paradigm developed by Ainsworth to assess the type of attachment relationship that exists between a child and parent. Its name derives from the strange situations in which children are placed to observe their responses.

Superego: Freud's term for the conscience and the ideals that are internalized from society. The superego is often irrational.

Symbol: A thing or mental action that stands for something else, the *referent*.

Vicarious reinforcement: The expectancy one develops that he will be reinforced for behaving the same way that a model did who was reinforced for her behavior.

Zone of proximal development: Vygotsky's term for the range of tasks and challenges that a person is currently trying to master. This range is the area of the child's current development.

Biographical Notes

Ainsworth, Mary (born, 1913 in Ohio; died, 1999 in Virginia). Ainsworth received her Ph.D. in 1939 from the University of Toronto; she was a major in the Canadian Army in World War II; she studied mother-child relationships in Uganda, then developed and tested the *strange situation task* in Baltimore; she was then a professor at the University of Virginia. With John Bowlby, she developed attachment theory.

Bandura, Albert (born, 1925 in Canada). Bandura received his Ph.D. in 1952 from the University of Iowa; he then became a professor at Stanford University, where he is today. He developed social learning theory and self-efficacy theory.

Bowlby, John (born, 1907 in England; died, 1990 in England). Bowlby was trained as a physician in child psychiatry and Freudian psychoanalysis; after World War II, he directed the Tavistock Clinic and did research in children's hospitals. With Mary Ainsworth, he developed attachment theory.

Erikson, Erik (born, 1902 in Germany; died, 1994 in Massachusetts). Erikson's parents were Danish, but he was raised as a German Jew; he received only a high school diploma; he wandered around Europe and tried out various jobs; and studied psychoanalysis with Anna Freud in Austria. He came to the United States in 1933; he was the first child psychoanalyst in Boston; at various times, he was at Harvard University, Yale University, and the University of California at Berkeley. He developed the psycho-social theory of development, the first theory to describe adult development.

Freud, Sigmund (born, 1856 in Moravia; died, 1939 in England). Freud lived most of his life in Vienna; he received his M.D. in 1881; he initiated the practice of psychoanalysis in Vienna; he was a refugee of Nazism and immigrated to England. He developed the psychodynamic theory.

Piaget, Jean (born, 1896 in Switzerland; died, 1980 in Switzerland). Piaget studied biology and philosophy and published his first paper at age 10; he received his Ph.D. in 1917 from the University of Neuchatel; he worked on intelligence tests in Paris; in 1921, he became director of the Jean-Jacques Rousseau Institute at the

University of Geneva. He developed the cognitive-developmental theory.

Vygotsky, Lev (born, 1896 near Minsk; died [of tuberculosis], 1934 in Russia). Vygotsky graduated from Moscow University in 1917; his first publications were on the psychology of art; he worked most of his life in Moscow; most of his work consisted of posthumous publications. He developed the cognitive-mediation theory.

©2002 The Teaching Company Limited Partnership

Bibliography

Ainsworth, Mary D.S. "Infant-Mother Attachment." *American Psychologist* 34 (10) (1979), pp. 932–937. An excellent, brief review of Ainsworth and Bowlby's main theoretical ideas.

Ainsworth, Mary D.S., M.C. Blehar, Everett Waters, and S. Wall. *Patterns of Attachment.* Hillsdale, NJ: Lawrence Erlbaum, 1978. The best full account by Ainsworth of her theory and research.

Ames, Louise Bates. *Arnold Gesell—The Themes of His Work.* New York: Human Sciences Press, 1989. A good review of Gesell's conceptions of maturational stages by one of his collaborators.

Aries, Philippe. *Centuries of Childhood: A Social History of Family Life.* New York: Vintage/Random House, 1962. An insightful history of practices and attitudes toward children.

Bandura, Albert. *Social Learning Theory.* Englewood Cliffs, NJ: Prentice-Hall, 1977. The most complete account of his entire theory.

————. *Social Foundations of Thought and Action.* Englewood Cliffs, NJ: Prentice-Hall, 1986. A book laying out Bandura's research and ideas, including his cognitive concepts.

————. *Self-Efficacy: The Exercise of Control.* New York: Freeman, 1997. A good account of Bandura's self-efficacy theory, which includes applications to development and influences in old age.

Bandura, Albert, and Richard H. Walters. *Social Learning and Personality Development.* New York: Holt, Rinehart, and Winston, 1963. This classic book provides descriptions of Bandura's earliest studies of imitation, including characteristics of models that will elicit imitation.

Berk, L.E., and A. Winsler. *Scaffolding Children's Thinking: Vygotsky and Early Childhood Education.* Washington, DC: National Association for the Education of Young Children, 1995. A good application of Vygotsky's theory to early education, demonstrating the current influence of his theory.

Blurton-Jones, N. *Ethological Studies of Child Behavior.* Cambridge, England: Cambridge University Press, 1972. An account of the application of ethology theory to a study of child development (not just attachment), written by a well-known ethologist and developmentalist.

Bowlby, John. *Attachment and Loss*, Vol. I: *Attachment*. New York: Basic Books, 1969. The first of his trilogy of important books on attachment; perhaps the most important book to read by Bowlby.

————. *Attachment and Loss*, Vol. II: *Separation, Anxiety and Anger*. New York: Basic Books, 1973. The second of Bowlby's trilogy, with a focus primarily on what happens when a child is separated from an attached person.

————. *Attachment and Loss*, Vol. III: *Loss*. New York: Basic Books, 1980. The third of his trilogy, dealing primarily with loss of an attached figure.

Bretherton, Inge. "The Origins of Attachment Theory: John Bowlby and Mary Ainsworth." *Developmental Psychology* 28 (5) (1992), pp. 759–775. An excellent history and description of attachment theory, which includes an account of how Ainsworth and Bowlby interacted with and influenced each other; written shortly after Bowlby's death by one of Ainsworth's main students.

Bretherton, Inge, and Everett Waters, eds. "Growing Points of Attachment Theory and Research." In *Monographs of the Society for Research in Child Development*, S.N. 209, Vol. 50, Nos. 1–2, 1985. A detailed set of research reports of important findings as of the early 1980s; included is an excellent overview of the theory.

Chodorow, Nancy. *The Reproduction of Mothering: Psychoanalysis and the Socialization of Gender*. Berkeley, CA: University of California Press, 1978. An account of developmental and psychological issues from a feminist perspective; provides a challenge to Erikson's male-oriented account of the stages of identity and intimacy.

Chukovsky, Kornei. *From Two to Five*. Berkeley, CA: University of California Press, 1963. A delightful and insightful account of many anecdotes illustrating preschool children's developing symbol use, imagination, and poetic sense. The author was a well-known author of books for children in the Soviet Union.

Cleverly, John, and D.C. Phillips. *Visions of Childhood: Influential Models from Locke to Spock*. New York: Teachers College Press, 1986. An excellent review of the history of ideas regarding child development and human nature; includes most of the primary historical influences that have occurred.

Coles, Robert, ed. *The Erik Erikson Reader*. New York: W.W. Norton, 2001. An excellent compilation of Erikson's writings on a number of topics, including his stages.

Erikson, Erik H. *Childhood and Society*, 2nd ed. New York: W.W. Norton, 1963. The most important book by Erikson, in which he laid out his eight stages of development; also included are his studies of some other cultures and examples of identity development in some famous people, such a Hitler. The second edition includes the fully elaborated stage theory.

————. *Identity: Youth and Crisis*. New York: W.W. Norton, 1968. A follow-up description, including more details of the stage of identity development; includes a discussion of psychopathological development.

————. *Dimensions of a New Identity*. New York: W.W. Norton, 1974. A monograph-length essay on the life and development of Thomas Jefferson that includes primarily an application of Erikson's theory of identity development to the development of a national identity of the United States and our culture. The last chapter provides excellent summaries and insights into many of Erikson's important ideas and shows his writing at its best.

Freud, Sigmund. *On Dreams*. New York: W.W. Norton, 1980 (originally published, 1901). One of the most important of Freud's books because it shows his revolutionary thinking about the unconscious and the conflicts within us, his account of the functions of dreams and why we dream what we do is still as good as any.

————. *The Sexual Enlightenment of Children*. New York: Collier, 1963 (originally published, 1907–1913). A collection of separate essays regarding sex and sexual behavior in young children. Included is Freud's account of the phobias of Little Hans, which provided his most important empirical evidence for the Oedipus complex; one can see extreme biases in the objectivity of the observations and interviews with the boy, which were done by the boy's father.

————. *Beyond the Pleasure Principle*. New York: W.W. Norton, 1961 (originally published, 1920). Freud lays out principles of the development of personality.

————. *The Ego and the Id.* New York: W.W. Norton, 1962 (originally published, 1923). A further account of the development of personality and psychological functions, including the development of the superego.

————. *Civilization and Its Discontents.* New York: W.W. Norton, 1961 (originally published, 1930). An account of the influence of society and civilization on personality development, including some of the problems that can occur; includes a scathing criticism of the role of religion in development.

————. *New Introductory Lectures on Psychoanalysis.* New York: W.W. Norton, 1964 (originally published, 1933). Freud's second summary account of much of his theory, providing a description of his fully developed thinking.

————. *An Outline of Psycho-Analysis.* New York: W.W. Norton, 1949 (originally published, 1940). Another short summary of his entire theory, written at the end of his life and, thus, describing his final thinking on human nature and development.

Gay, Peter. *Freud: A Life for Our Time.* New York: W.W. Norton, 1988. Perhaps the most accessible and interesting biography of Freud's life and work by someone who knows his work well.

————, ed. *The Freud Reader.* New York: W.W. Norton, 1989. A book of selected readings by Freud; perhaps the best single book to obtain a sampling of some of his important works.

Goldhaber, Dale E. *Theories of Human Development: Integrative Perspectives.* Mountain View, CA: Mayfield, 2000. An excellent review of many of the theories discussed in this course; presented in terms of major worldviews (such as mechanistic and organismic).

Hall, Calvin S. *A Primer of Freudian Psychology.* New York: Mentor/New American Library, 1954. An excellent, brief description of Freud's theory for beginners. Written by a leading personality psychologist at a time when behaviorism dominated psychology; therefore, some of the description facilitates understanding of Freud by integrating behaviorist ideas.

Hazan, Cindy, and Phillip Shaver. "Romantic Love Conceptualized as an Attachment Process." *Journal of Personality and Social Psychology* 52 (3) (1987), pp. 511–524. The initial description of the authors' theory of attachment styles applied to adult romantic love, with empirical evidence to support their conceptualization.

Hwang, C. Phillip, Michael E. Lamb, and Irving E. Sigel, eds. *Images of Childhood.* Mahwah, NJ: Lawrence Erlbaum, 1996. A collection of writings that provides an excellent complementary description to the theories discussed in the course; these articles discuss child development and human nature as seen in, and through a comparison of, other cultures, including Japan, Zambia, Brazil, Sweden, and Navajo society.

Inhelder, Barbel, and Jean Piaget. *The Early Growth of Logic in the Child.* New York: W.W. Norton, 1969 (originally published, 1964). A detailed account of development in young and elementary-school-age children presented by Piaget and one of his most important collaborators. One should note that most of Piaget's writings are complicated and not clear, though the details of observation and the insights are excellent.

Kagan, Jerome. *Three Seductive Ideas.* Cambridge, MA: Harvard University Press, 1998. One of the foremost current developmental psychologists argues persuasively against some of the common assumptions we hold regarding development and human nature, including some that are part of many of the theories we have studied.

Kessen, William. *The Child.* New York: Wiley, 1965. One of the most insightful and excellent histories and commentaries about the development of ideas and interest in the study of children. Contains many excerpts from primary source writings, including excellent selections from John Locke, Jean-Jacques Rousseau, Charles Darwin, John Watson, and Arnold Gesell. Unfortunately, this book is out of print and only available in libraries.

Kozulin, A. *Vygotsky's Psychology: A Biography of Ideas.* Cambridge, MA: Harvard University Press, 1990. An account of Vygotsky's history and theory, written by a Russian psychologist while he was a visitor at Harvard University after the opening up of the former Soviet Union. The work describes Vygotsky as he was perceived and known to Russian developmentalists.

Miller, Neal E., and John Dollard. *Social Learning and Imitation.* New Haven, CT: Yale University Press, 1941. The initial conceptualization of social learning and modeling and imitation that influenced Bandura's theory. This conceptualization is more tied to traditional learning theory than is Bandura's theory.

Miller, Patricia H. *Theories of Developmental Psychology*, 4th ed. New York: Worth, 2002. One of the best reviews and summaries of various theories of human development, including reviews of the contributions and weaknesses of the theories; well written.

Pepper, Stephen C. *World Hypotheses: A Study of Evidence.* Los Angeles: University of California Press, 1961. A philosopher's account of various worldviews that we use as metaphors to guide our thinking; a discussion of the mechanistic and organismic worldviews.

Phillips, J.L. *Piaget's Theory: A Primer.* San Francisco: Freeman, 1981. An introductory account of Piaget's entire theory; a good way to begin.

Piaget, Jean. *The Origins of Intelligence in Children.* New York: W.W. Norton, 1963 (originally published, 1952). One of the most influential books ever published about human development. The first book of a trilogy that offers a theoretical account of Piaget's processes, with abundant detailed observations, primarily of his own three children; covers development from birth to the preschool years and lays out the sub-stages of the sensory-motor period. Again, keep in mind that Piaget's writing is often dense and unclear, though rewarding.

―――――. *The Construction of Reality in the Child.* New York: Ballantine, 1971 (originally published, 1954). The second book in his trilogy about early development; provides detailed descriptions of the development of the notion of object permanence and other important concepts.

―――――. *Play, Dreams and Imitation in Childhood.* New York: W.W. Norton, 1963. The third book in Piaget's trilogy; originally entitled in French *The Development of the Symbol in the Young Child.* Discusses the transition to symbol use and provides an excellent discussion of the development of symbolic play and functions of play in childhood; purported to be the best translation of any of his trilogy.

―――――. *Six Psychological Studies.* New York: Random House, 1968. A collection of various essays; includes some valuable discussion of equilibration and operations.

 ©2002 The Teaching Company Limited Partnership

Piaget, Jean, and Barbel Inhelder. *The Psychology of the Child.* New York: Basic Books, 1969. A summary of Piaget's entire theory of child development that includes a chapter on each of the four periods; excellent review but not for those with only a beginning knowledge of his theory.

Rogoff, Barbara. *Apprenticeship in Thinking: Cognitive Development in Social Context.* New York: Oxford University Press, 1990. An excellent account of the contextual approach to development, which includes the concept of co-construction; research and theory based on Vygotsky's cognitive-mediation theory.

Shaver, Phillip R., and Cindy Hazan. "Adult Romantic Attachment: Theory and Evidence." In *Advances in Personal Relationships,* edited by D. Perlman and W.H. Jones. London: Jessica Kingsley, 1993. A good summary of their theory and empirical research regarding adult attachment styles.

Siegler, Robert S. *Emerging Minds: The Process of Change in Children's Thinking.* New York: Oxford University Press, 1996. An excellent account of Siegler's research and theory regarding variability and overlapping strategies in children's cognitive development; written by one of the foremost current researchers and theorists in cognitive development.

Vygotsky, Lev S. *Mind in Society: The Development of Higher Psychological Processes.* Cambridge, MA: Harvard University Press, 1978. A compilation of some of his writings on various topics but all related to his basic theory of development in a social context. Discusses the child's incorporation of psychological tools from adults; also includes a description of the concept of a zone of proximal development and an excellent chapter on the value of symbolic play.

Waters, Everett, B.E. Vaughn, G. Posada, and K. Kondo-Ikemura, eds. "Caregiving, Cultural, and Cognitive Perspectives on Secure-Base Behavior and Working Models: New Growing Points of Attachment Theory and Research." In *Monographs of the Society for Research in Child Development,* S.N. 244, Vol. 60, Nos. 2–3, 1995. A series of research reports demonstrating the current evidence for, and thinking about, attachment theory, especially the relation of early attachments to adult attachments and relationship styles; Waters is one of Ainsworth's main students.

Wertsch, James V. *Voices of the Mind: A Sociocultural Approach to Mediated Action.* Cambridge, MA: Harvard University Press, 1991. A good account of Vygotsky's theory with applications to various areas of research.

 ©2002 The Teaching Company Limited Partnership